Wissenschaftliche Beiträge aus dem Tectum Verlag

Reihe Rechtswissenschaft

Wissenschaftliche Beiträge
aus dem Tectum Verlag

Reihe Rechtswissenschaft
Band 127

Cansu D. Burkhalter

Legal and Regulatory Framework of European Energy Markets

Competition Law and Sector-Specific Regulations

Tectum Verlag

Abdruck der der Rechtwissenschaftlichen Fakultät der Universität Zürich vorgelegten Dissertation.

Cansu D. Burkhalter
Legal and Regulatory Framework of European Energy Markets.
Competition Law and Sector-Specific Regulations
Wissenschaftliche Beiträge aus dem Tectum Verlag
Reihe: Rechtswissenschaft; Bd. 127
Zugl. Diss. Universität Zürich 2019

ISBN 978-3-8288-4429-2
ePDF 978-3-8288-7440-4
ePub 978-3-8288-7441-1
ISSN 1861-7875

Druck und Bindung: CPI buchbücher.de, Birkach
Printed in Germany

Besuchen Sie uns im Internet
www.tectum-verlag.de

Bibliografische Informationen der Deutschen Nationalbibliothek
Die Deutsche Nationalbibliothek verzeichnet diese Publikation in der Deutschen Nationalbibliografie; detaillierte bibliografische Angaben sind im Internet über http://dnb.d-nb.de abrufbar.

Foreword

It is impossible to name all the people who have contributed to this thesis.

I am very grateful to my main supervisors Prof. Dr. Rolf Weber and Prof. Dr. Andreas Heinemann who have guided and supported this project from the start. Their supervision and comments on the various drafts of chapters are greatly appreciated and have improved the final product markedly.

I must express my very profound gratitude to Hélène Koller for providing me with unfailing support and continuous encouragement. This accomplishment would not have been possible without her. Her valuable input and rich experience have truly made this thesis a viable and original piece of academic work.

I also would like to thank my mother, Prof. Dr. Emine Koban, for patiently answering all of my queries on how to write a better PhD thesis.

I reserve a very special note of thanks to my husband (Tim Burkhalter) for his extensive support, encouragement and unconditional love. My special thanks are extended to my parents (Emine and Engin Koban), parents-in-law (Theres and Thomas Burkhalter) and friends as well as colleagues for their support and endless patience.

Inhaltsverzeichnis

List of Abbreviations

ACER	Agency for the Cooperation of Energy Regulators
bcm	billion cubic metres
BER	Block Exemption Regulation
CCS	Carbon Capture and Storage
CDM	Clean Development Mechanism
CFI	European Court of First Instance
CHP	Combined Heat and Power Generation
CJ	Court of Justice (European Court of Justice)
CIS	Commonwealth of Independent States
CO_2	carbon dioxide
CRM	Capacity Remuneration Mechanism
DG COMP	Directorate-General for Competition
DSO	Distribution System Operator
EC	European Community
EC Treaty	Treaty establishing the European Community
ECSC	European Coal and Steel Community
EEA	European Economic Area
EEA	European Environment Agency
EEC	European Economic Community
ENISA	European Union Agency for Network and Information Security
ENTSO-E	European Network of Transmission System Operator for Electricity
ENTSO-G	European Network of Transmission System Operator for Gas
ERG	European Regulators Group
ERGEG	European Regulators Group for Electricity and Gas
ESA	Euratom Supply Agency
ESTEP	European Steel Technology Platform
EU	European Union
EURACOAL	European Association for Coal and Lignite
EURATOM	European Atomic Energy Community
EUREL	Convention of National Associations of Electrical Engineers of Europe
GBER	General Block Exemption Regulation

IAEA	International Atomic Energy Agency
IAR	International Authority for the Ruhr
ICN	International Competition Network
IEA	International Energy Agency
IEM	Internal Energy Market
IGC	Intergovernmental Conference
InterEnerStat	Intersecretariat Working Group on Energy Statistics
ISO	Independent System Operator
ITO	Independent Transmission Operator
LNG	Liquefied Natural Gas
MCR	Merger Control Regulation
NGLs	Natural Gas Liquids
NO_x	Nitrogen oxides
NRAs	National Regulatory Authorities
NTPA	Negotiated Third-Party Access
OECD	Organisation for Economic Co-operation and Development
OPEC	Organisation of the Petroleum Exporting Countries
OU	Ownership Unbundling
Para.	Paragraph
RECs	Renewable Energy Certificates
RES	Renewable Energy Sources
RTPA	Regulated Third-Party Access
SEA	Single European Act
SGEI	Services of General Economic Interest
SMEs	Small and Medium Sized Enterprises
SO_2	sulfur dioxide
SOEs	State-owned Entities
TEC	Treaty establishing the European Community
TEN-E	Trans European Energy Networks
TEU	Treaty on European Union
TFEU	Treaty on the Functioning of the European Union
TPA	Third-Party Access
TSO	Transmission System Operator

Bibliography

AAI, 2005. *Comments of The American Antitrust Institute Working Group on Regulated Industries.* Washington, DC: The American Antritrust Institute.

Advocacy Working Group, 2002. *Advocacy and Competition Policy.* Naples: International Competition Network.

Ahner, N., 2011. The Framework for Supporting Renewable Energy in Europe: Implementing Directive 2009/28/EC. In: M. M. Roggenkamp & U. Hammer, eds. *European Energy Law Report VIII.* Antwerp: Intersentia, pp. 93–116.

Akman, P., 2012. *The General Court's judgment in Telefónica: has the Atlantic Ocean just got wider?* (Online) Available at: https://competitionpolicy.wordpress.com/2012/04/17/the-general-courts-judgment-in-telefonica-has-the-atlantic-ocean-just-got-wider/ (accessed 1 June 2019).

Akman, P., 2015. *The Concept of Abuse in EU Competition Law: Law and Economic Approaches.* 2nd ed. Oxford: Hart Publishing.

Alexiadis, P., 2008. Informative and Interesting: The CFI Rules in Deutsche Telekom v. European Commission. *Global Competition Policy Magazine,* 1 May, pp. 1–16.

Alexiadis, P., 2012. Balancing the Application of Ex Post and Ex Ante Disciplines under Community Law in Electronic Communications Markets: Square Pegs in Round Holes? In: E. Buttigieg, ed. *Rights and Remedies in a Liberalised and Competitive Internal Market.* Msida: University of Malta, pp. 137–164.

Almunia, J., 2010. *Competition v Regulation: where do the roles of sector specific and competition regulators begin and end?* (Online) Available at: europa.eu/rapid/press-release_SPEECH-10-121_en.pdf (accessed 1 June 2019).

Alter, K. & Steinberg, D., 2007. The Theory and Reality of the European Coal and Steel Community. In: S. Meunier & K. McNamara, eds. *Making History: European Integration and Institutional Change at Fifty.* Oxford: Oxford University Press, pp. 89–105.

Andersen, S., 2001. Energy Policy: Interest Interaction and Supranational Authority. In: S. Andersen, ed. *Making Policy in Europe.* London: Sage Publishing, pp. 106–124.

Ardiyok, Ş. & Oguz, F., 2010. Competition Law and Regulation in the Turkish Telecommunications Industry: Friends or Foes? *Telecommunications Policy,* 34(4), pp. 233–243.

Armenteros, M. F. & Lefevere, J., 2001. European Court of Justice, 13 March 2001, Case C-379/98, PreussenElektra Aktiengesellschaft v. Schleswag Aktiengesellschaft. *Review of European Community & International Environmental Law*, 10(3), pp. 344–347.

Arnold, R., 2006. Régulation économique et démocratie politique. In: M. Lombard, ed. *Régulation économique et démocratie.* Paris: Dalloz, pp. 83–96.

Aronson, E. & Stern, P. C., 1984. *Energy Use: The Human Dimension,* New York: W. H. Freeman and Company.

Baldwin, R., Cave, M. & Lodge, M., 2012. *Understanding Regulation Theory, Strategy, and Practice.* Oxford: Oxford University Press.

Baldwin, R., Scott, C. & Hood, C., 1998. Introduction. In: R. Baldwin, C. Scott & C. Hood, eds. *A Reader on Regulation.* Oxford: Oxford University Press, pp. 1–55.

Banks, F. E., 1983. *Resources and Energy: An Economic Analysis.* Lexington: Lexington Books.

Barros, P. P. & Hoernig, S., 2018. Sectoral Regulators and the Competition Authority: Which Relationship is Best? *Review of Industrial Organization*, 52(3), pp. 451–472.

Bartok, C. et al., 2006. A combination of gas release programmes and ownership unbundling as remedy to a problematic energy merger: E.ON / MOL. *Competition Policy Newsletter*, 13(2), pp. 73–83.

Battista, J., Gee, A. & Koppenfels, U. v., 2009. Commission imposes heavy fine on two major European gas companies for operating a market-sharing agreement. *Competition Policy Newsletter*, 16(3), pp. 38–40.

Bebr, G., 1953. The European Coal and Steel Community: A Political and Legal Innovation. *The Yale Law Journal*, 63(1), pp. 1–43.

Bechtold, R., 2000. Modernisierung des EG-Wettbewerbsrechts: Der Verordnungs-Entwurf der Kommission zur Umsetzung des Weißbuchs. *Betriebs-Berater*, 17(48), pp. 2425–2430.

Bellamy, C. & Child, G. D., 1987. *Common Market Law of Competition.* London: Sweet & Maxwell.

Bellamy, C. & Child, G. D., 2013. *European Community Law of Competition.* 7th ed. London: Sweet & Maxwell.

Bengtsson, M., 1998. *Climates of Competition.* Amsterdam: Harwood Academic Publishers.

Better Regulation Task Force, 2003. *Principles of Good Regulation,* London: BRTF.

Bishop, M., Kay, J. & Mayer, C., 1995. Introduction. In: M. Bishop, J. Kay & C. Mayer, eds. *The Regulatory Challenge.* Oxford: Oxford University Press.

Bishop, S. & Walker, M., 2010. *Economics of EC Competition Law: Concepts, Application and Measurement.* 3rd ed. London: Sweet & Maxwell.

Black, J., 2005. What is Regulatory Innovation? In: J. Black, M. Lodge & M. Thatcher, eds. *Regulatory Innovation: A Comparative Analysis.* Cheltenham: Edward Elgar, pp. 1–16.

Blakey, S., 2013. *Long-term Outlook for Gas to 2035.* Brussels: Eurogas.

Börner, A. R., 2002. Negotiated Third Party Access in Germany: Electricity and Gas. *Journal of Energy & Natural Resources Law,* 20(1), pp. 27–39.

Boscheck, R., 2009. The EU's Third Internal Energy Market Legislative Package: Victory of Politics over Economic Rationality? *World Competition,* 32(4), pp. 593–608.

BP, 2015. *Energy Outlook to 2035.* London: BP Publications.

BP, 2016. *Statistical Review of World Energy.* London: BP Publications.

Brakman, S., Marrewijk, C. V. & Witteloostuijn, A. v., 2009. *Market liberalization in the European Natural Gas Market: The importance of capacity constraints and efficiency differences.* Utrecht: Tjalling C. Koopmans Research Institute.

Brennan, T. J., 2005. Regulation and Competition as Complements. In: M. A. Crew & M. Spiegel, eds. *Obtaining the Best from Regulation and Competition.* Boston: Kluwer Academic Publishers, pp. 1–21.

Brennan, T. J., 2008. Essential Facilities and Trinko: Should Antitrust and Regulation Be Combined? *Federal Communications Law Journal,* 61(1), pp. 133–147.

Breyer, S. G., 1982. *Regulation and Its Reform.* Cambridge: Harvard University Press.

Breyer, S. G., Stewart, R. B., Sunstein, C. R. & Vermeule, A., 2006. *Administrative Law and Regulatory Policy: Problems, Text and Cases.* New York: Aspen Publishers.

Buigues, P. A., 2006. *Competition Policy and Sector-Specific Regulation in Network Industries: The EU Experience.* Geneva: UNCTAD.

Burger, M., Graeber, B. & Schindlmayr, G., 2014. *Managing Energy Risk: An Integrated View on Power and Other Energy Markets.* 2nd ed. Chichester: Wiley.

Buschle, D., 2013. Unbundling of State-owned Transmission System Operators – Effective Remedy or Eyewash? *European Networks Law and Regulation Quarterly,* 1(1), pp. 49–64.

Buts, C., Jegers, M. & Juris, T., 2011. Determinants of the European Commission's State Aid Decisions. *Journal of Industry, Competition and Trade,* 11(4), pp. 399–426.

Cabau, E., 2016. The relevant product market – Gas. In: E. Cabau, ed. *The Internal Energy Market.* 4th ed. Leuven: Claeys & Casteels, pp. 105–124.

Cabau, E. & Sandberg, L., 2016. Unbundling of Transmission System Operators. In: C. Jones, ed. *EU Energy Law: The Internal Energy Market.* Deventer: Claeys & Casteels, pp. 91–191.

Cameron, P. D., 2007. *Competition in Energy Markets: Law and Regulation in the European Union.* Oxford: Oxford University Press.

Cameron, P. D., 2010. *International Energy Investment Law: The Pursuit of Stability.* Oxford: Oxford University Press.

Capece, G., Pillo, F. D., Gastaldi, M. & Levialdi, N., 2007. The European gas market: the effects of liberalization on retail prices. *WIT Transactions on Ecology and the Environment*, 105, pp. 417–442.

Cardoso, R. et al., 2010. The Commission's GDF and E.ON Gas decisions concerning long-term capacity bookings: Use of own infrastructure as possible abuse under Article 102 TFEU. *Competition Policy Newsletter*, 17(3), pp. 8–11.

Carlton, D. W. & Picker, R. C., 2007. *Antitrust and Regulation.* Cambridge: The National Bureau of Economic Research.

Chalmers, D., Davies, G. & Monti, G., 2010. *European Union Law Cases and Materials.* Cambridge: Cambridge University Press.

Chauve, P. et al., 2009. The E.ON electricity cases: an antitrust decision with structural remedies. *Competition Policy Newsletter*, 16(1), pp. 51–54.

Chemtob, S. M., 2007. *The Role of Competition Agencies in Regulated Sectors.* Beijing, Chinese Academy of Social Sciences.

Clark, J. M., 1940. Toward a Concept of Workable Competition. *The American Economic Review*, 30(2), pp. 241–256.

Coal Mines Committee, 1947. *General Report.* Geneva: International Labour Organisation.

Colangelo, M., 2013. The Interface between Competition Rules and Sector-Specific Regulation in the Telecommunications Sector: Evidence from Recent EU Margin Squeeze Cases. *Competition and Regulation in Network Industries*, 14(3), pp. 214–240.

Colomo, P. I., 2016. *EU Competition Law in the Regulated Network Industries.* London: London School of Economics and Political Science.

Cook, B. A., 2001. *Europe since 1945: An Encyclopedia, Volume II.* New York: Garland Publishing.

Cook, P., 2002. *Competition and Its Regulation: Key Issues.* Manchester: Centre on Regulation and Competition.

Cook, P., Kirkpatrick, C., Minogue, M. & Parker, D., 2004. Competition, Regulation and Regulatory Governance: An Overview. In: P. Cook, C. Kirkpatrick, M. Minogue & D. Parker, eds. *Leading Issues in Competition, Regulation and Development.* Cheltenham: Edward Elgar, pp. 3–39.

Cottier, T., Matteotti-Berkutova, S. & Nartova, O., 2010. *Third Country Relations in EU Unbundling of Natural Gas Markets: The "Gazprom Clause" of Directive 2009/73 EC and WTO Law.* Bern: National Centre of Competence in Research on Trade Regulation.

Council of Economic Advisers, 2016. *Benefits of Competition and indicators of market power.* (Online) Available at: https://obamawhitehouse.archives.gov/sites/default/files/page/files/20160414_cea_competition_issue_brief.pdf (accessed 1 June 2019).

Courivaud, H., 2004. *L'ouverture à la concurrence des marchés de l'énergie.* Ankara: Turkish Competition Authority.

CPS, 2011. *EU Acquis Guide Related to Steel Sector.* Brussels: MESS.

CPS, 2012. *EU Acquis Guide Related to Competition.* Brussels: MESS.

Crampton, P., 2002. *Striking the Right Balance between Competition and Regulation: The Key Is Learning from Our Mistakes.* Jesu Island, OECD.

Dabbah, M. M., 2003. *The Internationalisation of Antitrust Policy.* Cambridge: Cambridge University Press.

Dabbah, M. M., 2004. *EC and UK Competition Law: Commentary, Cases and Materials.* Cambridge University Press: Cambridge.

Dabbah, M. M., 2010. *International and Comparative Competition Law.* Cambridge: Cambridge University Press.

Dabbah, M. M., 2011. The Relationship between Competition Authorities and Sector Regulators. *The Cambridge Law Journal,* 70(1), pp. 113–143.

Dahl, C. A., 2015. *International Energy Markets: Understanding Pricing, Policies, and Profits.* 2nd ed. Tulsa: PennWell.

Davies, S. & Price, C. W., 2007. Does Ownership Unbundling Matter? Evidence from UK Energy Markets. *Intereconomics,* 42(6), pp. 297–301.

Davis, L. W. & Muehlegger, E., 2010. Do Americans Consume Too Little Natural Gas? An Empirical Test of Marginal Cost Pricing. *The RAND Journal of Economics,* 41(4), pp. 791–810.

De Bronett, G.-K., 2003. Die Verordnung Nr. 17. In: H. Schröter, T. Jakob & W. Mederer, eds. *Kommentar zum europäischen Wettbewerbsrecht.* Baden-Baden: Nomos, pp. 1016–1136.

De Clercq, G., 2014. *Insight: Europe's utilities squeezed by creeping nationalization.* (Online) Available at: http://www.reuters.com/article/us-utilities-unplugged-renationalisation-idUSBREA0I03720140119 (accessed 1 June 2019).

Delvaux, B., 2007. The Gas Transmission Regulation 1775/2005: Has a Genius been born? In: M. M. Roggenkamp & U. Hammer, eds. *European Energy Law Report IV.* Antwerp: Intersentia, pp. 41–70.

Department of the Taoiseach, 2004. *Regulating Better.* Dublin: Department of the Taoiseach.

Diathesopoulos, M., 2010. *Third Party Access and Refusal to Deal in European Energy Networks: How Sector Regulation and Competition Law Meet Each Other.* Tilburg: Tilburg Law and Economics Center.

Diathesopoulos, M., 2011. *Competition Law and Sector Regulation in the European Energy Market after the Third Energy Package: Hierarchy and Efficiency.* Tilburg: Tilburg University.

Dogan, S. L. & Lamley, M. A., 2009. Antitrust Law and Regulatory Gaming. *Texas Law Review,* pp. 685–730.

Drauz, G., Chellingsworth, T. & Hyrkas, H., 2010. Recent Developments in EC Merger Control. *Journal of European Competition Law & Practice*, 1(1), p. 12–26.

Dube, C., 2008. *Competition Authorities and Sector Regulators: What is the Best Operational Framework?* Jaipur: Cuts International.

Dunne, N., 2015. *Competition Law and Economic Regulation: Making and Managing Markets.* Cambridge: Cambridge University Press.

Dziadykiewicz, E., 2007. Refusal to Grant Third-Party Access by an Electricity Transmission System Operator – Overview of Competition Law Issues. *Journal of Energy & Natural Resources Law*, 25(2), pp. 114–149.

EFET, 2000. *Unbundling as a crucial factor in the completion of European Electricity and Gas Market Liberalisation.* Amsterdam: EFET.

Ehlermann, C.-D. & Laudati, L. L., 1998. Introduction. In: C.-E. Ehlermann & L. L. Laudati, ed. *European Competition Law Annual 1997: Objectives of Competition Policy.* Oxford: Hart Publishing, pp. vii–xviii.

Ehlers, E., 2010. *Electricity and gas supply network unbundling in Germany, Great Britain and The Netherlands and the law of the European Union.* Intersentia: Portland.

ENISA, 2011. *Desktop Research on Public Private Partnership.* Athens: ENISA.

Erbach, G., 2019. *Common rules for the internal electricity market.* Brussels: European Parliamentary Research Service.

ERG, 2009. *Transition from Sector Specific Regulation to Competition Law.* Brussels: ERG.

ESTEP, 2013. *State-Owned Enterprises in the European Union: ensuring level playing field.* Brussels: ESTEP.

Euracoal, 2011. *Coal Industry across Europe.* Brussels: European Association for Coal and Lignite.

Euracoal, 2013. *Coal Industry across Europe.* Brussels: European Association for Coal and Lignite.

Euracoal, 2017. *Coal Industry across Europe.* Brussels: European Association for Coal and Lignite.

EUREL, 2013. *Electrical Power Vision 2040 for Europe.* Brussels: EUREL General Secretariat.

European Commission, 1997. *Commission Notice on the definition of relevant market for the purposes of Community competition.* Brussels: EC.

European Commission, 1999. *White Paper on Modernisation of the Rules Implementing Articles 85 and 86 of the EC Treaty.* Brussels: EC.

European Commission, 2001. *Commission Staff Working Paper: First benchmarking report on the implementation of the internal electricity and gas market.* Brussels: EC.

European Commission, 2004. *Green Paper on Public Private Partnerships.* Brussels: EC.

European Commission, 2004. *Green Paper on public-private partnerships and Community law on public contracts and concessions.* Brussels: EC.

European Commission, 2004. *Guidelines on the application of Article 81(3) of the Treaty.* Brussels: EC.

European Commission, 2004. *Guidelines on the effect on trade concept contained in Articles 81 and 82 of the Treaty.* Brussels: EC.

European Commission, 2005. *DG Competition discussion paper on the application of Article 82 of the Treaty to exclusionary abuses.* Brussels: EC.

European Commission, 2006. *Annex to the Green Paper: A European Strategy for Sustainable, Competitive and Secure Energy.* Brussels: EC.

European Commission, 2006. *Competition: Commission has carried out inspections in the EU gas sector in five Member States.* (Online) Available at: http://europa.eu/rapid/press-release_MEMO-06-205_en.htm (accessed 1 June 2019).

European Commission, 2007. *Accompanying the legislative package on the internal market for electricity and gas – Impact Assessment.* Brussels: EC.

European Commission, 2007. *Commission Report on the Application of Council Regulation (EC) No 1407/2002 on State Aid to the Coal Industry, COM(2007) 253 final.* Brussels: EC.

European Commission, 2007. *Sustainable power generation from fossil fuels: aiming for near-zero emissions from coal after 2020.* Brussels: EC.

European Commission, 2009. *Antitrust: Commission fines E.ON and GDF Suez €553 million each for market-sharing in French and German gas markets.* (Online) Available at: http://europa.eu/rapid/press-release_IP-09-1099_en.htm?locale=fr (accessed 1 June 2019).

European Commission, 2010. *Europe 2020 – A strategy for smart, sustainable and inclusive growth.* Brussels: EU.

European Commission, 2010. *Frequently Asked Questions – Coal Regulation.* (Online) Available at: http://europa.eu/rapid/press-release_MEMO-10-348_en.htm (accessed 1 June 2019).

European Commission, 2010. *The Unbundling Regime.* Brussels: EC.

European Commission, 2014. *European energy security strategy.* Brussels: EU.

European Commission, 2014. *Quarterly Report on European Gas Markets.* Brussels: EU.

European Commission, 2015. *Antitrust: Commission sends Statement of Objections to Gazprom for alleged abuse of dominance on Central and Eastern European gas supply markets.* (Online) Available at: http://europa.eu/rapid/press-release_IP-15-4828_en.htm (accessed 1 June 2019).

European Commission, 2015. *Renewable Energy Package: New Renewable Energy Directive and bioenergy sustainability policy for 2030.* Brussels: EU.

European Commission, 2015. *Renewable energy progress report.* Brussels: EU.

European Commission, 2016. *State aid: Commission opens in-depth investigation into support for Romanian petrochemical company Oltchim.* (Online) Available at: http://europa.eu/rapid/press-release_IP-16-1321_en.htm (accessed 1 June 2019).

European Commission, 2016. *State-Owned Enterprises in the EU: Lessons Learnt and Ways Forward in a Post-Crisis Context.* Brussels: EU.

Eurostat, 2015. *Electricity production and supply statistics.* (Online) Available at: https://ec.europa.eu/eurostat/statistics-explained/ (accessed 1 June 2019).

Eurostat, 2016. *Energy saving statistics.* (Online) Available at: https://ec.europa.eu/eurostat/statistics-explained/ (accessed 1 June 2019).

Evrard, S. J., 2004. Essential Facilities in the European Union: Bronner and Beyond. *Columbia Journal of European Law*, 10(3), pp. 491–526.

Eydeland, A. & Wolyniec, K., 2003. *Energy and Power Risk Management: New Developments in Modeling, Pricing, and Hedging.* New Jersey: Wiley Finance.

Ezrachi, A., 2018. *EU Competition Law: an analytical guide to the leading cases.* 6th ed. Oxford: Hart Publishing.

Faella, G. & Pardolesi, R., 2010. Squeezing Price Squeeze under EC Antitrust Law. *European Competition Journal*, 6(1), pp. 255–284.

Faull, J., Kjolbye, L., Leupold, H. & Nikpay, A., 2014. Article 101. In: J. Faull & A. Nikpay, eds. *The EU Law of Competition.* Oxford: Oxford University Press, pp. 183–328.

Fodorova, K., Lovasova, E. & Sabová, Z., 2014. Interplay between Competition Law and Sector-Specific Regulation – What Is the Role of the Ne Bis in Idem Principle. *Common Law Review*, 13, pp. 46–43.

Friedmann, W., 1954. *The Public Corporation: A comparative symposium.* London: Stevens and Sons.

Fumagalli, C., Motta, M. & Calcagno, C., 2018. *Exclusionary Practices: The Economics of Monopolisation and Abuse of Dominance.* Cambridge: Cambridge University Press.

Fusaro, P. C., 1998. *Energy Risk Management: Hedging Strategies and Instruments for the International Energy Markets.* New York: McGraw-Hill.

Gao, A. M.-Z., 2009. The Third European Energy Liberalization Package: Does Functional and Legal Unbundling in the Gas Storage Sector Go Too Far? *Competition and Regulation in Network Industries*, 10(1), pp. 17–44.

Gao, A. M.-Z., 2010. *Regulating Gas Liberalization. A Comparative Study on Unbundling and Open Access Regimes in the US, Europe, Japan.* Austin: Wolters Kluwer.

Gauer, C., Dalheimer, D., Kjolbye, L. & Smijter, E. D., 2003. Regulation 1/2003: A modernised application of EC competition rules. *Competition Policy Newsletter*, 10(1), pp. 3–8.

Gauer, C. & Kjolbye, L., 2014. Energy. In: J. Faull & A. Nikpay, eds. *The EU Law of Competition.* Oxford: Oxford University Press, pp. 1581–1646.

Geradin, D., 2011. *Refusal to Supply and Margin Squeeze: A Discussion of Why the "Telefonica Exceptions" are Wrong.* Tilburg: TILEC.

Geradin, D., Layne-Farrar, A. & Petit, N., 2012. *EU Competition Law and Economics.* Oxford: Oxford University Press.

Geradin, D. & O'Donoghue, R., 2005. *The Concurrent Application of Competition Law and Regulation: the Case of Margin Squeeze Abuses in the Telecommunications Sector.* Bruges: The Global Competition Law Centre.

Gillingham, J., 1991. *Coal, steel, and the rebirth of Europe, 1945–1955.* Cambridge: Cambridge University Press.

Girdis, D., 2001. *Power and Gas Regulation Issues and International Experience.* Washington, DC: The World Bank.

Gómez, L. & Murray, G., 2015. *Competition Regime: State Measures and Public Bodies under EC Law.* (Online) Available at: http://us.practicallaw.com/5-107-4648?q=Private (accessed 1 June 2019).

Goyder, D., Goyder, J. & Albors-Llorens, A., 2009. *Goyder's EC competition law.* 5th ed. Oxford: Oxford University Press.

Graells, A. S., 2015. *Public Procurement and the EU Competition Rules.* 2nd ed. Oxford: Hart Publishing.

Granville, L. & Irvine, H., 2015. The impact of regulation on competition in telecommunications and piped gas. *The African Journal of Information and Communication,* 2015(14), pp. 1–14.

Gräper, F., Schoser, C. & Papsch, J., 2016. Third Party Access. In: C. Jones, ed. *EU Energy Law: The Internal Energy Market.* Leuven: Claeys & Casteels, pp. 27–89.

Groot, K., 2013. *European Power Utilities under Pressure.* The Hague: Clingendael International Energy Programme (CIEP).

Guayo, I. d., Kühne, G. & Roggenkamp, M. M., 2010. Ownership Unbundling and Property Rights in the EU Energy Sector. In: A. McHarg, B. Barton, A. Bradbrook & L. Godden, eds. *Property and the Law in Energy and Natural Resources.* Oxford: Oxford University Press, pp. 326–360.

Haghighi, S. S., 2007. *Energy Security: The external legal relations of the European Union with major oil- and gas-supplying countries.* Oxford: Hart Publishing.

Hahn, H. J., 1958. Euratom: The Conception of an International Personality. *Harvard Law Review,* 71(6), pp. 1001–1056.

Hall, D., 2013. *Re-municipalising municipal services in Europe.* London: Public Services International Research Unit.

Hancher, L. & Klasse, M., 2018. Aid to Nuclear and Coal. In: L. Hancher, A. d. Hauteclocque & F. M. Salerno, eds. *State Aid and the Energy Sector.* Oxford: Hart Publishing, pp. 201–235.

Hancher, L. & Vlam, R. D., 2004. Mergers in the Electricity Sector – Relevant Markets and Related Issues. In: M. M. Roggenkamp & U. Hammer, eds. *European Energy Law Report I.* Antwerp: Intersentia, pp. 29–73.

Hauteclocque, A. d., 2009. Legal Uncertainty and Competition Policy in European Deregulated Electricity Markets: the Case of Long-term Exclusive Supply Contracts. *World Competition,* 32(1), pp. 91–112.

Hauteclocque, A. d., 2016. Article 102 TFEU – Abuse of a dominant position. In: C. Jones, ed. *EU Competition Law and Energy Markets.* Deventer: Claeys & Casteels, pp. 283–375.

Hauteclocque, A. d. & Hancher, L., 2011. The Svenska Kraftnät case: introduction of bidding zones in Sweden. *Network Industries Quarterly,* 13(1), pp. 20–22.

Hauteclocque, A. d. & Talus, K., 2011. *Capacity to Compete: Recent Trends in Access Regimes in Electricity and Natural Gas Networks.* Florence: Robert Schuman Centre for Advanced Studies.

Heimler, A., 2010. Is a Margin Squeeze an Antitrust or a Regulatory Violation? *Journal of Competition Law & Economics,* 6(4), pp. 879–891.

Hellwig, M., 2008. *Competition Policy and Sector-Specific Regulation for Network Industries.* Bonn: Max Planck Institute for Research on Collective Goods.

Hey, C., 2005. EU Environmental Policies: A Short History of the Policy Strategies. In: S. Scheuer, ed. *EU Environmental Policy Handbook.* Utrecht: International Books, pp. 15–30.

Höffler, F. & Kranz, S., 2011. Legal unbundling can be a golden mean between vertical integration and ownership separation. *International Journal of Industrial Organization,* 29(5), pp. 576–588.

Hofmann, M., 2013. *Regulierung und Wettbewerb: Koordinationsmechanismen im europäischen Energiesektor.* Zürich: Schulthess.

Holland, J. & Luoma, A., 2010. Decision-Making Powers and Institutional Design in Competition Cases: The Application of Competition Rules by Sectoral Regulators in the United Kingdom. *Competition Policy International,* 10(1), pp. 92–109.

Horstmann, N., 2011. Agency for the Cooperation of Energy Regulators: Its Particularities and Its Role in Enhancing the Cooperation of National Energy Regulators. In: M. M. Roggenkamp & U. Hammer, eds. *European Energy Law Report VIII.* Antwerp: Intersentia, pp. 43–58.

Hospers, G.-J. & Groenendijk, N. S., 2003. The European Coal and Steel Community. In: A. Prinz, A. E. Steenge & A. Vogel, eds. *Grenzüberschreitende Wirtschafts- und Finanzpolitik.* Münster: Lit, pp. 87–109.

Hossenfelder, S. & Lutz, M., 2003. Die neue Durchführungsverordnung zu den Artikeln 81 und 82 EG-Vertrag. *Wirtschaft und Wettbewerb,* 2003/2, pp. 118–129.

Hulst, R. & Montfort, A. v., 2007. *Inter-Municipal Cooperation in Europe.* Dordrecht: Springer.

Hyde-Smith, P., 1983. Legal Regulation of Pricing and Competition in the European Coal and Steel Community. *Journal of Energy & Natural Resources Law*, 1(3), pp. 176–185.

ICF Consultancy Services & DIW Berlin, 2016. *The economic impact of enforcement of competition policies on the functioning of EU energy markets.* Luxembourg: European Commission.

ICN, 2004. *Antitrust Enforcement in Regulated Sectors.* Seoul: International Competition Network.

IEA, 2014. *Energy Supply Security: The Emergency Response of IEA Countries.* Paris: IEA Publications.

IEA, 2015. *Medium Term Coal Market Report.* Paris: OECD/IEA.

IEA, 2015. *Medium Term Gas Market Report.* Paris: OECD/IEA.

IEA, 2015. *Oil Medium-Term Market Report.* Paris: OECD/IEA.

IEA, 2015. *World Energy Outlook: Factsheet Global energy trends to 2040.* Paris: OECD/IEA.

IEA, 2016. *Coal Information.* Paris: OECD/IEA.

IEA, 2016. *Electricity information.* Paris: OECD/IEA.

IEA, 2016. *Energy Policies of IEA Countries: Czech Republic.* Paris: OECD/IEA.

IEA, 2016. *Energy Policies of IEA Countries: Poland.* Paris: OECD/IEA.

IEA, 2016. *Key World Energy Statistics.* Paris: OECD/IEA.

IEA, 2016. *Medium Term Coal Market Report.* Paris: OECD/IEA.

IEA, 2016. *Oil Information.* Paris: OECD/IEA.

IEA, 2016. *Oil Market Report.* (Online) Available at: https://www.iea.org/oilmarketreport/omrpublic/ (accessed 1 June 2019).

Ilzkovitz, F., Dierx, A., Kovacs, V. & Sousa, N., 2007. *Steps towards a deeper economic integration: the Internal Market in the 21st century – A contribution to the Single Market Review.* Brussels: European Commission.

Immenga, U., 1993. The Development of European Energy Policy: From the ECSC Treaty to the Internal Market. In: E. J. Mestmäcker, ed. *Natural Gas in the Internal Market: a review of energy policy.* London: Graham & Trotman, pp. 47–58.

Immenga, U. & Mestmäcker, E.-J., 2012. *EU-Wettbewerbsrecht.* 5th ed. München: Beck.

InterEnerStat, 2008. *Harmonisation of Definitions of Energy Products and Flows.* Paris: IEA.

Jaag, C. & Trinkner, U., 2009. *A General Framework for Regulation and Liberalization in Network Industries.* Zurich: Swiss Economics.

Jakovac, P., 2012. Electricity Directives and Evolution of the EU Internal Electricity Market. *Economic Thought and Practice*, 1(11), pp. 315–338.

Joekes, S. & Evans, P., 2008. *Competition and Development.* Ottawa: International Development Research Centre.

Johnston, A., 1999. Maintaining the Balance of Power: Liberalisation, Reciprocity and Electricity in the European Community. *Journal of Energy & Natural Resources Law*, 17(2), pp. 121–150.

Johnston, A. & Block, G., 2012. *EU Energy Law.* Oxford: Oxford University Press.

Jones, A. & Sufrin, B., 2016. *EU Competition Law: Text, cases, and materials.* 6th ed. Oxford: Oxford University Press.

Jones, C., 2016. Introduction. In: C. Jones, ed. *EU Energy Law: The Internal Energy Market.* Deventer: Claeys & Casteels, pp. 1–14.

Jones, D. & Gutmann, K., 2015. *End of an Era: Why Every European Country Needs Coal Phase-out Plan.* London: Greenpeace.

Jordana, J. & Levi-Faur, D., 2004. The politics of regulation in the age of governance. In: J. Jordana & D. Levi-Faur, eds. *The Politics of Regulation: Institutions and Regulatory Reforms for the Age of Governance.* Cheltenham: Edward Elgar, pp. 1–31.

Jungjohann, A. & Morris, C., 2014. *The German Coal Conundrum: The status of coal power in Germany's energy transition.* Washington, DC: Heinrich Böll Stiftung.

Kahl, W., 2009. Die Kompetenzen der EU in der Energiepolitik nach Lissabon. *Europarecht*, 5(44), pp. 601–621.

Kahn, A. E., 1998. *The Economics of Regulation: Principles and Institutions.* Massachusetts: MIT Press.

Kanai, M., 2010. *Putting a Price on Energy: International Coal Pricing.* Brussels: Energy Charter Secretariat.

Kavalov, B. & Peteves, S. D., 2007. *The Future of Coal.* Petten: DG JRC Institute for Energy.

Kekelekis, M., 2006. *The EC Merger Control Regulation – Rights of Defence: A critical analysis of DG COMP practice and Community Courts' jurisprudence.* Alphen aan den Rijn: Kluwer Law International.

Khemai, S. & Waverman, L., 1997. Strategic Alliances: A threat to competition? In: *Competition Policy in the Global Economy: Modalities for Co-operation.* London: Routledge, pp. 121–157.

Kikeri, S., Nellis, J. & Shirley, M., 1992. *Privatization: The lessons of experience.* Washington DC: The World Bank.

Kilian, L., 2015. Energy Price Shocks. In: S. N. Durlauf & L. E. Blume, eds. *The New Palgrave Dictionary of Economics.* Basingstoke: Palgrave Macmillan.

Kirchner, C., 2004. Competition policy vs. regulation: administration vs. judiciary. In: M. Neumann & J. Weigand, eds. *The International Handbook of Competition.* 1st ed. Cheltenham: Edward Elgar, pp. 306–321.

Kirchner, C., 2006. Regulating towards what? The concepts of competition in sector-specific regulation, the likelihood of their realisation and of their sustainability, and their relationship to rendering public infrastructure services. In: H. Ullrich, ed. *The Evolution of European Competition Law: Whose regulation, which competition?* Cheltenham: Edward Elgar, pp. 241–256.

Kirschen, D. & Strbac, G., 2005. *Fundamentals of Power System Economics.* Chichester: Wiley & Sons.

Kishimoto, S., Petitjean, O. & Steinfort, L., 2017. *Reclaiming Public Services: How cities and citizens are turning back privatisation,* Amsterdam: Transnational Institute.

Kjolbye, L., 2016. Horizontal Agreements. In: C. Jones, ed. *EU Competition Law and Energy Markets.* Leuven: Claeys & Casteels, pp. 157–220.

Klein, M., 1996. *Competition in Network Industries.* Washington, DC: The World Bank.

Kloc-Evison, K. & Koska, D., 2012. Competition Law Mechanism as Additional Tool of the III Energy Package Implementation. In: R. Zajdler, ed. *EU Energy Law: Constraints with the Implementation of the Third Liberalisation Package.* Newcastle: Cambridge Scholars, pp. 27–53.

Koch, N., 1959. Das Verhältnis der Kartellvorschriften des EWG-Vertrages zum Gesetz gegen Wettbewerbsbeschränkungen. *Betriebs-Berater,* 1959, pp. 241–248.

Koch, O. & Gauer, C., 2011. Energy Liberalisation and Competition Law – the Commission's Recent Antitrust Case Practice. In: D. Buschle, S. Hirsbrunner & C. Kaddous, eds. *European Energy Law.* Bâle: Helbing Lichtenhahn, pp. 209–249.

Koch, O., Nagy, K., Pucinskaite-Kubik, I. & Tretton, W., 2009. The RWE gas foreclosure case: Another energy network divestiture to address foreclosure concerns. *Competition Policy Newsletter,* 16(2), pp. 32–34.

Kohl, W. L., 1978. Energy Policy in the Communities. *The Annals of the American Academy of Political and Social Science,* 440(1), pp. 111–121.

Kotlowski, A., 2007. Third-party Access Rights in the Energy Sector: A Competition Law Perspective. *Utilities Law Review,* 16(3), pp. 101–109.

Kratz, B. & Kreuzer, F., 2011. Ownership Unbundling – A Swiss Perspective. In: D. Buschle, S. Hirsbrunner & C. Kaddous, eds. *European Energy Law.* Bâle: Helbing Lichtenhahn, pp. 51–77.

Kroes, N., 2005. *European Competition Policy – Delivering Better Markets and Better Choices.* (Online) Available at: http://europa.eu/rapid/press-release_SPEECH-05-512_en.htm (accessed 1 June 2019).

Kroes, N., 2006. *Towards an Efficient and Integrated European Energy – First Findings and Next Steps.* Brussels, European Commission Conference.

Kroes, N., 2007. Improving Competition in European Energy Markets through Effective Unbundling. *Fordham International Law Journal,* 35(1), pp. 1387–1441.

Kroes, N., 2008. *Consumers at the heart of EU Competition Policy.* (Online) Available at: http://europa.eu/rapid/press-release_SPEECH-08-212_en.htm?locale=en (accessed 1 June 2019).

Kühne, G., 1994. GATT and EC Subsidies and State Aids: The Coal Sector. *Journal of Energy & Natural Resources Law*, 12(1), pp. 83–94.

Laffont, J. J. & Tirole, J., 2000. *Competition in Telecommunications.* Cambridge: MIT Press.

Landes, V., 2016. Jurisdiction: When does a merger fall under the Merger Regulation? In: C. Jones, ed. *EU Competition Law and Energy Markets.* Leuven: Claeys & Casteels, pp. 437–473.

Lang, J. T., 2007. *The Use of Competition Law Powers for Regulatory Purposes.* Oxford, Regulatory Policy Institute.

Liesen, R., 1999. Transit under the 1994 Energy Charter Treaty. *Journal of Energy & Natural Resources Law*, 17(1), pp. 56–73.

Lindroos, M., Schichel, D. & Svane, L. P., 2002. Liberalisation of European Gas Markets – Commission settles GFU. *Competition Policy Newsletter*, 9(3), pp. 50–52.

Littlechild, S. C., 1983. *Regulation of British Telecommunications' Profitability.* London: Department of Industry.

Liu, H., 2010. *Liner Conferences in Competition Law: A Comparative Analysis of European and Chinese Law.* Berlin: Springer-Verlag.

Lohmann, H., 2009. *The German Gas Market post 2005: Development of Real Competition.* Oxford: Oxford Institute for Energy Studies.

London Economics, 1997. *The Single Market Review, Sub-series V: Impact on Competition and Scale Effects. Vol. 3: Competition Issues.* London: Earthscan.

Loring, A., 1979. *OPEC Oil.* Cambridge Mass: Oelgeschlager Gunn & Hain.

Lowe, P., 2003. *Applying EU Competition Law to Newly Liberalised Energy Markets.* Brussels, Mentor Group – Forum for EU-US Legal-Economic Affairs.

Lucas, N., 1977. *Energy and the European Communities.* London: Europa Publications.

Lyons, P. K., 1998. *What is energy Policy? EC Inform – EU Energy Policies towards the 21st Century.* Surrey: EC Inform.

Mabry, R. H. & Ulbrich, H. H., 1989. *Introduction to Economic Principles.* New York: McGraw-Hill.

Maier-Rigaud, F., Manca, F. & Koppenfels, U. v., 2011. Strategic underinvestment and gas network foreclosure – the ENI case. *Competition Policy Newsletter*, 18(1), pp. 18–23.

Majone, G., 2003. *Deregulation, Liberalization and Regulatory Reform in the European Union.* Mexico City, Public Administration and Development Management UN.

Mallard, G., 2008. Can the Euratom Treaty Inspire the Middle East? The Political Promises of Regional Nuclear Communities. *The Nonproliferation Review*, 15(3), pp. 459–477.

Malmendier, B. & Schendel, J., 2006. Unbundling Germany's Energy Networks. *Journal of Energy & Natural Resources Law*, 24(3), pp. 362–383.

Mankabady, S., 1990. *Energy Law*. London: Euromoney Books.

Mäntysaari, P., 2015. *EU Electricity Trade Law: The Legal Tools of Electricity Producers in the Internal Electricity Market*. Cham: Springer International Publishing.

Martin, S. & El-Agraa, A. M., 2004. Energy Policy and Energy Markets. In: A. M. El-Agraa, ed. *The European Union Economics and Policies*. New Jersey: Prentice Hall, pp. 270–288.

Martin, S. & El-Agraa, A. M., 2011. Energy policy and energy markets. In: A. M. El-Agraa, ed. *The European Union Economics and Policies*. Cambridge: Cambridge University Press, pp. 257–288.

Mason, H. L., 1955. *The European Coal and Steel Community – Experiment in Supranationalism*. The Hague: Martinus Nijhoff.

Mateus, A. M., 2010. Competition and Development: Towards an Institutional Foundation for Competition Enforcement. *World Competition: Law and Economics Review*, 33(2), pp. 275–299.

Mathieu, G., 1970. The history of the ECSC: good times and bad. *Le Monde*, 9 May, p. 874.

Mathijsen, P., 1961. Problems Connected with the Creation of Euratom. *Law and Contemporary Problems*, 26(3), pp. 438–453.

Mathijsen, P., 1966. Some Legal Aspects of Euratom. *Common Market Law Review*, 3(3), pp. 326–343.

Matláry, J. H., 1997. *Energy Policy in the European Union*. Basingstoke: Macmillan Press.

Maugeri, L., 2006. *The Age of Oil: The Mythology, History, and Future of the World's Most Controversial Resource*. Westport: Prager.

Meeus, L., Purchala, K. & Belmans, R., 2005. Development of the Internal Electricity Market in Europe. *The Electricity Journal*, 18(6), pp. 25–35.

Merlino, P. & Faella, G., 2013. Strategic Underinvestment as an Abuse of Dominance under EU Competition Rules. *World Competition*, 36(4), pp. 513–539.

Mestmäcker, E. J., 1993. Energy Policy for Natural Gas in the Internal Market. In: E. J. Mestmäcker, ed. *Natural Gas in the Internal Market: a review of energy policy*. London: Graham & Trotman, pp. 1–18.

Mete, G., 2015. Analysis of the Term 'Transit' in Cross-Border Energy Transport: A Comparative Study of Regulatory Frameworks in the Eurasian Context. In: D. Buschle & K. Talus, eds. *The Energy Community: A new energy governance system*. Cambridge: Intersentia, pp. 591–619.

Midttun, A., 2001. Deregulation and Reconfiguration of Infrastructure Industry: Theoretical Reflections on Empirical Patterns from Nordic Markets. *Journal of Network Industries*, 2(1), pp. 25–68.

Mills, S. J., 2010. *Prospects for coal, CCTs and CCS in the European Union.* Paris: IEA.

Mitchell, R. A., 1999. The Electricity Directive of the European Union: What Can the Member States Learn from the Experiences of Privatized England and Wales? *American University International Law Review*, 14(3), pp. 761–803.

Moisejevas, R. & Novosad, A., 2013. Some Thoughts Concerning the Main Goals of Competition Law. *Jurisprudencija*, 20(2), pp. 627–642.

Molle, W., 1991. *The Economics of European Integration: Theory, practice, policy.* Aldershot: Dartmouth.

Monti, G., 1996. Oligopoly: Conspiracy? Joint Monopoly?, Or Enforceable Competition? *World Competition*, 19(3), pp. 59–102.

Monti, G., 2002. Article 81 and Public Policy. *Common Market Law Review*, 39(5), pp. 1057–1099.

Monti, G., 2017. Article 102: sources of interpretation. In: P. L. Parcu, G. Monti & M. Botta, eds. *Abuse of Dominance in EU Competition Law: Emerging Trends.* Cheltenham: Edward Elgar, pp. 34–52.

Monti, M., 2003. *Competition and Regulation in the New Framework.* Brussels, European Commission.

Möschel, W., 2002. The Relationship between Competition Authorities and Sector-Specific Regulators. *European Business Organization Law Review*, 3(4), pp. 823–831.

Motta, M., 2009. *Competition Policy: Theory and Practice.* Cambridge: Cambridge University Press.

Mukhigulishvili, G. & Margvelashvili, M., 2012. *Competition and Monopoly in Internal Energy Markets.* Tblisi: World Experience for Georgia.

Mulder, M., Shestalova, V. & Lijesen, M., 2005. *Vertical Separation of the Energy-Distribution Industry: An Assessment of Several Options for Unbundling.* The Hague: CPB Netherlands Bureau for Economic Policy Analysis.

Murphy, A., 2014. *Juggling Geopolitics and Competition Law – an Analysis of the Role Geopolitics Plays in the Application of Competition Law in Upstream Gas Contracts.* Natolin: College of Europe.

Nanes, A., 1958. The Evolution of Euratom. *International Journal*, 13(1), pp. 12–20.

Neresian, R. L., 2016. *Energy Economics: Markets, History and Policy.* London: Routledge.

Newbery, D. M., 1999. *Privatization Restructuring and Regulation of Network Utilities.* Cambridge: MIT Press.

Newbery, D. M., 2002. Regulating Unbundled Network Utilities. *The Economic and Social Review*, 33(1), pp. 23–41.

Newbery, D. M. G., 2004. *Privatising Network Industries.* Munich: CESifo (Center for Economic Studies and Ifo Institute).

Nieburg, H. L., 1963. EURATOM: A Study in Coalition Politics. *World Politics*, 15(4), pp. 597–622.

Noguera, J., 2017. The Seven Sisters versus OPEC: Solving the mystery of the petroleum market structure. *Energy Economics*, 64(4), pp. 298–305.

Oberthür, S. & Pallemaerts, M., 2010. The EU's External and Internal Climate Policies: an Historical Overview. In: S. Oberthür & M. Pallemaerts, eds. *The New Climate Policies of the European Union: Internal Legislation and Climate Diplomacy.* Brussels: VUBPRESS, pp. 27–64.

O'Donoghue, R., 2008. Regulating the Regulated: Deutsche Telekom v. European Commission. *Global Competition Policy*, 1 May, pp. 1–24.

O'Donoghue, R. & Padilla, J., 2013. *The Law and Economics of Article 102 TFEU.* 2nd ed. Oxford: Hart Publishing.

Odudu, O., 2002. A new economic approach to Article 81(1)? *European Law Review*, 27(1), pp. 100–105.

Odudu, O., 2006. *The Boundaries of EC Competition Law.* Oxford: Oxford University Press.

OECD, 1996. *The Essential Facilities Concept.* Paris: OECD.

OECD, 1998. *Relationship between Regulators and Competition.* Paris: OECD.

OECD, 2000. *Privatisation, Competition and Regulation.* Paris: OECD.

OECD, 2001. *Restructuring Public Utilities for Competition.* Paris: OECD.

OECD, 2005. *Guiding Principles for Regulatory Quality and Performance.* Paris: OECD.

OECD, 2006. *OECD Economic Surveys: Germany.* Paris: OECD.

OECD, 2009. *OECD Guidelines for Fighting Bid Rigging in Public Procurement.* Paris: OECD.

OECD, 2010. *Regulatory Policy and the Road to Sustainable Growth.* Paris: OECD.

OECD, 2011. *Emission Permits and Competition.* Paris: OECD.

OECD, 2012. *Recommendation of the Council on Principles for Public Governance of Public-Private Partnerships.* Paris: OECD.

OECD, 2014. *Economic, Environmental and Social Statistics.* Paris: OECD.

OECD, 2015. *OECD Guidelines on Corporate Governance of State-Owned Enterprises.* Paris: OECD.

Ogus, A., 2004. *Regulation: Legal Form and Economic Theory.* Oxford: Hart Publishing.

Ordover, J. A., Pittman, R. W. & Clyde, P., 1994. Competition policy for natural monopolies in a developing market economy. *Economics of Transition*, 2(3), pp. 317–343.

Pace, L. F. & Seidel, K., 2013. The Drafting and the Role of Regulation 17: A Hard-Fought Compromise. In: K. K. Patel & H. Schweitzer, eds. *The Historical Foundations of EU Competition Law.* Oxford: Oxford University Press, pp. 54–89.

Palasthy, A., 2002. Third Party Access in the Electricity Sector: EC Competition Law and Sector-Specific Regulation. *Journal of Energy & Natural Resources Law,* 20(1), pp. 1–26.

Papadopoulos, A. S., 2010. *The International Dimension of EU Competition Law and Policy.* Cambridge: Cambridge University Press.

Park, P., 2013. *International Law for Energy and the Environment.* 2nd ed. Boca Raton: CRC Press.

Parker, C. & Braithwaite, J., 2005. Regulation. In: M. Tushnet & P. Cane, eds. *The Oxford Handbook of Legal Studies.* Oxford: Oxford University Press, pp. 119–146.

Parret, L., 2009. *Do we (still) know what we are protecting? The discussion on the objectives of competition law from different perspectives.* Tilburg: TILEC.

Parret, L., 2010. Shouldn't We Know What We Are Protecting? Yes We Should! A Plea for a Solid and Comprehensive Debate About the Objectives of EU Competition Law and Policy. *European Competition Journal,* 6(2), pp. 339–376.

Peeperkorn, L. & Verouden, V., 2014. The Economics of Competition. In: J. Faul & A. Nikpay, eds. *The EU Law of Competition.* New York: Oxford University Press, pp. 3–90.

Peltzman, S., 1989. The Economic Theory of Regulation after a Decade of Deregulation. *Brookings Papers on Economic Activity,* 1989, pp. 1–41.

Penttinen, S.-L., 2014. The role of the Court of Justice of the European Union in the energy market liberalization. In: K. Talus, ed. *Research Handbook on International Energy Law.* Cheltenham: Edward Elgar, pp. 241–275.

Pepe, L. S. d., 2014. European Union climate law and practice at the end of the Kyoto era: unilateralism, extraterritoriality and the future of global climate change governance. In: *Global Environmental Law at a Crossroads.* Cheltenham: Edward Elgar, pp. 279–294.

Pielow, J.-C., Brunekreeft, G. & Ehlers, E., 2009. Legal and Economic Aspects of Ownership Unbundling in the EU. *Journal of World Energy Law & Business,* 2(2), pp. 96–116.

Pielow, J.-C. & Ehlers, E., 2008. Ownership Unbundling and Constitutional Conflict: A Typical German Debate? *European Review of Energy Markets,* 2(3), pp. 55–88.

Pielow, J.-C. & Lewendel, B. J., 2011. The EU Energy Policy after the Lisbon Treaty. In: A. Dorsman, W. Westerman, M. B. Karan & Ö. Arslan, eds. *Financial Aspects in Energy: A European Perspective.* Berlin: Springer, pp. 147–167.

Pielow, J.-C. & Lewendel, B. J., 2012. Beyond 'Lisbon': EU Competences in the Field of Energy Policy. In: K. Talus & B. Delvaux, eds. *EU Energy Law and Policy Issues.* Cambridge: Intersentia, pp. 261–300.

Piergiovanni, M., 2009. Competition and regulation in the energy sector in Europe in the post-sector inquiry era. *Competition Law International*, 1(7), pp. 3–9.

Pisarkiewicz, A. R., 2018. *Margin Squeeze in the Electronic Communications Sector.* Alphen aan den Rijn: Wolter Kluwer.

Poelmans, E., 2012. Changes in the Structure of Coal and Steel Industries under the ECSC (1952–1967): Was West Germany Kept 'Small'? *Essays in economic and business history: the journal of the economic and business historical society*, 30(1), pp. 5–30.

Pollitt, M. G., 2007. Vertical Unbundling in the EU Electricity Sector. *Intereconomics*, 42(6), pp. 292–296.

Posner, R. A., 1999. *Natural Monopoly and Its Regulation.* Washington: Cato Institute.

Praduroux, S. & Talus, K., 2008. The Third Legislative Package and Ownership Unbundling in the Light of the European Fundamental Rights Discourse. *Competition and Regulation in Network Industries*, 9(1), pp. 3–29.

Proedrou, F., 2012. *EU Energy Security in the Gas Sector Evolving Dynamics, Policy Dilemmas and Prospects.* Farnham: Ashgate.

Prosser, T., 2005. *The Limits of Competition Law: Markets and Public Services.* Oxford: Oxford University Press.

Quigley, C., 2009. *European State Aid Law and Policy.* 2nd ed. Portland: Hart Publishing.

Quigley, C., 2015. *European State Aid Law and Policy.* 3rd ed. Portland: Hart Publishing.

Raalte, E. v., 1952. The Treaty Constituting the European Coal and Steel Community. *The International and Comparative Law Quarterly*, 1(1), pp. 73–85.

Rakova, E., 2008. *Economic Aspects of the Energy Sector in CIS Countries.* Warsaw: Centre for Social and Economic Research.

Ratliff, J. & Grasso, R., 2012. *Unilateral conduct in the energy sector: An overview of EU and national case law.* Brussels: E-competitions.

Ratliff, J. & Grasso, R., 2014. EPEX Spot, NPS, and OPCOM: the European Commission Fines Three Power Exchanges for Breach of EU Competition Law. *Journal of European Competition Law & Practice*, 5(6), pp. 371–372.

Ratner, M., Belkin, P., Nichol, J. & Woehrel, S., 2013. *Europe's Energy Security: Options and Challenges to Natural Gas Supply Diversification.* Washington, DC: Congressional Research Service.

Ray, G. F. & Dean, A., 1975. Possible Approaches to a Common European Energy Policy. In: F. A. M. A. V. Geusau, ed. *Energy in the European Communities.* Leyden: A. W. Sijthoff, pp. 166–182.

Renda, A. & Schrefler, L., 2006. *Public-Private Partnerships: National Experiences in the European Union.* Brussels: Centre for European Policy Studies.

Reuters, 2009. *Factbox – 18 countries affected by Russia-Ukraine gas row.* (Online) Available at: http://www.reuters.com/article/uk-russia-ukraine-gas-factbox-id UKTRE5062Q520090107?sp=true (accessed 1 June 2019).

Reynolds, P. A., 1952. The European Coal and Steel Community. *The Political Quarterly*, 23(3), pp. 282–292.

Ritter, L. & Braun, W. D., 2004. *European Competition Law: A practitioner's guide.* 3rd ed. The Hague: Kluwer Law International.

Robinson, D. et al., 2000. *The Impact of Higher Oil Prices on the Global Economy.* Washington, DC: International Monetary Fund.

Rodríguez, M. A. U., 2014. *Analysis of Distribution System Operator Unbundling.* Madrid: Universidad Pontificia Comillas.

Roggenkamp, M. M. & Boisseleau, F., 2005. The Liberalisation of the EU Electricity Market and the Role of Power Exchanges. In: M. M. Roggenkamp & F. Boisseleau, eds. *The Regulation of Power Exchanges in Europe.* Antwerp: Intersentia, pp. 1–31.

Roncaglia, A., 1985. *The International Oil Market: A Case of Trilateral Oligopoly.* London: Macmillan.

Rudianto, E., 2006. *Coal in Europe: what future? Prospects of the coal industry and impacts study of the Kyoto protocol.* Paris: École Nationale Supérieure des Mines de Paris.

Sadowska, M. M., 2011. Energy Liberalization in Antitrust Straitjacket: A Plant Too Far? *World Competition: Law and Economics Review*, pp. 449–476.

Sadowska, M. & Willems, B., 2012. *Market Integration and Economic Efficiency at Conflict? Commitments in the Swedish Interconnectors Case.* Tilburg: Tilburg University.

Sadowska, M. & Willems, B., 2012. *Power Markets Shaped by Antitrust.* Tilburg: Tilburg University.

Salter, J. R., 1994. Third Party Access to Gas and Electricity Transmission Systems in the Community: Third Party Access – Your Flexible Friend? In: D. S. M. Dougall & T. W. Wälde, eds. *European Community Energy Law.* London: Graham & Trotman, pp. 85–98.

Sandbergy, L. & Davies, L., 2016. The Relevant Geographic Market-Electricity. In: C. Jones, ed. *EU Competition Law and Energy Markets.* Leuven: Claeys & Casteels, pp. 43–104.

Schaub, A., 1997. *Competition Policy Objectives.* Oxford, Hart Publishing, pp. 9–10.

Schaub, A., 2000. Modernization of EC Competition Law: Reform of Regulation No. 17. *Fordham International Law Journal*, 23(3), pp. 752–777.

Schmitt, H. A., 1964. The European Coal and Steel Community: Operations of the First European Antitrust Law, 1952–1958. *The Business History Review*, 38(1), pp. 102–122.

Schnichels, D. & Valli, F., 2003. Vertical and horizontal restraints in the European gas sector: lessons learnt from the DONG/DUC case. *Competition Policy Newsletter*, 9(2), pp. 60–63.

Schülke, C., 2010. *The EU's Major Electricity and Gas Utilities since Market Liberalization.* Paris: IFRI.

Selznick, P., 1985. Focusing Organizational Research on Regulation. In: R. G. Noll, ed. *Regulatory Policy and the Social Sciences.* Berkeley: University of California Press, pp. 363–367.

Shapiro, S. A. & McGarity, T. O., 1991. Not So Paradoxical: The Rationale for Technology-Based Regulation. *Duke Law Journal*, 40(3), pp. 739–742.

Shively, B. & Ferrare, J., 2010. *Understanding Today's Electricity Business.* Laporte: Enerdynamics LLC.

Sidak, G. & Spulber, D. F., 1998. *Deregulatory Takings and the Regulatory Contract: The Competitive Transformation of Network Industries in the United States.* Cambridge: Cambridge University Press.

Slocock, B., 2002. The Market Economy Investor Principle. *Competition Policy Newsletter*, 9(2), pp. 23–26.

Smijter, E. D. & Sinclair, A., 2014. The Enforcement System under Regulation 1/2003. In: J. Faull & A. Nikpay, eds. *The EU Law of Competition.* Oxford: Oxford University Press, pp. 91–181.

Spanjer, A., 2009. Long-Term Contracts and Competition on European Gas Markets – Has the Commission Struck the Right Balance? *Competition and Regulation in Network Industries*, 10(2), pp. 189–204.

Stern, J. P., 2005. *The Future of Russian Gas and Gazprom.* Oxford: Oxford University Press.

Stigler, G. J., 1971. The Theory of Economic Regulation. *Bell Journal of Economics*, 2(1), pp. 3–21.

Stigler, G. J., 1975. *The Citizen and the State: Essays on Regulation.* Chicago: University of Chicago Press.

Stockmann, K., 2006. Comments on Regulating towards what? The concepts of competition in sectorspecific regulation, the likelihood of their realisation and of their sustainability, and their relationship to rendering public infrastructure services. In: H. Ullrich, ed. *The Evolution of European Competition Law: Whose regulation, which competition?* Cheltenham: Edward Elgar, pp. 256–263.

Stoft, S., 2002. *Power System Economics: Designing Markets for Electricity.* New Jersey: IEEE Press, Wiley-Interscience.

Stork, J., 1973. *Middle East Oil and the Energy Crisis: Part One.* Washington, DC: MERIP Reports.

Strange, S., 2009. *The Retreat of the State: The Diffusion of Power in the World Economy.* Cambridge: Cambridge University Press.

Stucke, M. E., 2012. What is competition? In: D. Zimmer, ed. *The Goals of Competition Law.* Cheltenham: Edward Elgar, pp. 27–53.

Stucke, M. E., 2013. Is competition always good? *Journal of Antitrust Enforcement*, 1(1), pp. 162–197.

Subiotto, R., Little, D. R. & Lepetska, R., 2016. The Application of Article 102 TFEU by the European Commission and the European Courts. *Journal of European Competition Law & Practice*, 7(4), pp. 288–296.

Sunstein, C. R., 1990. Remaking Regulation. *The American Prospect*, pp. 73–82.

Sunstein, C. R., 1991. Administrative Substance. *Duke Law Journal*, 40(3), pp. 607–646.

Talus, K., 2009. Public-private partnerships in energy – Termination of public service concessions and administrative acts in Europe. *Journal of World Energy Law & Business*, 2(1), pp. 43–67.

Talus, K., 2011. Long-term natural gas contracts and antitrust law in the European Union and the United States. *Journal of World Energy Law and Business*, 4(3), pp. 260–315.

Talus, K., 2011. *Vertical Natural Gas Transportation Capacity, Upstream Commodity Contracts and EU Competition Law.* Alphen Aan Den Rijn: Wolters Kluwer.

Talus, K., 2013. *EU Energy Law and Policy: A Critical Account.* Oxford: Oxford University Press.

Tapia, J. & Mantzari, D., 2013. The Regulation/Competition Interaction. In: I. Lianos & D. Geradin, eds. *Handbook on European Competition Law: Substantive Aspects.* Cheltenham: Edward Elgar, pp. 588–629.

Thatcher, M., 2014. European Commission merger control: combining competition and the creation of larger European firms. *European Journal of Political Research*, 53(3), pp. 443–464.

The World Bank, 2004. *Doing Business in 2004: Understanding Regulation,* Washington, DC: The World Bank.

Thieme, D. & Rudolf, B., 2002. PreussenElektra AG v. Schleswag AG. Case C-379/98. *The American Journal of International Law*, 96(1), pp. 225–230.

Thomas, S., 2003. The Seven Brothers. *Energy Policy*, 31(5), pp. 393–403.

Thomas, S., 2007. *Unbundling of Electricity Transmission Networks: Analysis of the European Commission's position.* London: PSIRU.

Thomas, S. D., 2006. Electricity industry reforms in smaller European countries and the Nordic experience. *Energy*, 31(6–7), pp. 788–801.

Torti, V., 2016. *Intellectual Property Rights and Competition in Standard Setting: Objectives and Tensions.* London: Routledge.

Toth, A., 2005. *Relationship between Competition Law and Sector Specific Regulation regarding the Abuse of Dominant Position.* Budapest, OECD.

Train, K. E., 1997. *Optimal Regulation: The Economic Theory of Natural Monopoly.* Cambridge: MIT Press.

Tugendhat, C., 1968. *Oil: The Biggest Business.* New York: G. P. Putnam's Sons.

Ubertazzi, B., 2004. The End of the ECSC. *European Integration Online Papers*, 8(20), pp. 1–36.

Uchelen, W. v. & Roggenkamp, M. M., 2004. Regulatory Reforms in the Norwegian Gas Industry. *Journal of Energy & Natural Resources Law*, 22(4), pp. 450–464.

Ugarte, S. & Di Masi, L., 2016. EU: Energy. *The European, Middle Eastern and African Antitrust Review*, 2016, pp. 22–28.

Vedder, H., Roggenkamp, M. M., Ronne, A. & Guayo, I. d., 2016. EU Energy Law. In: M. Roggenkamp, C. Redgwell, A. Ronne & I. d. Guayo, eds. *Energy Law in Europe*. 3rd ed. Oxford: Oxford University Press, pp. 187–366.

Vertessy, Z., 2015. The Court of Justice's Judgment in the Telefonica Case: Margins, Markets and Judicial Restraint. *European Networks Law and Regulation Quarterly*, 3(1), pp. 39–48.

Vickers, J., 2009. *Competition Policy and Property Rights*. Oxford: University of Oxford.

Vijver, T. v. d., 2012. Third Party Access Exemption Policy in the EU Gas and Electricity Sectors: Finding the Right Balance between Competition and Investments. In: M. M. Roggenkamp, ed. *Energy Networks and the Law: Innovative Solutions in Changing Markets*. Oxford: Oxford University Press, pp. 333–353.

Vogelaar, T., 1964. *Euratom, its relations to the other European Communities and its regulatory responsibilities*. Arlington: The Federal Bar Association.

Wägenbaur, R. & Wainwright, R., 1996. European Community Energy and Environment Policy. *Yearbook of European Law*, 16(1), pp. 59–86.

Waloszyk, M., 2014. *Law and Policy of the European Gas Market*. Cheltenham: Edward Elgar.

Wårell, L., 2006. Market Integration in the International Coal Industry: A Cointegration Approach. *The Energy Journal*, 27(1), pp. 99–118.

Weber, R. H., 2012. *Energy Law in Switzerland*. Bern, Alphen aan den Rijn: Stämpfli, Wolters Kluwer.

Weber, R. H. & Kratz, B., 2009. *Stromversorgungsrecht: Ergänzungsband Elektrizitätswirtschaftsrecht*. Bern: Stämpfli.

Werner, P., 2012. *European commission v Electricité de France: the private investor test and state aid*. (Online) Available at: http://www.lexology.com/library/detail.aspx?g=01eb1ceb-ff0f-4cb0-aa84-04b1598abd0d (accessed 1 June 2019).

Wesseling, R., 1997. The Commission Notices on decentralisation of E.C. antitrust law: in for a penny, not for a pound. *European Competition Law Review*, 18(2), pp. 94–97.

Whish, R. & Bailey, D., 2018. *Competition Law*. 9th ed. Oxford: Oxford University Press.

Wilde, M., 2010. *European Union policies and strategies related to the use of coal*. Moscow, European Commission.

Wood, J., 2007. *Nuclear Power.* London: The Institution of Engineering and Technology.

World Energy Council, 2016. *World Energy Resources.* London: WEC.

World Trade Organization, 1998. *Energy Services – Background Note by the Secretariat.* Geneva: WTO.

Wright, K., Waddams, C. & Davies, L., 2005. *Experience of Privatisation, Regulation and Competition: Lessons for Governments.* Norfolk: ESRC Centre for Competition Policy.

Wurmnest, W., 2012. Case C-52/09, Konkurrensverket v. TeliaSonera Sverige AB, Judgment of the Court of Justice (First Chamber) of 17 February 2011. *Common Market Law Review*, 49(2), pp. 721–736.

Yarrow, G., 1994. The Economics of Regulation. In: V. V. Ramanadham, ed. *Privatization and After: Monitoring and Regulation.* London: Routledge, pp. 35–47.

Yu, M., 2010. *Liberalization of the European Natural Gas Market and Achieving Energy Security: An Internal Solution to an External Problem.* Pennsylvania: Dickinson College.

Zafirova, Z., 2007. Unbundling the Network: the Case for Ownership Unbundling? *International Energy Law & Taxation Review*, 2, pp. 29–36.

Introduction

The European Union (EU) traces its origins to the European Coal and Steel Community (ECSC), which was founded by the Treaty of Paris, signed on 18 April 1951. The foundation of the ECSC was based on the Schuman Plan (within the framework of the Schuman Declaration), which, in 1950, proposed the formation of a single authority to control the coal as well as the steel production of Germany and France, wherein the participation of other European nations was allowed. The Schuman Declaration led to the establishment of the ECSC.

Quite soon after the creation of the ECSC, the European Economic Community (EEC) and the European Atomic Energy Community (Euratom) were established in 1957. While the EEC focused on economic integration, Euratom was concerned with finding alternative energy resources in an effort to prevent the increasing dependency of European countries on Middle East petroleum. Contrary to the Euratom, the EEC Treaty contained neither specific provisions regarding energy policy in general nor any policies for oil, gas and electricity. The founding fathers of the Treaty appear to have believed that the application of its general principles in the energy sector would be sufficient and appropriate to deal with any problems that might arise.

Aside from coal, being specific to the ECSC Treaty, and nuclear energy, being specific to the Euratom Treaty, it can be stated that there has never been an explicit legal basis for energy in primary EU law. Until the late 1980s, EU common energy policy was virtually non-existent even though the aforementioned Treaties obviously dealt with energy matters and set up certain instruments with the aim of maintaining minimum standards for the security of oil and gas supplies.

The original state of affairs has undergone a transformation with the Lisbon Treaty and the adoption of a new article specific to energy (Article 194 TFEU). For the first time the EU's constitutive Treaties included energy policy as an area of the EU's competence. Article 194 TFEU codifies the existing objectives and instruments of European energy policy and subsequently links them in an explicit manner. It further aims at enabling the proper functioning of the energy markets, thereby covering topics with pertinence to the competitive energy markets. Today, the EU's established energy policy is based on three-pillars: competitive markets, sustainability and secure energy supply. The main focus of this thesis pertains to the competitive energy markets.

The European energy markets have significantly changed during the past two decades. Europe has been struggling to establish a competitive as well as a fully integrated European internal energy market since the beginning of the 1990s. Until the early 1990s, the European energy markets consisted of national monopolies possessing vertically integrated structures, and they were still nationally segregated. Moreover, the idea that the electricity and gas sectors could be operated by private undertakings under competitive conditions was, at that time, inconceivable. It was generally assumed that there was no other way to provide a reliable and secure supply of electricity and gas to customers under reasonable conditions. However, the EU took a decision to open European energy markets (especially electricity and gas markets) to competition in a gradual manner and subsequently to establish an internal energy market.

Through liberalisation, the electricity and gas markets have been transformed from national markets controlled by vertically integrated monopolies to more competitive markets. At present, the competitive segments (production and retail) and the regulated segments (transmission and distribution) are segregated from each other in most Member States.

Upon an analysis of the background of liberalisation studies in energy markets since the 1990s, it can be asserted that the EU aims at establishing an internal energy market based on the principle of free competition. The main objectives of liberalisation are to introduce competition, abolish the national measures, enable efficiency in energy markets and increase the security of supply. In order to achieve these goals, the EU has established legislative and regulatory frameworks.

The European Commission (in the following "the Commission") set up a three-step process to establish an internal energy market. In 1990, as first measure, the EU initially adopted three directives – the so-called pre-liberalisation Directives (Directive 90/377/EEC, Directive 90/547/EEC and Directive 91/296/EEC) – with the aim of integrating the European energy markets.As a second step, the Directive on the conditions for granting and using authorisations for the prospection, exploration and production of hydrocarbons (Directive 94/22/EC) was adopted on 30 May 1994.

After these first steps towards the integration of the European energy markets, the Commission enacted the first Electricity Directive (Directive 96/92/EC) in 1996 and the first Gas Directive (Directive 98/30/EC) in 1998, which constituted the cornerstone with regard to the liberalisation of the electricity and gas markets. The main objectives of the aforementioned Directives were to create a competitive environment in terms of the electricity and gas markets so as to achieve the requisite objectives of liberalisation, transparency, free access to energy networks and, lastly, supply security. The Directives aimed at moving from markets consisting of vertically integrated undertakings, mostly with supply monopolies, to markets that were to be segregated between segments where competition was feasible and segments being natural monopolies to which third parties would have access in a fair, reasonable and non-discriminatory manner. When the first Directives proved insufficient in order to reach the aforementioned objectives, new electricity and gas Directives were enacted in 2003 (respectively 2003/54/EC and 2003/55/EC). These Directives were equipped with new provisions in order to realise the objective of establishing an internal energy market functioning in a competitive environment. With respect to the aforementioned scope, enhanced unbundling and third-party access regimes were implemented.

Not having obtained the desired results from the second Directives, the EU enacted the third Electricity and Gas Directives (respectively 2009/72/EC and 2009/73/EC). In conjunction with these, several other regulations were also introduced. The new Directives contained vital provisions regarding unbundling and third-party access regimes. Unbundling and third-party access are considered to be the most important issues involved in the process of energy market liberalisation.

The Commission expended an immense amount of effort to achieve rapid results through this new energy package. In addition to the aforementioned legislative measures, it started to use the full range of competition tools to pursue cases setting precedents which can significantly improve competition in energy markets. The Commission initiated extensive competition investigations against undertakings within the electricity and gas sectors and, subsequently, enforced strict measures against them. The authority of the Commission, needed to initiate investigations, is derived from its position as the enforcer of competition rules in the TFEU. The Commission, therefore, has implemented general competition law rules in numerous antitrust cases and imposed strict structural remedies. With this, the problem arose with relation to the particular cases that tend to demand the implementation of sector-specific regulations versus general competition law. According to the Commission, the most effective solution is to implement sector-specific regulations as well as competition law collectively and also to impose the structural measures on the basis of the aforementioned co-ordination. This solution is considered to be the most appropriate method for the purpose of overcoming the obstacles that are opposed to establishing the internal energy markets.

The European energy markets are controlled by a dual structure consisting of two different regulatory frameworks with two different procedures and their respective supervisory bodies. Competition law is comprised of general legal norms set out in the EU Treaty and can be implemented within any industry. These legal norms can be enforced only when an infringement (*ex post*) has taken place. Sector-specific regulations, however, are particular to the sector they encompass and can regulate the sector *ex ante* prior to the occurrence of an infringement.

The present thesis aims at analysing the development of the European energy markets and policies from both the perspective of competition law and sector-specific regulations, thus identifying the problems regarding the introduction of competition into the energy markets.

The problem of understanding the relationship between competition law and sector-specific regulations can be observed in various industries undergoing liberalisation, especially the energy industry. Therefore, the present research is expected to provide a useful framework with respect to the role of sector-specific regulations and competition law within the energy markets.

As a result, the present thesis endeavours to seek solutions to the following questions:

- What is the evolutionary development process that established the legal framework of European energy markets?
- In which manner did the structural and legislative features of European energy markets develop?
- What type of role do the competition instruments (competition law and sector-specific regulations) play in the liberalisation process of European energy markets?
- What is the nature of the relationship between competition law and sector-specific regulations? Under which circumstances can competition law affect particularly those issues which are the subject matter of the authority of sector-specific regulations in energy markets?

By analysing legal norms and case law, the present research will apply doctrinal methodologies concerning the development as well as the formulation of the doctrinal parameters that will define a model of cooperation between competition law and sector-specific regulations. This research will be primarily normative, since its objectives are to put forth the facts in the field under research (European energy sector) and to indicate the manner in which the regulation model could undergo improvement. Moreover, the description and analysis of the current frameworks of competition law and sector-specific regulations will comprise a major part of this study. The results of the analysis will provide the material for the formulation of a new hybrid model.

The methodology of the present research endeavour will be based on the examination of core provisions of EU energy law and competition law. In the first part, the definition of energy companies and energy markets is specified inasmuch as they are the main subjects which are affected by EU law and sector-specific regulations. The second part encompasses the EU Energy Acquis. Within the ambit of its chapters, the origin of the energy acquis and a sectoral legal framework are examined in detail. The following two chapters of part three provide an overview of competition law and sector-specific regulations and the relation between them. The fourth part consisting of three chapters encompasses a detailed analysis of the interaction between competition tools and energy markets. These chapters illustrate how competition law and sector-specific regulations have affected energy markets. Part five presents the conclusions of the study.

Part 1 The Fundamentals of Energy Markets and Energy Companies

§ 1. Distinction of Energy Markets

Energy in all its forms can help people live an easier and more comfortable life.[1] It is a main driving force of all economies. Adequate energy resources, sustainable energy infrastructure and robust energy markets are among the essential needs of a successfully functioning society.[2] In order to ensure people's well-being and sustainable growth as well as the competitiveness of EU industry, access to a reliable, steady and secure supply of energy at competitive and affordable prices is crucial.[3]

Energy is often considered to be a commodity[4] and energy markets include many different commodities that are quite distinct in nature. In principle, energy markets can be classified into the three following categories:

a) coal markets
b) oil and natural gas markets
c) electricity markets[5]

This classification roughly corresponds to the historical pace at which these markets were opened to competition.[6]

1 Dahl, 2015, p. 1.
2 Mukhigulishvili & Margvelashvili, 2012, p. 1.
3 ICF Consultancy Services & DIW Berlin, 206, p. 2.
4 Aronson & Stern, 1984, p. 15.
5 Electricity markets including renewable energy markets.
6 Eydeland & Wolyniec, 2003, p. 2.

I. Coal Market

A. World

Coal is one of the three major forms of fossil fuels, consisting of carbonised vegetal matter.[7] It is primarily used for electricity generation and steel production worldwide. There are various types of coal with different physical and chemical characteristics.[8] These characteristics determine the price of coal and its suitability for various uses.[9]

Inasmuch as coal is the most abundant fossil fuel and thus affordable, many developed and developing countries choose coal for electricity generation. In Europe, coal helps to maintain energy markets competitive. The industrial and residential electricity consumers in the EU would be faced with much higher energy prices without inter-fuel competition from coal.[10]

The international coal industry has undergone fundamental changes during the past fifty years. In the 1960s, the coal market was considered rather local. Production was almost exclusively aimed at national usage, and international coal trade was rare. The high transportation costs involved in shipping and handling coal constituted a natural obstacle to the development of a global coal market. However, the oil crises in 1973 and 1979, which led to rises in oil prices, enhanced the position of coal, and the demand for coal increased substantially. Due to significant reductions in shipping costs during this period, the economic attractiveness of coal increased.[11]

The coal prices tend to be relatively stable and are not drastically altered or affected by pertinent international events because of the prevalence of longer-term supply and purchase commitments in this market.[12] The belief in the non-exhaustible nature of coal supply is substantiated by the fact that there exists a well-developed infrastructure in the world in terms of coal, because it can in a quintessentially

---

7 InterEnerStat, 2008, p. 5.
8 There are three main categories of coal: hard coal, sub-bituminous coal and brown coal (also called lignite). Ibid., p. 5.
9 Burger et al., 2014, p. 7.
10 Euracoal, 2017, p. 9.
11 Wårell, 2006, pp. 99–100.
12 Robinson et al., 2000, p. 45; Kilian, 2015.

easy manner be stored and brought to the market. Consequently, coal prices did not witness an imminent hike, as was the case with oil prices during the first and second oil crisis. Coal prices were quite stable and were not linked to oil prices until recently.[13] Furthermore, in comparison with the alternative fossil fuels, the coal sector lacks a price-fixing institution such as the Organisation of the Petroleum Exporting Countries (OPEC); as a consequence, coal prices have been determined in a free manner in the market for the past thirty years.

B. Europe

In Europe[14], the economic significance of coal has witnessed an increase as a result of the enlargement of the EU in 2004 and, also, 2007. In 2013, 28% of electricity generation in the EU was coal-based.[15] Furthermore, in several EU Member States the share of coal in energy generation amounts to over 50%, for instance 59% in the Czech Republic and 53% in Greece.[16]

Since the beginning of 2004 coal production began to decrease in then existing Member States as the imported coal was considered to be relatively economical. However, coal remains one of EU's most important energy sources, meeting 15.5% of EU primary energy demand in 2016.[17]

Among Member States, Germany can be considered as the primary leader in coal production. As a result, Germany ranks at position eight in global coal production after China, the USA, India and Indonesia.[18] However, notwithstanding such high coal production, Germany's domestic coal demand constitutes only a share of 3% in the

13 Kanai, 2010, pp. 8–9.

14 About 80% of Europe's fossil fuel reserves comprise hard coal and lignite, and most EU Member States have access to reserves of one or both.

15 In Europe, aside from energy generation, coal is used in various sectors such as iron and steel manufacture and cement production.

16 Mills, 2010, p. 1.

17 Euracoal, 2017, p. 9; EEA, Primary energy consumption by fuel, 2018, https://www.eea.europa.eu/ (accessed: 1 June 2019).

18 In Germany, the most extracted form of coal is lignite, whereas it imports solid coal from countries such as Russia, Colombia and the USA. IEA, Coal Information, 2016, p. xi.

market—which is an insignificant share compared to the 48% consumption rate of China along with the 11% consumption rate of the USA.[19] Nevertheless the aforementioned observation, the currently increasing natural gas prices and also the nuclear phase-out have led Member States to look to alternative energy resources, whereby one of the primary alternative resources is coal. The main advantage of coal is its security of supply and its competitive price. Energy produced by coal is cheaper and more affordable than other energy sources. Moreover, coal is the most abundant fossil fuel on earth.

There are, however, some significant disadvantages to using coal. The unremitting use of coal by numerous Member States brought a multitude of environmental concerns such as the greenhouse gas emissions. The combustion of coal involves harmful by-products which cause pollution and contribute to global warming. For this reason, the EU has been struggling to decrease the amount of carbon emissions resulting from coal use and, thereby, takes into consideration studies such as CCS and EU ETS.

The rapidly burgeoning concerns with respect to global warming and greenhouse gas emissions have fuelled a broad range of initiatives focusing on reducing CO_2 produced from coal-fired power plants. Therefore, in all coal-consuming Member States several on-going activities centred on the development and application of clean coal technologies alongside carbon capture and storage which have come into being. Thus, it can be empirically observed that the long-term future of coal use necessitates the utilisation of CCS[20], and the future of coal consumption in Member States will depend heavily on the increasing use of high-efficiency power plants coupled with the widespread deployment of CCS.[21]

As part of the above-mentioned studies, in 2007 the *Communication on Sustainable Power Generation from Fossil Fuels*[22] was published within the scope of the EU energy package with the objective to decrease the carbon emissions. The communication examined the man-

19 Jungjohann & Morris, 2014, p. 5.

20 Wilde, 2013.

21 Mills, 2010, p. 73.

22 European Commission, Sustainable power generation from fossil fuels: aiming for near-zero emissions from coal after 2020, 2007.

ner in which the development of energy security could be fostered and also the particular manner in which the greenhouse gas emissions could be decreased. It included an addendum outlining the existing CCS strategies and the related programmes in the EU. Eventually, in 2009, the *European Carbon Dioxide Capture and Storage (CCS) Demonstration Project Network* was implemented.

II. Oil and Natural Gas Market

A. Oil Market

1. World

The oil market is certainly the most prominent among the energy markets since oil remains the world's leading fuel, accounting for 32.9% of total global energy consumption.[23] Crude oil[24] is a liquid found in reserves spread across particular regions of the earth, where it can be accessed from the surface.[25]

Oil, as a basic energy resource, can be considered as immensely significant in the lives of human beings. That fact is magnified by a fundamental truism, namely that nearly every sector of the economy, national or international, depends on this natural resource. For such reason, oil is distinct from the other energy resources in the world and subsequently occupies a strategic position. High-energy density and the ease of handling for storage and transport are the main advantages of oil as an energy carrier compared with other primary energy sources. Today, crude oil is still the main source of energy in the transportation sector and plays an important role in the chemical industry and power generation.[26]

---

23 World Energy Council, 2016, p. 14; BP, Energy Outlook to 2035, 2015.

24 Chemically, crude oil is a mixture of hydrocarbons with different molecular weights. For actual usage, crude oil is transformed via a refinery process into different petroleum products, such as fuel oil or gasoline. Because of oil's great economic importance historically, oil markets have always been subject to political regulations and interventions. Burger et al., 2014, p. 7.

25 Ibid.

26 Ibid.

The oil market has a complex and very broad structure including exploration, transportation, processing and marketing. It is also a dynamic structure due to its reliance on many independent as well as interdependent political, economic, socio-cultural and technological factors.

The use of oil for commercial purposes dates back to the mid-19th century. Edwin L. Drake is known to have established the first modern, commercial oil well in 1859, near Titusville, Pennsylvania, and also to have launched the export of oil from Philadelphia to London through a ship named Elizabeth Watts. This was an important move to make the oil industry vital in world economy.[27]

In 1863, John D. Rockefeller established an oil processing company and pioneered the transportation of oil through pipes. In the following period, it was realised by Rockefeller that in the future he couldn't compete with the small oil refineries; for this reason, he founded the Standard Oil Co. in Cleveland, Ohio, during 1870. Within one year of incorporation the Standard Oil Co. gained control of 10% of the American oil industry. With the passage of time, it came to wield control over 80% of the oil processing industry and also 90% of pipeline transportation. The Standard Oil Co. subsequently monopolised oil processing as well as the distribution areas within the USA.[28] It, furthermore, controlled the entire oil industry with the aid of its thirty-seven subsidiaries. It began to swallow up competitors or drive them out of business. The Standard Oil Co.'s tactics included negotiating freight discounts from railroads, undercutting prices of competitors and controlling pipelines. By 1880, it controlled about 90% of the US oil product market through the refining sector, although it was not integrated backwards to oil production.[29] As a result of lawsuits brought pursuant to the "Sherman Antitrust Act"[30], the components of the company were divided into thirty-eight regional joint stock companies in 1911.[31]

27 Banks, 1983, pp. 6–7; Roncaglia, 1985, p. 81.
28 Tugendhat, 1968, pp. 30–31.
29 Dahl, 2015, p. 153.
30 The Sherman Antitrust Act of 1890 was the first legal measure passed by the U.S. Congress to prohibit abusive monopolies. In 1914, the Clayton Act supplemented the Sherman Act and made mergers restraining competition also illegal.
31 Loring, 1979, p. 27.

This litigation constituted a milestone in the history of the antitrust movement.[32] Following the forced demerger of the Standard Oil Company, five American companies (Exxon, Mobil, Chevron, Gulf, Texaco) and two European companies (Shell, BP), known as the "seven sisters", began dominating the world's oil market. Even though the intensity of their dominance decreased after the establishment of OPEC in the 1960s, their influence on the developing countries rendered them predominant in the oil market.

Since producer and consumer countries have rapidly accepted the strategic importance of oil as a universally significant energy resource, global economic development and growth have become immensely dependent on oil. Changes in the oil market followed by those in oil prices have affected both national economies and the world economy in a myriad of manners. The oil price is one of the most paramount indicators of economic performance. Naturally, the greater the increase in oil prices and the longer they prevail, the bigger the effect on the macroeconomy will be. The major factors affecting the world's oil supply and subsequently the price formation include the countries' strategic petroleum reserves[33], current stock status of the producer states, the costs of production and transportation, along with the environmental factors. Moreover, the strategies and also the investment policies of IEA, the USA and the large oil companies intrinsically affect the supply of the oil. Furthermore, factors affecting price formation in terms of demand include economic development, regional conflicts, political and military activity, expectations about energy supply security and, lastly, the increase in the requirement for oil products of higher quality in the transportation sector.

32 Maugeri, 2006, p. 18.

33 Strategic petroleum reserves refer to crude oil inventories (or stockpiles) held by the government of a particular country, as well as private industry, to safeguard the economy and to help maintain national security during an energy crisis. Austin, Stable oil prices herald sea change for Strategic Petroleum Reserve, http://www.oil-price.net/ (accessed: 1 June 2019).

2. Europe

With respect to oil as an energy resource, the EU is dependent on non-EU nations. In correlation with economic development, oil demand is witnessing a gradual increase. It can be observed that, because oil demand forever increases globally, oil will continue to hold its strategic importance in the future. The EU imports 90% of its crude oil. It is importing nearly 40% of its oil from the nation states which are members of OPEC, such as Saudi Arabia, Libya, Iran and Iraq.

The EU has attempted to protect its energy market which is dependent on external factors. Secure access to energy during a crisis is important. For this reason, the EU has made it mandatory to hold oil stocks in Member States.[34] The EU Member States must maintain emergency stocks which meet at least ninety days supply to cover internal consumption for three key product groups, namely, gasoline products, middle distillates (diesel oil, gas oil and jet fuels) and fuel oil. Stocks must be readily available so that in the event of a crisis they can be allocated quickly to where they are most needed.

3. OPEC

OPEC is one of the most important actors in the world oil industry. Founded in 1960, OPEC is a cartel established by thirteen nations which are net exporters of oil and possess two-thirds of the known world oil reserves.

OPEC members are divided into three main groups: founding members, full members and limited members. Founding countries are those which signed the agreement establishing OPEC in 1960 and include Saudi Arabia, Iran, Kuwait, Iraq and Venezuela. Full members refer to those nations which joined OPEC later and whose membership was approved by the founding countries and the Conference[35]. Finally, limited members refer to those who are not as influential as the full members and chosen by the Conference subject to special conditions. OPEC members, other than the founding members, include

34 European Commission, Annex to the Green Paper: A European Strategy for Sustainable, Competitive and Secure Energy, pp. 8–9.

35 OPEC Meetings of the Conference.

Qatar (1961), Libya (1962), Indonesia (1962), Ecuador (1963–1993), United Arab Emirates (1967), Algeria (1969), Nigeria (1971), Gabon (1975–1995) and Angola (2007).[36]

Prior to 1960, the world oil market was under the domination of the Seven Sisters[37] spearheaded by the USA. It can be observed that during this period, the oil industry was structured as a natural monopoly. After OPEC was established in 1960, the monopoly of the Seven Sisters in the oil market was challenged especially by the embargo of OPEC in 1973, which targeted the territories of the USA and the Netherlands.[38] Following the establishment of OPEC, new oil fields were opened to production, which enabled new companies to become market participants.[39] Middle Eastern countries came to wield substantial power with the establishment of OPEC and were able to exercise more influence on the international oil companies operating within their nations. It can be argued that the establishment of OPEC increased competition by opening the market to new players. Throughout emerging markets, dominance in the oil industry has shifted to the OPEC and state-owned oil companies, such as Gazprom, China National Petroleum Corporation (CNPC), Aramco, National Iranian Oil Company (NIOC), Petrobras.[40]

OPEC aims at regulating and coordinating the oil policies of Member States in order to protect their individual and collective interests. It enables price stability by preventing fluctuations in oil prices

36 For more information, see: OPEC, www.opec.org (accessed: 1 June 2019).

37 "Seven Sisters" was a term coined in the 1950s by businessman Enrico Mattei, then-head of the Italian state oil company Eni, to describe the seven oil companies which formed the "Consortium for Iran" cartel and dominated the global petroleum industry from the mid-1940s to the 1970s: Anglo-Iranian Oil Company (today's British Petroleum), Gulf Oil (most of which became part of British Petroleum and the other parts which joined Chevron), Standard Oil of California or SoCal (today's Chevron), Texaco (later a part of Chevron in a merger), London headquartered Royal Dutch Shell, Standard Oil Company of New Jersey (Esso, which became Exxon) and Standard Oil Company of New York or Socony (Mobil, which merged with Exxon to become ExxonMobil). https://www.financial-dictionary.info/terms/seven-sisters-oil-companies/ (accessed: 1 June 2019).

38 Stork, 1973, p. 14.

39 Noguera, 2017, p. 301.

40 The new Seven Sisters: oil and gas giants dwarf western rivals, https://www.ft.com/content/471ae1b8-d001-11db-94cb-000b5df10621 (accessed: 1 June 2019).

and, subsequently, aims at supplying regular, economic, efficient and stable oil to the oil consumer countries. Furthermore, OPEC also ensures the fair return to the oil market of the oil income it obtains.[41]

B. Natural Gas Market

1. World

Natural gas is a fairly clean fuel, and it is more plentiful than oil as far as energy content is concerned. North America is the largest producer and consumer of natural gas, followed by Russia. Russia holds one third of the world's discovered reserves of natural gas; the Middle East holds another one third.[42]

Since 1980, natural gas has exhibited the fastest consumption growth of all fossil fuels.[43] Today, natural gas ranks as the number three fuel, reflecting 24% of global primary energy, and it is the number two energy source for power generation, representing a 22% share.[44]

During the decade of the 1950s, natural gas originally was used solely for local purposes and comprised merely 10% of the energy consumption internationally. Since then the international use has witnessed a steady increment. The negative effects of the 1970s oil crises on the economies and air pollution resulting from increasing oil consumption constitute the most significant reasons for the increasing share of natural gas use.[45]

Since natural gas is susceptible of being supplied from different sources under numerous purchase conditions and the demand may require several different structures, gas systems are a complex phe-

---

41 For more information, see: OPEC, www.opec.org_(accessed: 1 June 2019).

42 Dahl, 2015, p. 213.

43 Following the oil crises which took place in the decade of 1970s, the consumption of gas witnessed a gradual increment. Since then natural gas has been considered as one of the most significant energy resources of the world.

44 World Energy Council, 2016, p. 14.

45 Reducing and/or eradicating pollution which is caused by the usage of energy is an increasingly significant issue with respect to the environmental policies. Environmentalism plays a central role with respect to the preference for natural gas, reportedly known for relatively lower polluting emissions as compared to the other fossil fuels.

nomenon. A natural gas system consists of several different layers including exploration, production, processing, transmission, distribution and consumption. Initial investment costs for natural gas systems are very high. However, their marginal costs are low.[46] The general structure of these systems is determined by three main factors, namely, supply resources, transmission and distribution systems, and the market.

It has been empirically observed that in order to meet the requirements of the market structure, the natural gas system is required to maintain integrity beginning from the production phase to its supply to the end users. Furthermore, a good organisational structure along with a communication network should be established in order to further the efficient operation of the system in a technically and economically viable fashion.

In terms of demand, the market structure of natural gas must take into account numerous factors such as consumer composition, the deployment of flexible measures and also affordable prices in order to be accepted by the consumer. Moreover, natural gas consumption is highly seasonal, with weather being a strong driver. The most prominent feature is the strong winter peak for heating, with a much smaller summer peak for natural gas to supply electricity generation for the cooling season. Prices also show a jagged tendency, with peaks often during the winter and troughs during the off season.

Inasmuch as natural gas has higher transportation costs as compared to oil, natural gas trade patterns have tended to be more regionally oriented, with regional markets in North America, South America and Western Europe.[47]

2. Europe

In 2014, natural gas accounted for a significant 21% of Europe's primary energy consumption.[48] There has been a decrease on the proportion of natural gas in EU primary energy consumption. This is partly the result of the increase in renewable energy.[49] Another reason for such

46 Davis & Muehlegger, 2010, p. 792.
47 Dahl, 2015, p. 213.
48 Blakey, 2013, p. 3.
49 EEA, Primary energy consumption by fuel, 2017.

temporary decrease can be attributed to the warm winter season compared to the climatic conditions in the previous years.

Natural gas also plays a significant role in the EU's plan with respect to reducing emissions and climate change. Furthermore, as compared to the other traditional energy resources, natural gas is one of the cleanest resources because it emits 50% less CO_2. Due to its higher hydrogen-to-carbon ratio, the combustion of natural gas results in 25 to 30% less CO_2 than is the case for oil and 40 to 50% less than for coal per unit of energy produced, depending on the process and fuel quality.[50]

Russia-Ukraine Gas Crises: In March 2005, it was reported that the prices and the transit costs of the supplied natural gas gave rise to a conflict between Russia and Ukraine. During the course of this conflict, Russia claimed that Ukraine had defaulted on payment for the gas that it had purchased. Ukraine illicitly and covertly deployed the particular gas stratum that was supposed to transport gas to the European continent. Even though *Naftohaz*, a Ukrainian oil and gas company, initially denied the claim, it later admitted to withholding the natural resource within its territory and deploying it for local purposes. However, the conflict undertook a severe turn on 1 January 2006, which was followed by Russia's withdrawal of its gas supply from Ukraine. Furthermore, on 4 January 2006, the parties made an agreement and gas supply was subsequently normalised and continued in the same manner until October 2007. However, post October 2007, Ukraine's debts were at issue again. Thereafter, this issue again led to disruptions in gas supply. By January 2009, the said conflict led to a multitude of gas disruptions in many European countries. 18 European countries complained that the requisite supply of natural gas to Ukraine decreased or rather wholly cut their supply.[51] In 2009, the conflict continued since the parties still could not agree upon gas prices and supply.

The said confrontation had major repercussions on the domains of trade, financial and energy relationships within the regions. As a result, supply security became the focal point of the agenda in the EU. Moreover, the EU authorities tried to find ways to decrease the EU's natural gas

50 EUROGAS, https://eurogas.org/knowledge_centre/about-gas/ (accessed: 1 June 2019).

51 Reuters, Factbox – 18 countries affected by Russia-Ukraine gas row, 2009.

dependency on Russia. Following the natural gas crises between Russia and Ukraine, issues such as the revision of energy policies, diversification of energy resources, energy transit, secure and uninterrupted energy, and determining effective procedures for solving transit disputes have become immensely significant.[52] Furthermore, the EU defined areas wherein certain decisions needed to be taken and outlined concrete actions implemented in the short, medium and longer term in order to address concerns regarding secure energy supply. The EU's new energy security strategy was based on the following key pillars[53]:

- increasing the energy capacity and energy production in the EU,
- moderating energy demand,
- strengthening emergency/solidarity mechanisms including coordination of risk assessments and contingency plans, and protecting strategic infrastructure,
- completing the creation of a well-functioning and fully integrated internal market,
- developing new energy technologies,
- diversifying supplier countries and routes,
- improving coordination between national energy policies.

This strategy aims at promoting a close cooperation which will be beneficial for all Member States while respecting national energy choices and is underpinned by the principle of solidarity.[54]

III. Electricity Market

A. World

Electricity is a secondary energy source. In other words, it is generated from the conversion of primary energy sources such as coal, natural gas, oil and nuclear power, but also renewable sources such as hydropower, solar energy and wind energy. Electricity is used for many purposes (e.g., lighting, heating, cooling, transportation, industrial

52 European Commission, European energy security strategy, 2014.

53 Ibid., p. 3.

54 Ibid.

purposes). It is convenient, versatile, easy to control and non-polluting at the location of its usage, particularly when used to produce heat, light and power.[55]

The source of electricity varies considerably across countries and regions. Coal dominates in China, India and a number of other countries. Natural gas is the primary source for power generation in many countries, e.g., Russia, United States and United Kingdom.[56] While hydropower dominates in Latin America, Europe has the highest proportion of nuclear power and renewable energy sources. The Middle East has the largest share of oil in electricity generation. North America remains the most electricity-intensive region of the world, followed by Europe, the former Soviet Union and the industrial countries of Asia and Oceania. The developing countries lag behind, especially in Africa. Such countries, however, are eager to catch up and provide very promising markets for new generation capacity.[57]

Inasmuch as electricity is generated from the conversion of primary energy sources, electricity markets and electricity prices are fundamentally linked to the markets for primary fuels and environmental conditions. It is essential to take into consideration the electricity generation process and the fuel markets to understand electricity markets and price mechanisms.[58]

Certain structural features of the electricity sector distinguish it from other energy markets. Electricity cannot be easily stored, and it requires large physical spaces. Most energy generated by electricity needs to be fully consumed immediately. Because of this, regardless of the production methods, the installed capacity of any power plant requires a capacity which can meet the highest demand. In other words, the generation and consumption of electricity should be equal with one other. Moreover, other technical parameters such as the voltage should be balanced. In the situation of an imbalance between the supply and demand for other goods, such an imbalance would usually not create a serious negative effect in the market. However, if imbalances between supply and demand cannot be managed properly within the

55 Burger et al., 2014, p. 27.

56 IEA Statistics, http://www.iea.org/statistics/ (accessed: 1 March 2019).

57 Dahl, 2015, p. 122.

58 Burger et al., 2014, p. 27.

electricity sector, the security of the entire system is likely to be endangered. In contrast to the other markets, a central system operator is needed in order to ensure the security of the system.[59] The system operator monitors the production, the consumption and the currents. It provides the coordination needed to eliminate the prevalent imbalances between supply and demand; if needed, it increases or decreases the energy taken from the necessary production units; and also, if need be, it activates or deactivates production units.

B. Europe

In 2016, the total net electricity generation in the EU totalled 3.1 million gigawatt hours (GWh). Among the EU Member States in 2013, Germany had the highest level of net electricity generation, accounting for 19.8% of the EU total, just ahead of France (17.2%). France was followed by the United Kingdom with 10.5% of the EU total.[60]

Considering the distribution of electricity consumption according to sectors, the highest electricity consumption is made by the industry with a share of 40.4%. The household sector follows industry with a ratio of 28.2%. Then the service sector comes with a share of 26.7%. The share of the transportation sector in the total electricity consumption is only 2.5%.[61] However, it is estimated that this will change with the advent of newly developed technologies, and the share of electricity in the transportation sector will slowly increase.

According to 2016 data, thermal power plants have the highest share in electricity generation in Europe, with a ratio of 48.7%. Nuclear power plants have a share of 25.7%, which is followed by the hydroelectric power plants having a share of 12.1%. The share of the new generation of renewable energy resources, such as wind and solar energy, only amounts to 13.2%.[62] The EU will continue to undertake pertinent research in the following ten years to increase the share of electricity generated by renewable energy sources to the maximum level.

59 Neresian, 2016, p. 36.

60 Eurostat, 2018, https://ec.europa.eu/eurostat/statistics-explained/index.php (accessed: 1 March 2019).

61 EUREL, 2013, p. 10.

62 Eurostat, Electricity production and supply statistics, 2015.

Amongst the renewable energy sources, wind and photovoltaic energy are expected to grow rapidly. However, it can be argued that the classic fossil and nuclear energy power plants will keep their absolute value for a long time in the future.[63]

§ 2. Organisational Distinction of Energy Undertakings

I. Public Undertakings

A. State-owned Undertakings

In the widest sense, state-owned undertakings constitute companies over which, for a variety of reasons, the state exercises control.[64] This definition encompasses joint stock companies, limited liability companies and also partnerships which are limited by shares.[65] Friedmann defines such an organisation as *"an institution operating a service of an economic or social character on behalf of the government, but as an independent legal entity, largely autonomous in its management, though responsible to the public, through government and Parliament and subject to some direction, by the government; equipped with independent separate funds of its own, and the legal and commercial attributes of a commercial enterprise."*[66]

State-owned undertaking is defined in the Financial Transparency Directive[67] as follows: *"any undertaking over which the public authorities may exercise directly or indirectly a dominant influence by virtue of their*

---

63 Eurostat, 2018, https://ec.europa.eu/eurostat/statistics-explained/index.php (accessed: 1 March 2019).

64 European Union, State-Owned Enterprises in the EU: Lessons Learnt and Ways Forward in a Post-Crisis Context, 2016, p. 1.

65 OECD, OECD Guidelines on Corporate Governance of State-Owned Enterprises, 2015, p. 14.

66 Friedmann, 1954, p. 541. *"Developing countries have created SOEs for many reasons: to balance or replace weak private sectors, to produce higher investment ratios and extract a capital surplus for investment in the economy, to transfer technology to strategic sectors, to generate employment, and to make goods available at lower cost."* Kikeri et al., 1992, p. 15.

67 Commission Directive 80/723/EEC of 25 June 1980 on the transparency of financial relations between Member States and public undertakings, OJ L 195, 29.7.1980,

ownership of it, their financial participation therein, or the rules which govern it.

A dominant influence on the part of the public authorities should be presumed when these authorities, directly or indirectly, in relation to an undertaking:

a) Hold the major part of the undertaking's subscribed capital; or
b) Control the majority of the votes attaching to shares issued by the undertaking; or
c) Can appoint more than half of the members of the undertaking's administrative, managerial or supervisory body".

In the Financial Transparency Directive[68], the Commission defines public undertaking in the widest sense as any undertaking within the ambit of which the public administration can exert preponderant direct or indirect controlling influence. In this regard, the related controlling influence could be construed as a result of the ownership, financial partnership or the rules governing the undertaking.[69] The presence of controlling influence can be assumed when the public administrations either directly or indirectly hold the majority of the capital of the undertaking or control the majority of the administration or organs of the undertaking. State-owned undertakings are generally organised as autonomous entities with separate legal bodies. In addition,

---

pp. 35–37. This Directive is extended in Directive 85/413/EEC of 1985. Some previously excluded private sectors are included again. For example, water administrations, energy companies, postal administrations and telecommunication administrations, transportation and finance institutions etc. Other than that, the Commission observed that the law on insuring public property only by public insurance companies was not in accordance with the provisions of European Community Treaty. See: OJ L 152/25. It was abolished by Commission Directive 2006/111/EC (OJ L 318, 17.11.2006).

68 The most important yield of the Financial Transparency Directive is the transparency it has brought to the accounts, which, in turn, breaks the competitive advantage of public undertakings against private undertakings.

69 The public characteristic of the undertakings has gained a different dimension with the privatisation process. A privatised undertaking passes from being public property to private property as a result of privatisation. However, the state may keep the "golden share" of the privatised undertaking in some cases. Authorities in control of "golden share" may be so important that this can lead a controlling influence of public administrations over the privatised undertaking. In such a case, the privatised undertaking may be considered to be a public undertaking at least according to Article 106(1).

when the public administration participates directly in the execution of an economic activity, it is considered a public undertaking.[70]

The scope of the public ownership in various sectors of the economy is particularly extensive in certain EU Member States such as France, Italy and Sweden, but also in certain new Member States such as Slovenia, Romania, Croatia and Poland.[71] The ownership and governance practise of large undertakings active in areas such as telecommunication, transportation, energy and postal services across Europe generally fall under the category of state-owned undertakings.[72] Although the rules concerning state-owned undertakings vary across Member States, issues related to state-owned undertakings such as state aid, public procurement and services of general economic interest (SGEI) are regulated at the EU-level.[73] Sometimes the EU files investigations against Member States, especially in relation to state aid provided to state-owned undertakings, in order to balance competition.[74]

As regards company ownership in the energy sector, it can be observed that a large number of utilities are partly state-owned today compared to the situation twenty years ago, when nearly all energy utilities were fully state-owned. This demonstrates that energy sector has undergone structural changes over the last decades.[75] The overall trend is clearly towards continuation of privatisation and liberalisation and, consequently, towards a decrease in state ownership. Currently,

70 For a CJ decision about this topic, see: Case 118/85, *Commission v Italian Republic*, [1987] ECR 2599, par. 11. *"In that regard, it must be pointed out, as the Court has frequently emphasised in its decisions, that having recourse to Member States' domestic law in order to limit the scope of provisions of Community law undermines the unity and effectiveness of that law and cannot, therefore, be accepted. Consequently, the fact that a body has, or has not, under national law, legal personality separate from that of the State is irrelevant in deciding whether it may be regarded as a public undertaking within the meaning of the Directive."* See: Gómez & Murray, p. 3.

71 Ibid., p. 6.

72 Estep, 2013, p. 3.

73 Ibid., p. 4.

74 *"The European Commission has opened an in-depth probe to verify whether debt write-offs by the Romanian State and continued supplies by State-owned enterprises in favour of Oltchim, despite the company's deteriorating financial situation, were in line with EU state aid rules."* European Commission, State aid: Commission opens in-depth investigation into support for Romanian petrochemical company Oltchim, 2016.

75 P79FSchülke, 2010, p. 10.

only one of the "seven brothers"[76] is still fully state-owned (Vattenfall).[77]

B. Municipal Utilities

Municipal utilities denote the entities which are owned by a single or several neighbouring municipalities. The municipal utility refers to a commercial corporate entity which encompasses its own budget, accounting and finance system, workforce, capital tools and an independent or semi-independent management organ.

These entities produce goods and services for general public consumption. There are two groups of entities:

- entities in which one or more local administrative bodies have at least 50% of shares; or
- entities in which the municipality retains a minority share but has special statutory powers.

Municipalities are considered to be the oldest and also the most durable elements of the European administration.[78] Local public companies in Member States operate in basic public services known as the network services (water, electricity, gas, waste, telecom, postal services, public transport, port and airport, etc.). Nonetheless, these companies can provide services in any area related to the general public interest.

General regulations pertaining to the organisational structures or the service areas of the local public companies are not created by the EU.[79] Therefore, the legal structures, organisations, service strategies and impact areas of the mentioned types of companies vary in nearly every EU Member State.

---

76 Europe's largest electricity and gas companies: E.ON, EDF, RWE, Vattenfall, GDF-Suez, Endesa and ENEL. Thomas, 2003.

77 Schülke, 2010, p. 10.

78 Hulst & Montfort, 2007.

79 One of the most important basic principles of the EU preventing it from taking binding decisions against Member States is the Subsidiarity Principle which is set forth by Article 5(3) of the Treaty on European Union (TEU) and Protocol (No 2). The Subsidiarity Principle states that staying at the closest level to the citizens is appropriate by considering the economic efficiency principle in dealing with problems of the EU and producing public services.

Within Member States, there exist local public companies which are fully owned by the municipalities and which carry out joint ventures with the private sector. These joint ventures develop in the course of partnership between the different municipalities and private companies operating internationally (particularly in the energy sector). For instance, the German municipalities Mainz, Wiesbaden and Darmstadt have established a co-operative (e.g., Kraftwerke Mainz-Wiesbaden & HEAG) in order to produce and offer basic public services so as to compete with large energy groups.[80] Graz, Linz, Salzburg and Innsbruck, municipalities in Austria, have established a consortium (Citykom Ltd) in the energy and transportation areas and founded a joint venture by selling 50% of the shares to international companies.

In general, the municipalities perform their duties in two distinct ways. They may have their own generation facilities and produce their indigenous power, or they may transfer energy generation activity to a third company through a contract. In both cases, the municipalities provide energy distribution locally. For example, since consumers are also local when it comes to electricity, the municipalities do not need to transmit electricity through high-voltage electricity lines.

Municipal utilities are particularly present in Germany, which has more than 900 distribution grid operators, most of which belong to Stadtwerke (Municipal Utilities). Stadtwerke is constrained solely by the principle of territoriality. Furthermore, they are responsible for the operation of the local electricity networks and the distribution of energy to the local consumers. Stadtwerke can also determine its own strategies and thus may threaten the market share of main EU energy firms in Germany.[81]

As a consequence of the liberalisation of energy markets, numerous companies have become privatised and the new privately-owned companies have had the opportunity to enter into the market. However, recently the remunicipalisation movement has begun in Europe. The underlying reasons for this tendency are the cheaper services provided by local authorities, the private sector's failure, reflected in high energy prices, poor service quality and the lack of addressing public

80 HEAG remained in this union until 2007 before selling all its shares.
81 Groot, 2013, p. 31.

demand for a renewable energy transition, and the termination of the concessions given to private companies.[82] In Germany alone, more than 60 new Stadtwerke have been established since 2007, and privileges related to energy distribution networks and service offering have returned to public hands.[83] Apart from Germany, the remunicipalisation movement can also be observed in countries such as France, the UK and Finland.

II. Public-Private Partnerships (PPP)

In a general sense, public-private partnership (PPP) can be defined as *"long term contractual arrangements between the government and a private partner whereby the latter delivers and funds public services using a capital asset, sharing the associated risks"*.[84] PPP refers to a general term which assimilates various collaboration types between the public and the private sectors. The quality and quantity of the services which are required from the private partner are specified by the government in a PPP contract. The private partner may undertake financing, design, construction, operation, maintenance and management of a capital asset required for service delivery as well as the delivery of a service to the government, or to the public, using that asset.[85]

The EU acquis communautaire lacks a comprehensive PPP definition. PPP thus are characterised by the duration of the relationship between the contracting parties, the role of partners in the definition of objectives, design, completion, implementation, financing, the method of funding the project and the distribution of risks. The Commission has attempted to formalise a homogenous definition of PPP in its Green Paper on Public Private Partnerships.[86] According to this document, PPP refers to forms of cooperation between public authorities and the world of business which aim at ensuring the funding, con-

82 De Clercq, 2014; Kishimoto et al., 2017, p. 121.

83 Hall, 2013, p. 10.

84 OECD, Recommendation of the Council on Principles for Public Governance of Public-Private Partnerships, 2012, p. 18.

85 Ibid.

86 European Commission, Green Paper on Public Private Partnerships, 2004, p. 3.

struction, renovation, management or maintenance of an infrastructure or the provision of a service.

There is a dual distinction regarding PPP in the Green Paper on Public-Private Partnerships[87]:

- Contractual PPP: PPP is of a pure contractual nature, i.e., the cooperation between the public and the private sector is solely based on the contractual links.
- Institutional PPP: PPP has an institutional character; in other words, it involves the establishment of a distinct entity jointly held by the public and the private sector.

The PPP mostly aims at the implementation of infrastructure projects and also the provision of public services. These classes of contracts require complex legal and financial agreements encompassing the private operators and also their public bodies. They are widely used in the transportation, energy, infrastructure, public security, waste management and water distribution sectors.[88]

Certain relevant studies have been conducted with pertinence to the legal framework of the PPP practices, the importance of which is gradually increasing within the ambit of the EU. Since 2000, the Commission has conducted a series of studies to define PPP, clarify its practical issues and render its practices a commonality.[89] The results of these studies constituted the origin of the basic legal framework of PPP.

With respect to this term and its scope, the Directives regulating public procurement[90] have been modernised. Directive 2014/24/EU[91],

87 Ibid., p. 44.
88 Talus, 2009, p. 43.
89 ENISA, Desktop Research on Public Private Partnerships, 2011.
90 Directive 2004/18/EC of the European Parliament and of the Council of 31 March 2004 on the coordination of procedures for the award of public works contracts, public supply contracts and public service contracts, OJ L 134, 30.4.2004, pp. 114–240. Directive 2004/18/EC has been repealed by Directive 2014/24/EU. Directive 2004/17/EC of the European Parliament and of the Council of 31 March 2004 coordinating the procurement procedures of entities operating in the water, energy, transport and postal services sectors, OJ L 134, 30.4.2004, pp. 1–113. Directive 2004/17/EC has been repealed by Directive 2014/25/EU.
91 Directive 2014/24/EU of the European Parliament and of the Council of 26 February 2014 on public procurement and repealing Directive 2004/18/EC, OJ L 94, 28.3.2014, pp. 65–242.

which regulates classic public procurement, and Directive 2014/25/EU[92], which regulates energy, transportation, water and postal services, have been implemented. Directive 2014/24/EU introduced a new procedure, designated as "competitive dialogue", allowing the public authorities to hold discussions with the applicant businesses in order to identify the solutions best suited to their needs.

In this context, a platform was created at the initiative of the Commission to determine how and to what extent public procurement Directives can be applied to different types of PPP forms, to clarify the current legal framework with respect to the PPP models and to decide whether they need to be elaborated. During the consultation process it was determined that sufficient competition was not given in most of Member States. It was also emphasised that alternative policies and regulations ought to be developed in order to solve the numerous problems associated with public procurement and privileges.

Different partnership regulations aim at transferring the activities which normally constitute the responsibilities of the governments. This course of action is a manner of attracting private sector financing to the public sector. A number of reasons can be given for the increasing interest in partnerships between the state and the private sectors, including expected efficiency gains, limited effect on the budget and private sector know-how. The effect on budgeting is especially important for the most recent EU Member States and the candidate countries. This fact also reflects a deep transformation in the ideology at the foundation of the state's role from a direct operator to a supervisor and regulator. The paradigm shift from state to market creates an economy financed and operated by the private sector. The role of the state in such an economy is to enable the functioning and reliability of the system.

As a result of the studies conducted by the EU to create a fully liberalised internal market with a free competitive environment, the importance of PPP gradually is increasing.[93]

92 Directive 2014/25/EU of the European Parliament and of the Council of 26 February 2014 on procurement by entities operating in the water, energy, transport and postal services sectors and repealing Directive 2004/17/EC, OJ L 94, 28.3.2014, pp. 243–374.

93 "*The financial crisis has had a major impact on the capacity of European businesses and governments to finance investment and innovation projects. To accomplish its objectives for Europe 2020, a regulatory environment that renders financial markets both effective*

III. Privately Held Undertakings

A privately held entity refers to a commercial enterprise that is owned by private investors.

The developments in the direction of the free market economy worldwide have influenced the restructuring of the public sector. The most effective tool to reduce the role of government in the national economy is privatisation.

Today, the provider of energy services is not always a state-owned company, as the task can also be entrusted to private undertakings.[94] The advent of liberalisation throughout the last decades paved the way for a far more critical role for the energy industry. The energy sector was characterised by natural monopolies. In order to open the energy sector to competition, a restructuring of the sector was necessary. Over the last 30 years many countries have drastically reduced their share of state ownership in the energy sector. Therefore, the governments' role in the energy sector has been limited in the last decades. In many countries, strenuous efforts are being made to privatise state-owned undertakings and to put both the development and the production processes into private hands.[95]

According to *Proedrou*, the private energy companies that have emerged cannot be treated analytically in the same way as state-owned and state-controlled companies. These new actors are autonomous players in the market, driven foremost by their interests in survival and economic profitability. Since they have to serve their shareholders' interests, their policies, interests and strategies frequently deviate from those of their governments.[96]

---

and secure is key. Europe must also do all it can to leverage its financial means, pursue new avenues in using a combination of private and public finance, and in creating innovative instruments to finance the needed investments, including public-private partnerships (PPPs)." European Commission, Europe 2020 – A strategy for smart, sustainable and inclusive growth, 2010, p. 20.

94 Penttinen, 2014, p. 264.

95 Strange, 2009, p. 53.

96 Proedrou, 2012, p. 50; Strange, 2009, p. 143.

Part 2 The European Union's Energy Acquis

§ 3. Origins of the Energy Acquis

I. European Coal and Steel Treaty

In the past, coal constituted the most important resource fulfilling Europe's energy needs in the decade of 1950s.[97] During the period following World War II, Germany's neighbouring nations were concerned that Germany would again come to dominate the steel and coal industry, thus disrupting their access to steel and coal necessary for the rebuilding of their economies. Taking advantage of the occupation of Germany, allied powers established the International Authority for the Ruhr (IAR) in 1949 to control the coal and steel industry of the Ruhr Area and to regulate steel and coal production as well as trade practices in West Germany.

Accordingly, in a press conference in 1950, Robert Schuman suggested establishing a community which would end Germany's domination of the coal and steel industry.[98] It was also stated that other European countries would be free to join this community creating a single authority to control the coal and steel production of Germany and France. The objective of this plan was to build a peaceful Europe and prevent the conflict between Germany and other European countries, especially France.[99] Schuman expressed this aim in his speech as follows: "*by pooling basic production and by instituting a new High Authority, whose decisions will bind France, Germany and other member countries, this proposal will lead to the realisation of the first concrete*

97 Kohl, 1978, pp. 111–121.
Lang, 1957, p. 761.

98 Germany's market dominance over Europe was feared, especially due to the scarcity of steel in the market at that time. Such dominance would have caused difficulties for other countries which yearned to rebuild their own economies.

99 Reynolds, 1952, p. 282.

foundation of a European federation indispensable to the preservation of peace."[100] Another important reason was to undertake an initial step in facilitating the economic and political integration in Europe.

The coal sector was organised in a different manner in each nation. While Germany, France and Belgium were predominantly the main producers, Italy and Luxembourg had limited local production. West Germany and France could be considered the largest producers of coal, followed by Belgium and the Netherlands. Furthermore, the Netherlands were de facto self-sufficient in the days leading up to the war. However, after World War II, the Netherlands became dependent on imports of coal.

Ownership concepts differed from nation to nation. For example, in France the mining industry was nationalised. The nationalisation of the French coal mines began in 1944 and was completed in 1946.[101] Private coal companies were reorganised into the public mining company Charbonnages de France. Due to general political reasons, the coal prices were pegged at a low level and the resulting deficits were covered by subsidies. In the Netherlands, two-thirds of the mines belonged to the state, and, based on the 1908 Law, the state-owned companies controlled the industry.[102] In Italy, the coal industry was partially nationalised. Furthermore, the coal industry in France, Italy and the Netherlands was immensely concentrated, and it was characterised by a number of large companies and a few smaller firms.[103] In Belgium[104] and Germany[105] with little-to-no nationalisation, coal mines were controlled by small to medium-size private companies and by relatively

100 The Schuman Declaration, 9 May 1950.

101 On May 1946, the Coal Mines and Mineral Fuels Nationalisation Act was adopted, and nationalization became effective for the entire coal mining industry. Coal Mines Committee, 1947, p. 37.

102 Schmitt, 1964, p. 103.

103 Poelmans, 2012, p. 17.

104 Belgium alone boasted undiluted private ownership of its mines, half of the production of which, however, was controlled by two enterprises, the Société Générale and Launoit. In addition, a sales cartel, the Comptoir Beige des Charbons (COBECHAR), controlled 60% of the national output and the prices of the remaining independents as well.

105 *"While the overwhelming majority of Ruhr shafts remained in private hands, at least 80 per cent of their product fell under the control of a sales cartel founded in 1893 with the approval of the German government. In 1934, the same organisation*

few large or very small companies. The coal industry was not particularly concentrated.[106] The authors of the Schuman Plan thus sought to establish a common, competitive market for coal and steel.

Upon the suggestion of Schuman, Jean Monnet undertook the preparation of a draft treaty in order to establish the ECSC. During the Treaty negotiations in Paris, it was in fact taken into account that the real purpose of the countries was not the establishment of a coordinated sectoral structure; rather, their main intention was to access the resources which would in the future help them to rebuild their economies and their local industries. While production companies in France were fighting for easier access to German coal[107], the companies from Belgium, the Netherlands and Italy requested adjustment subsidies and asked for more time to rebuild their own industries.[108] The Netherlands was wholly against the independent supranational institution proposed by Monnet and insisted on establishing a Council of Ministers to control the High Authority. After several negotiations lasting for more than one year, the final Treaty exhibited a different picture as compared to the first draft which was prepared by Schuman.[109]

The Treaty of Paris, which founded the ECSC, was signed on 18 April 1951 and became effective on 23 July 1952. It was to be valid for 50 years, and it was superseded by the EC Treaty on 23 July 2002. Alongside France and Germany, Italy, Belgium, the Netherlands and

---

(Rheinisch-Westfalisches Kohlensyndikat) extended its sway over the output of the Aachen area." Schmitt, 1964, p. 104.

106 Poelmans, 2012, p. 17.

107 *"Monnet's proposed coal and steel pool has rather to be seen as a means to protect French security and promote economic reconstruction through the international control of Germany's heartland of heavy industry, the Ruhr. With France being—at the time—the world's largest importer of coal and coke, a common market for coal and steel promised to ensure sufficient and cheap supply of German combustible for French industry and for the realisation of the French economic modernisation plan. The motivation of the French governing elite to tie Germany's coal and steel industry to a supranational coal and steel pool was not driven by the sector- or issue-specific demands articulated by organised interests but rather by domestic economic policy objectives which were spelled out in the Monnet Plan."* Gillingham, 1991, p. 229.

108 Alter & Steinberg, 2007, p. 3.

109 *"The outlines of Monnet's original design were left intact in the treaty, with the High Authority remaining the exclusive source of executive power."* Alter, 2007, p. 89.

Luxembourg were participants.[110] The Treaty aimed at contributing to the economic expansion, growth of employment and a rising standard of living, through establishing a common market for coal and steel.[111] With its comprehensive economic regulations, the ECSC constitutes an important phase of the post-war economic reconfiguration struggles. It has been described as *"a new structure in the marches between internal and international law."*[112] It can be construed as the first supranational structure established by the European countries.[113] Member States transferred a part of their sovereignty to a supranational institution, namely the High Authority. The ECSC did not only form a customs union, but also the production volume and the selling price of coal and steel were decided by the supranational High Authority.

The ideas of the Schuman Plan were reflected in the following principles and purposes of the ECSC Treaty[114]:

- to secure the presence of a systematic market, and
- to provide a common market freely accessible to all member nations and to promote the development of the coal and steel industry as a whole by abolishing discriminative practices and trade barriers.

Since coal and steel require high-cost infrastructure investments, they were considered as immensely sensitive, which, in turn, led to limitative practices and amalgamations. Hence, more than simply creating a competitive environment, the Treaty aimed at producing sustainable results. The removal of national trade barriers could not alone assure the benefits to be gained from competition. The authors of the Treaty subsequently recognised that the introduction of detailed regulations

---

110 Although Schuman's proposal was addressed to all European nations which produced coal or steel, including the UK, the UK refused to be part of this plan. The reason for this was that the UK was not ready to sacrifice its national jurisdiction. According to Schuman, another reason is that the UK applies Anglo-Saxon law and does not prefer a written constitution. See: Mason, 1955, p. 9.

111 Article 2 of the ECSC Treaty.

112 Raalte, 1952, p. 74.

113 Belgium and Netherlands rejected the supranational structure proposed in the Schuman Plan at the Paris Conference in 1950; because of this reason the negotiation process lasted longer. See: Hospers & Groenendijk, 2003, p. 96. It could be argued that the High Authority was supranational, but the ECSC as a whole was largely intergovernmental.

114 Hyde-Smith, 1983, p. 176.

regarding pricing and competition was indispensable for the creation of an effective competitive environment. Furthermore, the members of the ECSC were aware that without these regulations the coal and steel industries could continue to fix prices, restrict production and technology, and allocate markets and raw materials.[115]

Politically, one must acknowledge that the ECSC advanced the process of integration. Economically, the ECSC achieved early success. The years 1952 to 1959 can be considered the golden age of the ESCS. It did a significant work removing the trade barriers, controlling pricing practices, harmonising national policies and restricting the development of cartels.[116] It can be argued that the ECSC was successful both in the market management and in the struggle against the economic crisis during that particular period. Following the creation of the ECSC, production of steel and iron increased by 75% in Member States, and industrial production increased by 58%. Moreover, when the overproduction of coal (especially in Belgium) became a problem[117] and the competitiveness of European coal was jeopardised due to availability of other fuels and imported coal after 1959, the ECSC helped to reduce coal-producing capacity and introduced programmes aiming at retraining miners and developing new industries.[118]

Although the coal-producing capacity and the employment in this sector decreased, the importance attributed to technological development, security and environmental issues increased. Moreover, security of supply increased along with better prices for consumers. Cross-border collaborations between companies from different countries increased.

However, the ECSC failed to achieve several fundamental goals of the Treaty of Paris and also to establish a common market for coal and steel.[119] The expectation had been that the ECSC would prevent a resurgence of large coal and steel groups such as the "Konzerne". Nevertheless, coal and steel industries became more concentrated. Ten

115 Bebr, 1953, pp. 6–7.

116 Cook, 2001, p. 1125.

117 Poelmans, 2012, p. 11.

118 European Commission, Expiry of the European Coal and Steel Community (ECSC) Treaty: an overview, 2002.

119 Alter & Steinberg, 2007, p. 90.

years after the establishment of the ESCS a shift towards fewer undertakings of all sizes with the larger undertakings accounting for a greater share of the total production could be ascertained.[120] In the Cold War trade-offs, the cartels and major companies re-emerged, leading to ostensible price fixing which was intended to be tackled by the ESCS.[121]

II. Euratom Treaty

The decision to create the Treaty establishing the European Atomic Energy Community (Euratom[122]) was taken during the Messina Conference in 1955.[123] In line with this decision, the intergovernmental committee headed by Henri Spaak was appointed to prepare a draft.[124] There were military[125] as well as economic and political reasons be-

120 Poelmans, 2012, p. 25.

121 Mathieu, 1970, p. 874.

122 *"Euratom can be defined as a union of sovereign states, based upon an international treaty, with institutions of its own, acting independently from the Member States, endowed in the field of nuclear energy with powers not only within the Community, but also competent to act as an international legal person."* Mathijsen, 1961, p. 438.

123 *"The Messina Conference, attended by the Foreign Ministers of the six Member States of the European Coal and Steel Community (ECSC), took place from 1 to 3 June 1955. In Messina, the Foreign Ministers expressed their wish to start negotiations at both levels at once: while forms of new, partial integration — especially in the areas of transport, conventional energy and nuclear energy — needed to be examined, another objective was the creation of a common market. The Six adopted a resolution in which they stated their determination to make 'further progress [...] towards the setting up of a united Europe by the development of common institutions, the gradual merging of national economies, the creation of a common market and the harmonisation of their social policies'."* The Messina Conference (1 to 3 June 1955), http://www.cvce.eu/ (accessed: 1 June 2019).

124 The foundations of EURATOM were laid in the first Spaak Report of 1956. *"The Spaak Report proposed to establish in EURATOM a common organisation which would not only promote the formation and rapid growth of the nuclear industry, but which would help with the transition of the whole economy from a coal to nuclear base."* Lucas, 1977, p. 16.

125 It was observed that, compared to the United States or the Soviet Union, Western Europe fell behind in terms of nuclear technology. The fact that this situation had the possibility of putting Western Europe in a bad state in the international military-political arena led Member States to take action in this area. Nanes, 1958, p. 12. See also: Vogelaar, 1960, p. 12.

hind the establishment of Euratom. The primary motivation which led Member States to focus intensely upon atomic energy was the energy deficits which occurred due to the existing political problems concerning secure import of petroleum from the Middle East (the main cause was the Suez Crisis[126]).[127]

Initially, the main objective of the Treaty was to find alternative energy resources in an effort to prevent the increasing dependency of European countries on Middle East petroleum.[128] The Community also gave particular importance to the development of nuclear energy for peaceful purposes. Moreover, in view of the devastating effects of the atomic bombs dropped over Japan during the Second World War, the Community tried to prevent the use of nuclear technology for military purposes. The Euratom Treaty also provided an incentive for Western European nations to place their nuclear development under the supranational authority of the Euratom Commission.[129]

III. Treaty on the Functioning of the European Union

As mentioned above, the European integration began in the 1950s through the establishment of three treaties: the ECSC Treaty, the Euratom Treaty and the EEC Treaty.

The original EEC Treaty has been amended several times. The Single European Act of 1986 (SEA) brought the first major reform as it set the

126 *"The Suez crisis in November 1956, precipitated by Egyptians seizure of the Canal, accelerated the timetable. Western Europe hoped to find a future source of power to replace Middle Eastern oil. More important the US. role in the crisis tended to confirm the French charge that American interest diverged from those of Europe that Europe could not base its strategic defence on U.S. nuclear weapons and that progress toward genuine European federation based on European interests alone, was imperative. This recognition strengthened French leadership on the Continent."* Nieburg, 1963, pp. 597–622.

127 However, following later agreements, the supply of petroleum from Africa began and petroleum prices did not increase significantly until the 1970. This development created the biggest obstacle for the development of Euratom.

128 In order to realise this goal, the Community has assumed the duty of developing nuclear technology and making it a useful energy source from which all humanity can benefit safely, from the first days of its establishment up until today.

129 Mallard, 2008, pp. 459–477.

objective of achieving the internal market by 1992 and introduced qualified majority voting in the Council, thus facilitating the adoption of internal market harmonising legislation. The SEA also supplemented the EEC Treaty with new provisions on economic and social cohesion, research and technological development. Moreover, it provided a legal basis for the Community. EU action within the environmental area in pursuit of defined policy objectives, such as the "prudent and rational utilisation of natural resources", became possible.

Soon thereafter, the Maastricht Treaty was concluded in 1992. It was significant in several ways. First it brought the three Communities (ECSC, Euratom and EEC) under one umbrella. The original three treaties remained in force, but the EEC was renamed and became the European Community (EC). Secondly, in Article 3(u) of EC Treaty[130], the energy area was considered to be in the competency of the Community; hence the authority to make regulations in this content was given to the Community.[131] However, other than in this article, the Treaty did not contain any specific chapter about energy except for the regulations on the environment within the SEA.[132] Another place where energy was mentioned was the Declaration No. 1 attached to the Treaty on the European Community.[133] It stated that the Treaty revision negotiations, to start in 1996, should again consider the question of energy (as well as tourism and civil protection) on the basis of a Commission proposal.[134]

130 Ex-Article 3(t).

131 Wägenbaur & Wainwright, 1996, p. 60.

132 Due to the fact that Member States have refused and continue to refuse to give up sovereignty over energy issues, the separate energy chapter could not be inserted in the Maastricht Treaty. "*The tension between national interests and the EU is the main reason why energy did not formally become a field of common policy during the treaty revisions in Maastricht and Amsterdam. When it was proposed during the negotiations over the Maastricht Treaty, Britain was against it as part of a strategy to limit the scope of supranational authority.*" Andersen, 2001, p. 122.

133 Lyons, 1998, p. 9.

134 On 3 April 1996, the Commission published a report regarding civil protection, tourism and energy. It was concluded that the Community does have a policy (as regards coal and nuclear energy) and specific or general instruments for implementing that policy; however, these instruments are scattered across the three treaties. Therefore, there was a need for the consolidation of this policy and these instruments. Report from the Commission to the Council on civil protection, tourism and energy. SEC (96) 496 final, 3 April 1996.

Moreover, Article 129b[135] of the EC Treaty authorised the EC to create Trans-European networks including energy and to support them financially. Both electricity lines and energy pipelines in liquid and gas state are also considered within the scope of Trans-European networks. The objectives cited in the EC Treaty might only be imposed on Member States, while the concept of Trans-European networks refers to the need to create networks across all of Europe. Within this scope, cooperation with third-party countries was also officially ensured.

Following the Maastricht Treaty, the Treaty of Amsterdam was signed in October 1997 and came into force in May 1999. It further increased the powers of the EU, including amendments to the EC. It simplified and renumbered the articles of the treaties. The Treaty of Amsterdam was followed in 2001 by the Treaty of Nice with the main purpose being to reform the institutions, so that the EU could function efficiently after growing to 25 Member States. Although these treaties did not include specific energy provisions, they did contain provisions which have had an impact on the energy sector, such as the services of general economic interest and the principles of subsidiarity and proportionality. Subsequently, a body of European energy and environmental legislation emerged, covering a broad range of energy-related matters. According to the Commission, the overall energy acquis more than doubled in size during the five-year period from 31 December 1999 to 31 December 2004.[136]

Despite various deficiencies in the legal framework becoming readily apparent, the overall experience demonstrated that it has been possible to elaborate and update a fairly thorough legislative framework relating to the energy sector without having to rely upon the formality of an "energy chapter" in the Treaty. Nevertheless, there was an apparent need for a more formal approach, and the aim was to replace the founding Treaties of the EU with a European Constitution. The Constitutional Treaty for Europe included a provision on the EU energy policy. It was signed in Rome on 29 October 2004.

In 2007, the European Council decided to convene an Intergovernmental Conference (IGC) to adopt a new Treaty. The IGC concluded

135 New Article 170 TFEU.

136 Directorate General of Energy and Transport, Repertoire of the Acquis Communautaire, 2004.

its work in October 2007. The Treaty of Lisbon was signed at the European Council of Lisbon on 13 December 2007 and was ratified by all Member States. The Treaty, entered into force on 1 December 2009, did not replace the founding Treaties but only amended them, as did the Amsterdam Treaty and the Nice Treaty. Therefore, two founding Treaties of the EU still remain: The Treaty on the European Union (TEU) and the Treaty establishing the European Community. However, at Lisbon, the latter was renamed the Treaty on the Functioning of the European Union. It thus brought an end to the "European Community". It also provided for a new allocation of competencies between the EU and Member States, aiming at improvements of the decision-making process. Moreover, it reformed several of the EU's internal and external policies.

The Lisbon Treaty has led to profound reforms in the EU, especially to changes in the EU's institutional and organisational structure, and it has widened the boundaries of European integration pushing them to the next level. In particular, the energy policy has been subject to fundamental changes. The introduction of its own chapter in Article 194 TFEU, titled XXI "Energy", can be considered the cornerstone on the way to the creation of the common energy policy.[137]

Firstly, the topic of energy is addressed in Article 4, which provides a "shared" competence[138] between the EU and Member States in the energy sector. Secondly, energy is discussed in Article 194. According to this Article, the EU's energy policy has the following four main objectives:

- ensuring the functioning of the energy markets,
- encouraging the development of energy efficiency, energy savings, new and renewable energy resources,

---

137 Pielow & Lewendel, 2012, p. 147.

138 "Shared competence" means that, when the Treaties confer on the EU a competence shared with Member States in a specific area, the EU and Member States may legislate and adopt legally binding acts in that area (Article 2(2) TFEU). However, Member States exercise their own competence to the extent that the EU does not exercise, or has decided not to exercise, its own competence. European Commission, Division of competences within the European Union, 2016. Under the principle of conferral, the EU may only act within the limits of the competences conferred upon it by the EU countries in the Treaties to attain the objectives provided therein (Article 5 of the TEU).

- ensuring the security of energy supply in the EU, and
- supporting the connections of energy networks with each other.

Article 194(1) puts forth two important changes. Firstly, a clear statement was added which declared that the energy policy would be formulated "in a spirit of solidarity between Member States." This addition was largely made as a result of the Polish delegation's insistence. However, background reasons included:

- the dependency on Russia, which exports energy to Central and Eastern European countries;
- concrete dispute situations due to reasons such as the disruption of natural gas transport to Central European countries in 2007 because of the showdown between Russia and Ukraine; and
- the Baltic Sea Pipeline Project.

Secondly, it can be seen that encouraging the intermediary connections of energy networks is an objective of the European energy policy.[139] This change is essential for creating an energy internal market and ensuring energy supply security across the EU.[140]

Article 194(2) specifies how competence is to be shared and gives authority to the EU for fulfilling the objectives specified in the first paragraph. Hence, the EU becomes obliged to take necessary measures. In the view of the provisions of Articles 4 and 122 TFEU, these objectives are to be implemented in a spirit of solidarity between Member States and the EU. Accordingly, as a rule, the EU and Member States can act together in the legislative area; however, Member States can only use their authorities when the EU does not use its authority or when it decides that it will not use its authority anymore.[141]

However, Member States still have the opportunity for opting out of the EU's energy policy.[142] According to Article 194(2) and (3), the measures to be taken by the EU should not affect a Member State's right to determine the conditions for exploiting its energy resources, its choice between different energy sources and the general structure of its energy supply.

139 Article 194(1)(d) TFEU.
140 Kahl, 2009, p. 608.
141 Ibid., p. 607.
142 Pielow & Lewendel, 2011, p. 153.

Despite the aforementioned changes, the Article has been criticised since it lacks a provision regarding third parties.[143] Contrary to Article 191[144], which sets out the legal basis for environmental policy, Article 194 does not put in place any regulation for the cooperation of the EU and Member States with third countries.

§ 4. Energy Acquis on Sectoral Base

I. Coal

A. General

1. Expiry of the European Coal and Steel Community Treaty

The ECSC Treaty has been of historical importance because it emphasised the necessity of the tenets of cooperation and common interest in terms of coal as an energy resource. The Treaty marked the establishment of the EC and included the first steps for creating a common energy policy. Articles 1 and 2 of the ECSC Treaty highlighted the cooperation envisaged among members with common interests.

The ECSC has stated its objectives which go beyond cooperation in terms of coal and steel. These included the following:

- providing more rational production and distribution,
- creating a single market in six Member States by combining coal and steel markets,
- increasing productivity and reducing costs,
- leaving the control of coal and steel production and consumption to a supranational organ,
- enabling the continuity of peace among Member States, and
- pioneering similar unities in other areas of Europe.

---

143 Pielow & Lewendel, 2012, p. 264.

144 Article 191 TFEU: "*Within their respective spheres of competence, the Union and the Member States shall cooperate with third countries and with the competent international organisations. The arrangements for Union cooperation may be the subject of agreements between the Union and the third parties concerned.*"

According to Article 97 of the ECSC Treaty, *"the Treaty is concluded for a period of 50 years as of its entry into force"*. In Council Resolutions of 20 July 1998[145] and 21 June 1999[146], the Council and the Representatives of Member States decided not to renew the ECSC Treaty and instead to continue operating the coal and steel sectors under the EC Treaty.[147] Following the Protocol attached to the Nice Treaty[148], the assets and liabilities of the ECSC were transferred to the European Union. The net worth of these assets was allocated to the new "Research Fund for Coal and Steel" (RFCS).[149]

The RFCS's legal basis is the Council Decision 2008/376/EC of 29 April 2008. The Commission, Directorate-General for Research and Innovation, implements the fund's activities with the assistance of a programme committee and several advisory committees consisting of experts from Member States, industry as well as academia.

The RFCS programme's main objective is to establish a correlation between research, innovation and industrial applications by using a network of researchers and producers. Thus, it aims at increasing the competitiveness of the European coal and steel industry, contributing to its sustainable development and promoting the exchange of information and rapid transfer of technology. In order to guarantee the economic,

145 OJ C 247, 7.8.1998, p. 5.
146 OJ C 190, 7.7.1999, p. 1.
147 Ubertazzi, 2004, p. 2.
148 Protocol on the financial consequences of the expiry of the ECSC Treaty and on the research fund for coal and steel, OJ C 80, 10.3.2001, pp. 67–68.
149 According to the Protocol added to the Nice Treaty, net assets of ECSC and liabilities conveyed to the EU are allocated to the new "Research Fund for Coal and Steel". As of the termination date of the Treaty, the total amount of the fund was 1.6 billion Euros. The yearly interest of this amount reaches 60 million Euros. 72.8% of it is allocated to steel researches. This amounts to more than 43 million Euros for the research conducted in 2003 and 2004. The Research Fund for Coal and Steel aims to create a reciprocal relationship between research, renovation and industrial practices by using a network of researchers and producers. For this reason, it encourages information exchange and rapid transfer of technology. Although ECSC ended in July 2002, this programme still continues. The Council Decision 2008/376/EC adopted on 29 April 2008 is the legal basis of this programme. The commission made a proposal for amending this decision on 18 February 2016. For more information, see: Research Fund for Coal and Steel, http://ec.europa.eu/research/industrial_technologies/rfcs_en.html_(accessed: 1 June 2019).

clean and safe production of steel products, the RFCS programme focuses on the development of new or improved technologies.[150]

Concerning coal, research projects supported by the fund aim at enhancing the entire coal production chain including the optimisation of coal mining production, improvement of coal preparation techniques and development of clean combustion processes. In addition, these projects focus on climate change issues as well as on health and safety issues in mines.[151]

2. State-Aid Regulations for Coal

State incentives for the coal industry play a significant role in the EU's sectorial policies. The basic provision regarding state aids is contained in Article 4(c) of the ECSC Treaty. According to Article 4 (c), subsidies or state assistance, or special charges imposed by the state, in any form whatsoever shall be abolished and prohibited, as they are recognised to be incompatible with the common market for coal. Although Article 4 prohibited granting state aid to the coal industry, it becomes clear that, when the Treaty as a whole is systematically interpreted, aids can be granted to the coal sector under some conditions.[152]

Commission Decision 3632/93/ECSC[153], adopted in 1993, established community rules concerning state aid to the coal sector and remained effective from 1994 until 2002 when the ECSC Treaty expired.[154] Then, it was replaced by Council Regulation 1407/2002 (the so-called Coal Regulation)[155] on 24 July 2002.[156] The Coal Regulation allowed state aids in the coal sector (until 31 December 2010).

150 CPS, 2011, p. 47.

151 Research Fund for Coal and Steel, http://ec.europa.eu/research/industrial_technologies/rfcs_en.html (accessed: 1 June 2019).

152 Kühne, 1994, p. 85.

153 Commission Decision No 3632/93/ECSC of 28 December 1993 establishing Community rules for State aid to the coal industry, OJ L 329, 30.12.1993, pp. 12–18.

154 Quigley, 2009.

155 Council Regulation (EC) No 1407/2002 of 23 July 2002 on State aid to the coal industry, OJ L 205, 2.8.2002, pp. 1–8.

156 The most striking basic difference between these two regulations is that Council Regulation 1407/2002 gives its weight to energy security. Recital 3, 11 and 12 of the Directive mentioned energy security. While Recital 3 gives importance to the diversity of the energy resources for ensuring security of supply, according to

According to Article 3(1), only the aid granted to the coal industry which complies with the provisions of Chapter 2 of the Coal Regulation could be considered compatible with the proper functioning of the common market, without prejudice to state aid schemes concerning research and technological development, the environment and training. The Coal Regulation allowed for closure aid[157], investment aid[158] and operating aid.[159]

The coal industry was forced to undertake substantial restructuring measures involving major cutbacks in activity due to the competitive imbalance between the Community coal and imported coal. To overcome this imbalance, Council Regulation 1407/2002 allowed Member States to grant state aid to the coal sector.[160]

Under the Coal Regulation, 11 Member States continued to produce coal. These countries can be divided into the following three groups[161]:

- countries which stopped coal subsidies for mines in operation (Italy, France, and the Czech Republic)
- countries which granted investment aid (the United Kingdom, Slovakia, and Poland)
- countries which granted operating aid (Spain, Germany, Bulgaria, Romania, Hungary and Slovenia)

Since the Coal Regulation expired on 31 December 2010[162], the Council adopted a new Decision, the so-called Coal Decision[163], on 10 December 2010. The Coal Decision should not be considered a continuation of the Coal Regulation since the two pursue different aims. The Decision aims at facilitating the transition for the coal sector, from the application of sector-specific rules to the enforcement of general State

Recital 1 production of subsidised coal must be limited to what is strictly necessary to make an effective contribution to the objective of energy security. Johnston & Block, 2012, p. 360.

157 Article 4 of Regulation 1407/2002.

158 Article 5(2) of Regulation 1407/2002.

159 Article 5(3) of Regulation 1407/2002.

160 Recital 2 of Regulation 1407/2002.

161 European Commission, Commission Report on the Application of Council Regulation (EC) No 1407/2002 on State Aid to the Coal Industry, 2007, p. 3.

162 Article 14(3) of Regulation 1407/2002.

163 Council Decision 2010/787/EU on State aid to facilitate the closure of uncompetitive coal mines, OJ L 336, 21.12.2010, pp. 24–29.

aid rules.[164] According to the Decision, *"aid must be degressive"*. In other words, it was contemplated that the aid provided by the State should be decreased gradually and be totally abolished by 31 December 2018.

There are several technical, social and environmental reasons for the aforementioned gradual plan of the Commission. As for the enumeration of the technical reasons, after closing a mine staggered measures such as the removal of mining equipment, the cleaning-up of the site, underground safety work, the removal of wastewater and other measures are needed for rehabilitating the mining area. As for the social reasons, after closing a mine, many workers would become unemployed. Therefore, Member States should be able to take measures to alleviate the social consequences of the closure of mines.[165] Member States should provide financial support to workers who have lost or will lose their jobs due to closure of the mines by funding severance packages and social security benefits[166], such as paying social welfare benefits resulting from the pensioning-off of workers before they reach statutory retirement age, paying pensions and allowances outside the statutory system, supplying free coal and covering former miners' health insurance.[167]

The Coal Decision regulates the state aid granted to the coal industry within the framework of the closing of mines which are no longer competitive. The state aid may be deemed compatible with the internal market only if the aid is granted to cover costs concerning coal used for the electricity generation, the combined production of heat and electricity, the production of coke and the fuelling of blast furnaces in the steel industry, where such use takes place in the Union. With respect to the said scope, Member States can solely provide state incentives upon the closure of the production units with a deadline which does not extend beyond 31 December 2018. Beyond that date, it was decided that aid for exceptional costs of closure related to social welfare benefits, such as site rehabilitation or removal of wastewater, can be given until 31 December 2027 by Member States.

164 Recital 6 of Council Decision 2010/787/EU.
165 Recital 5 of Council Decision 2010/787/EU.
166 Case SA.34332, European Union v Spain, Aid to facilitate the closure of coal mines in Spain; Hancher & Klasse, 2018, p. 229.
167 Annex of Council Decision 2010/787/EU.

According to the Council Resolution, aids pertaining to the current production losses of production units are considered as compatible with the internal market solely if the conditions determined in Article 3 are met.[168] Article 7 of the Coal Decision states that Member States having an intention to grant closure aid must notify the Commission of their intention. Through this decision, the closure of uncompetitive mines is supported in a socially and politically acceptable way.[169] Since the Coal Decision entered into force, the Commission has dealt with a number of cases, some of which solely concerned aid for exceptional costs (Slovenia[170] and Poland[171]). However, the more significant aid volumes were in relation to the closure of coal mines which were no longer economically feasible, and they were related to covering production costs.[172]

As the deadline was approaching (31 December 2018), there was an increase in decisions concerning closure aid, including in relation to mines whose restructuring had proven unsuccessful in the past.[173] For instance, in May 2016 the Commission approved Spanish plans to grant €2.13 billion aid to support the operators of 26 coal mines that were supposed to be shut down by 2018.[174] However, since Spain could not reach its goal of having a subsidy-free coal sector, amendments were made to the Framework Plan in 2017.[175] Spain implemented an amended plan to gradually reduce coal mining subsidies by 2019.

---

168 Article 3 of Council Decision 2010/787/EU.

169 European Commission, Frequently Asked Questions – Coal Regulation, 2010.

170 Case SA.30907, *Slovenia Closure of mine Trbovlje Hrastnik Ltd*, [2011] OJ C294/3.

171 Case SA.33013, *Poland Coal plan for the period 2011–2015*, [2013] OJ Cl22/6.

172 Case SA.24642, *German Coal mine closure plan 2008–2018*, [2012] OJ C284/6 and Case SA.33033, *National Hard Coal Company Petrosani*, [2013] C23/3.

173 Hancher & Klasse, 2018, pp. 218–222.

174 Under Spain's National Coal Plan (2006–2012) this aid was initially expected to be phased out by the end of 2010. However, in 2013 the Spanish government reached an agreement with the domestic coal industry regarding the reduction of subsidies to the coal mining sector until the end of 2018. This plan only received approval by the European Commission in 2016. Case SA.34332, *Aid to facilitate the closure of coal mines in Spain*, [2016] OJ C471/1.

175 Financial measures under the amended Framework plan include the following (Decision 2010/787/EU): closure aid: for uncompetitive coal mines (2013–2018); exceptional aid: social aid for labour costs to cover lost working days and for advanced age workers, but also environmental aid for the rehabilitation of mining land (2013–2021); economic stimulation aid: financing of infrastructure and job creation projects for an alternative economic development of mining regions

In November 2016, the Commission agreed upon granting state aid of €1.8 billion to ensure the orderly closure of coal mines in Poland.[176] Similar to the Spanish scheme, the new aid was partially an extension of schemes that had been approved by the Commission but had meanwhile expired.[177]

Even though the deadline (31 December 2018) passed, some countries (i.e. Romania) continue to grant state aid to the coal sector.[178]

B. Directive 2009/31/EC[179]

1. Carbon Capture and Storage Technologies

In order to reduce the environmental problems due to coal usage, to increase the competitive capacity of coal and to enable its acceptance environmentally, large financial resources are allocated to R&D studies in the areas of developing modern, more efficient clean coal technologies and their implementation. For this purpose, during the ECSC period the budget of "Research and Technology Development Programme", which operated between 1957 and 2002, was dedicated to R&D studies.

Certain short-term and mid-term studies in the area of clean coal technologies have focused on decreasing current coal-based thermal power plant emissions by using control technologies (SO_2 and NO_x technologies, combined SO_2/NO_x technologies and dust emission reducing technologies), improving coal preparation technologies, supporting the launch of new thermal power plants based on highly-effi-

(2013–2021). Cutting Europe's lifelines to coal, https://www.odi.org/sites/odi.org.uk/files/resource-documents/11488.pdf (accessed: 1 August 2019).

176 Case SA.41161, *State Aid to Polish coal mining in the period 2015–2018*, [2017] OJ C51/1.

177 Case SA.33013, *Coal plan for the period 2011–2015*, [2013] OJ Cl22/6; Hancher & Klasse, 2018, p. 222.

178 Romania keeps giving state aid to coal even as it holds EU presidency, https://www.euractiv.com/section/energy/opinion/romania-keeps-giving-state-aid-to-coal-even-as-it-holds-eu-presidency/ (accessed: 1 August 2019).

179 Directive 2009/31/EC of the European Parliament and of the Council of 23 April 2009 on the geological storage of carbon dioxide and amending Council Directive 85/337/EEC, European Parliament and Council Directives 2000/60/EC, 2001/80/EC, 2004/35/EC, 2006/12/EC, 2008/1/EC and Regulation (EC) No 1013/2006; OJ L 140, 5.6.2009, pp. 114–135.

cient coal and bringing in CO_2 capture and storage technologies. The long-term aim is to commercially launch – with ongoing R&D studies – highly efficient thermal power plants which have nearly zero emission and to launch technologies of CO_2 capture and storage.

Generally, the concept of "clean coal technologies" refers to the efficiency and environmental dimensions of coal production, preparation and usage processes. These technologies aim at reducing emissions and wastes on the one hand and to increase the energy obtained from a unit of coal on the other hand. The main areas upon which the global coal industry recently has focused include increasing the efficiency of coal-based thermal power plants and decreasing the CO_2 emissions of these power plants. The expectation is for coal to obtain its leading position in the realm of energy and become once again a preferred fuel option as a result of technological developments.[180]

It can be observed that research efforts progress according to the general strategic framework adopted by industrialised Western countries which try to increase the efficiency of coal-based thermal power plants while limiting CO_2 emissions. Moreover, such efforts are based on the following three objectives:

- reaching the 44–45% efficiency level by enabling the use of the latest technologies (supercritical, ultra-supercritical) in current or newly established coal-based power plants (obtaining more efficiency from a unit of coal) and reducing CO_2 emissions by 1/3;
- reaching the 50–55% efficiency level by means of more advanced thermal power plant technologies and again reducing CO_2 emissions by 1/3; and
- reaching the 52–55% efficiency level by launching CO_2 capture and storage (CCS) technologies, and bringing to zero CO_2 emissions.

In this framework, the EU's energy policy bases the future of coal almost entirely on the development of CCS technologies.[181] In line with this policy, the accelerating development of the CCS demonstration facilities and the establishment of the infrastructure in this area have been important priorities for the EU. In this regard, a precondition for investing in CCS technologies seems to be the commercial-scale success

180 Kavalov & Peteves, 2007, p. 8.
181 Euracoal, 2011, p. 3.

of the trials which will establish the full chain defining CO_2 capture, compression, transport and proper storage and which will demonstrate the technical, economic and environmental performance of these technologies.

2. The CCS Directive

Directive 2009/31/EC (so-called: CCS Directive) constitutes the legal basis of CCS. The objectives of the CCS Directive can be specified as follows[182]

- providing a legal framework for the environmentally safe application of CO_2 storage;
- preventing or eliminating as far as possible negative effects and any risk to the environment and human health;
- ensuring that CCS technology would be deployed in an environmentally safe way;
- providing clarity, coherence and the stability necessary to enable market operators to invest in CCS facilities across the EU under comparable regulatory conditions;
- ensure the security of transport networks and storage spaces;
- minimising the risk of leakage and address the liability issues for leakage from storage sites during operation and post-closure.

The CCS Directive covers all the conditions that a storage space will need throughout its lifecycle. It also contains rules concerning extraction and transport together with the conditions of storage spaces.

The CCS Directive assigns the EU the duty of reviewing the implementation of the Directive with Article 38. Member States submitted reports on how the Directive would be applied between July 2011 and April 2013. As of September 2013, all Member States completed the transposition of the CCS Directive into their domestic laws. Some Member States found it sufficient to amend their current laws, while the rest preferred to create new regulations within their national legal framework. On 18 November 2015, the Commission prepared a report about the CCS Directive. In this report, it is concluded that the CCS

182 Johnston & Block, 2012, p. 366.

Directive properly serves its purpose and that it creates a regulatory framework for CO_2 capture, transport and storage.[183]

II. Natural Gas

A. Directives concerning Natural Gas

1. Directive 91/296/EEC

Directive 91/296/EEC[184], the so-called Natural Gas Transit Directive, entered into force with the aim of creating a common market in gas in order to accomplish the objective of establishing the European Common Market. It intended to make the energy trade between the various European States more efficient[185] and required Member States to take the measures necessary to facilitate the transit of natural gas between high-pressure transmission grids.[186]

According to the Directive, contracts concerning the natural gas transit between grids were to be negotiated between the undertakings responsible for those grids and the undertakings responsible for importing and exporting natural gas in Member States.[187] These contracts must not contain unfair clauses or unjustified restrictions and cannot include any provision which might endanger security of supply or quality of service.[188] Moreover, the conditions of transit should be non-discriminatory and fair for all parties concerned.

The Directive noted that greater natural gas transfers between grids can minimise the cost of investment involved in services related to this transit and ensure optimum use of the means of production and infrastructure.[189] Moreover, it stated that increased natural gas transfers between grids would also provide an incentive for natural gas

183 European Commission, Climate action progress report, 2015.
184 Council Directive 91/296/EEC of 31 May 1991 on the transit of natural gas through grids, OJ L 147, 12.6.1991, pp. 37–40.
185 Capece et al., 2007, p. 418.
186 Article 1 of Directive 91/296/EEC.
187 Article 3(1) of Directive 91/296/EEC.
188 Article 3(2) of Directive 91/296/EEC.
189 Haghighi, 2007, p. 127.

transmission undertakings to cooperate in order to find ways of improving natural gas transmission equipment which could lower the costs and consequently bring down the prices.[190]

2. Directive 98/30/EC

Directive 98/30/EC[191] came into force on 19 August 1998. It envisaged the implementation of common rules regarding transmission, distribution, supply and storage of the natural gas in Member States. It contained the essential provisions on the structure and the functioning of the natural gas markets, including access to the market, the operation of systems and procedures applicable to the granting of authorisations for transmission, distribution, supply and storage of natural gas.[192] Member States were expected to transpose Directive 98/30/EC into their internal laws within a two-year time frame.[193]

Unbundling: According to Directive 98/30/EC, vertically[194] or horizontally integrated[195] natural gas undertakings were required to keep separate accounting records for each of their activity areas.[196] Furthermore, where appropriate, they were to keep consolidated accounts for their non-natural gas related activities. The purpose of such a practice was to prevent integrated undertakings from discriminating and cross-subsidising and to avoid the distortion of competition.[197]

Moreover, the Directive included further provisions regarding confidentiality of commercially sensitive information, which is known as the

190 Recital 11 of Directive 91/296/EEC.

191 Directive 98/30/EC of the European Parliament and of the Council of 22 June 1998 concerning common rules for the internal market in natural gas, OJ L 204, 21.7.1998, pp. 1–12.

192 Article 1 of Directive 98/30/EC.

193 Article 29 of Directive 98/30/EC.

194 Article 2(16) of Directive 98/30/EC stated that "'*vertically integrated undertaking' means a natural gas undertaking performing two or more of the tasks of production, transmission, distribution, supply or storage of natural gas*".

195 Article 2(17) of the Directive 98/30/EC said that "'*horizontally integrated undertaking' means an undertaking performing at least one of the functions of production, transmission, distribution, supply or storage of natural gas, and a non-gas activity*".

196 Article 13 of Directive 98/30/EC.

197 Cameron, 2002, p. 181.

"Chinese Wall" principle[198]. Each transmission, storage, LNG and distribution undertaking was, in the context of sales or purchases of natural gas by the distribution undertaking or related undertakings, required to preserve the confidentiality of commercially sensitive information when such information was obtained in the course of carrying out its business.[199] Moreover, transmission and distribution undertakings were required not to abuse commercially sensitive information obtained from third parties in the context of providing or negotiating access to the system.[200] Along with the aforementioned measures, legislators aimed at precluding competition violations and preventing potential discrimination. However, it should be said that, in practice, it is not easy to identify whether the commercially sensitive information is abused or discrimination is taking place.[201]

System operator: Directive 98/30/EC did not envisage an obligation for appointing a transmission system operator in Member States. However, it can be stated that, in practice, the aforementioned situation emerged from the fact that vertically integrated undertakings operated within the ambit of natural gas supply activities by protecting their intrinsic structure.[202]

Access to networks: According to Directive 98/30/EC, non-discriminatory access to upstream pipeline networks was necessary. Member States were to allow certain gas customers to buy gas from the supplier of their choice and to have it transported through the existing pipeline network at negotiated or regulated rates.[203]

Directive 98/30/EC introduced two different access regimes: negotiated access[204] and regulated access.[205] Under the negotiated access, eligible customers could enter into negotiations with natural gas undertakings to determine the precise contractual terms for access to the gas network. Natural gas undertakings were obliged to publish their

198 An artificial barrier restricting the flow of information between different areas within an organization inasmuch as it could lead to conflicts of interest.
199 Cameron, 2002, p. 183.
200 Articles 8 and 11 of Directive 98/30/EC.
201 Cameron, 2002, p. 183.
202 Gräper & Schoser, 2004, p. 61.
203 Brakman et al., 2009, pp. 8–9.
204 Article 15 of Directive 98/30/EC.
205 Article 16 of Directive 98/30/EC.

main commercial conditions for access. Under the regulated access, eligible customers were to have a right of access on the basis of regulated and published tariffs and/or other terms and obligations for use of the network.

Eligible customer: Pursuant to Directive 98/30/EC, an "eligible customer" could be defined as a consumer who is eligible to enter into a commercial relationship with the suppliers of choice in the course of supplying natural gas within the national borders of a Member State. It is stated that Member States were to determine the necessary criteria for being eligible customers and subsequently publish it. Furthermore, Member States had to ensure that end consumers who consume approximately 25 million m^3 of natural gas annually and gas-fired power generators, irrespective of their annual consumption level, were designated as eligible customers.

According to the Directive, distribution undertakings, if not already specified as eligible customers, had the right to enter into commercial relationships with eligible customers regarding gas supply in regions over which they had distribution authority.[206]

The Commission might request a Member State to modify its specifications concerning eligible customers if they create obstacles to the correct application of the Directive as regards the smooth functioning of the internal market in natural gas.[207]

Directive 98/30/EC adopted a gradual approach in terms of the opening of markets. In this framework, Member States had to ensure that the definition of eligible customers would result in an opening of the market equal to at least 20% of the total annual gas consumption of the national gas market, increasing to 28% in 2003 and 33% in 2008.

Assessment: In 2001, the Commission published the first benchmarking report on the implementation of the internal electricity and gas market. According to the report, as of 2001, almost all Member States had implemented the Gas Directive into their national legislation and brought into force the laws, except France and Germany. The Commission launched infringement procedures against these countries.

---

206 Article 18 of Directive 98/30/EC.

207 Article 18(9) of Directive 98/30/EC.

However, the report also identified a number of competition-related issues[208]:

- Significant obstacles remained for eligible consumers and new entrants into the market.
- There was a high concentration in the gas production and import markets which made it difficult for new entrants to buy wholesale gas on reasonable terms.
- Third parties did not have flexibility to change their gas sources or their customer base without incurring higher costs due to network access tariffs based on distance and point-to-point capacity reservation.
- High network tariffs formed a barrier to competition in themselves by discouraging third-party access and provided revenue for cross subsidy of affiliated businesses in the competitive market.
- Network access tariffs and conditions which were not subject to *ex ante* approval created uncertainty and led to time consuming disputes.
- Balancing regimes were non-market-based and were unnecessarily stringent and not reflective of costs incurred.
- The level of unbundling was not sufficient and led to obscure discriminatory practices and cross subsidies.

According to the Commission, in order to achieve the goal of a fully functioning competitive internal gas market, concrete provisions were needed which would aim at reducing the risks of market dominance and predatory behaviour, ensuring non-discriminatory access to transmission and distribution networks on the basis of tariffs published prior to their entry into force and ensuring that the rights of customers are protected.[209]

208 European Commission, First benchmarking report on the implementation of the internal electricity and gas market, 2001, p. 4.

209 Recital 30 of Directive 2003/55/EC.

3. Directive 2003/55/EC

Directive 2003/55/EC[210] entered into effect on 4 August 2003. It required that Member States implement the Directive in their domestic laws through the key legal arrangements such as law, by-laws and regulations by 1 July 2004.[211] The Directive[212] aimed at creating a fully operational competitive internal gas market.[213]

Unbundling: The Directive envisaged three different forms of unbundling: accounting, legal and management. It aimed at preventing distortion of competition, cross-subsidisation and discrimination. The most radical shift in this Directive was the introduction of legal unbundling by requiring that transmission and distribution activities must be carried out by separate undertakings. In other words, the Directive required transmission and distribution system operators which were part of a vertically integrated undertaking to be independent, at least in terms of their respective legal forms, organisation and decision making, from other activities such as production or supply.[214]

Moreover, vertically integrated natural gas undertakings were required to keep separate accounts for their different activities, e.g., transmission, distribution, LNG and storage, as they would be required to do if the activities in question were carried out by separate undertakings.[215] Where appropriate, they were required to keep consolidated accounts for other, non-gas activities.

System operator: Directive 2003/55/EC required that a system operator should be designated by Member States or by the owners of the facilities wherein natural gas transmission, storage, distribution and LNG activities were conducted. According to the Directive, system operators (e.g., transmission, storage and/or LNG) were to avoid discriminating between system users, particularly in favour of their related

210 Directive 2003/55/EC of the European Parliament and of the Council of 26 June 2003 concerning common rules for the internal market in electricity and repealing Directive 98/30/EC, OJ L 176, 15.7.2003, pp. 57–78.

211 Article 33 of Directive 2003/55/EC.

212 Although the Directive was repealed by Directive 2009/73/EC, the most of main provisions were transposed into the new Directive.

213 Recital 30 of Directive 2003/55/EC.

214 Article 9 of Directive 2003/55/EC.

215 Article 17(3) of Directive 2003/55/EC.

undertakings, and not abuse commercially sensitive information or disclose it.

These system operators were to function, maintain and develop under economic conditions secure, reliable and efficient transmission, storage and/or LNG facilities, with due regard to the environment.[216] Moreover, each system operator were to provide any other system operator with sufficient information to ensure that the transport and storage of natural gas takes place in a manner compatible with the secure and efficient operation of the interconnected system.[217]

Furthermore, Article 15 of Directive 2003/55/EC allowed for operation of a combined transmission and distribution system operator. According to the Directive, transmission, LNG, storage and distribution activities could be combined under a single system operator as long as it was independent in terms of its legal form, organisation and decision making from other activities not relating to operations mentioned above.

Access to networks: Directive 2003/55/EC abandoned the "negotiated third-party access", and a more rigid "regulated third-party access" was adopted.[218] Regarding the regulated third-party access regime, the respective system operator was to publish tariffs, applicable to all eligible customers, including supply undertakings. Member States were required to ensure that these tariffs, or the methodologies underlying their calculation, are approved by a regulatory authority prior to their entry into force.[219] Tariffs were to be applied objectively and without discrimination between system users.

Access to storage facilities: The Directive realised two types of access regimes for storage facilities: regulated and negotiated third-party access. Member States had a choice as to which access regime to be introduced for storage facilities. However, both of above-mentioned options were to be implemented in accordance with objective, transparent and non-discriminatory criteria.[220]

216 Article 8 of Directive 2003/55/EC.
217 Ibid.
218 Article 18 of Directive 2003/55/EC.
219 Ibid.
220 Cameron, 2007, p. 185.

Eligible Customers: Directive 2003/55/EC required Member States to ensure that all non-household customers are eligible as 1 July 2004, and as of 1 July 2007 all customers are to be eligible.[221]

Assessment: Despite all the improvements introduced in the Directive, there were still a number of obstacles to the establishment of a fully competitive internal gas market. In order to address these issues, the Commission conducted an energy sector inquiry[222] in the electricity and gas markets in order to identify the main problems and find solutions. In the final report of the energy sector inquiry the Commission found the following shortcomings:

- At the wholesale level, the gas market remained national in scope and generally maintained a high level of concentration.
- Development of wholesale gas trade followed a slow pace, and the incumbents maintained their dominant position in their respective traditional markets by largely controlling upstream gas imports and/or domestic gas production.
- Despite the new unbundling provisions, new entrants often lacked effective access to networks, to storage and to liquefied natural gas terminals.
- Available capacity on cross-border import pipelines was limited.
- There was a lack of reliable and timely information on the markets.
- Competition at the retail level was often limited due to contracts with long or indefinite duration or contracts with tacit renewal clauses and long termination periods.
- LNG terminals must be open to third parties (to the extent such access does not eliminate the terminal constructor's incentives to build the terminal).

According to the energy sector inquiry, in order to address the aforementioned market shortcomings and to significantly improve the scope of competition it was essential to apply both competition- and regulatory-based remedies. Additionally, the report stated that, although competition law in the near future would contribute significantly, the imple-

221 Ibid., p. 193.

222 European Commission, Inquiry pursuant to Article 17 of Regulation (EC) No 1/2003 into the European gas and electricity sectors (Final Report) (SEC (2006) 1724), 2006.

mentation of competition law rules solely would not be sufficient for opening the gas market to competition and various regulatory measures should be taken for the solution of the problems detected by the energy sector inquiry.[223] The inquiry itself stated that competition law enforcement constitutes an effective tool to address some of the above-identified market shortcomings, namely[224]P market concentration, vertical foreclosure, market integration and market partitioning.

As the energy sector inquiry noted main concerns regarding the market structure, such as insufficient unbundling, as well as the regulatory environment, such as regulatory gaps specifically relating to cross border issues, it would have to be tackled in parallel in order to remedy the malfunctioning of the markets.[225]

4. Directive 2009/73/EC

The energy sector inquiry brought to light a wide range of important areas in which competition did not yet fully function in the EU energy markets. In order to address the ineffectiveness of the pre-existing EU Directive in achieving the goal of creating an internal gas market, the Commission proposed a new Directive.[226] Having not obtained the desired results from Directive 2003/55/EC, Directive 2009/73/EC[227] was enacted on 13 June 2009 within the scope of the Third Energy Package. It includes the following objectives:

- improving the functioning of the internal gas market in the EU,
- increasing the regulatory power and independence of national regulation institutions,
- providing more effective cooperation between transmission system operators,
- taking measures for increasing security of supply,

223 Ibid., p. 12.
224 Piergiovanni, 2009, p. 4; European Commission, Energy Sector Inquiry, 2007, pp. 12–13.
225 Energy Sector Inquiry, para. 52.
226 Johnston & Block, 2012, pp. 23–24.
227 Directive 2009/73/EC of the European Parliament and of the Council of 13 July 2009 concerning common rules for the internal market in natural gas and repealing Directive 2003/55/EC, OJ L 211, 14.8.2009, pp. 94–136.

- establishing the Agency for the Cooperation of Energy Regulators (ACER) to function as a coordination and consultation committee for cross-border transmission,
- establishing the European Network of Transmission System Operators for Gas to create a "network code" for cross-border transmission, and
- establishing a new distinguishing regime for Member States with three options.

Unbundling and system operator: Directive 2009/73/EC introduced three new unbundling mechanisms: ownership unbundling, independent transmission operator, independent distribution operator.

The Directive also emphasises that any unbundling system chosen by Member States should be effective in eliminating any conflict of interest between the producers, suppliers and also the system operators in order to create incentives for the necessary investments and to ensure that the new entrants can freely access the market under a transparent and efficient regulatory regime.[228] Moreover, it stresses that the system should not create an overly onerous regulatory regime for national regulatory authorities.

According to the Directive, each undertaking which owns a transmission system acts as a transmission system operator[229]; Member States may also choose to designate an independent system operator upon a proposal from the transmission system owner.[230]

Further, the Directive also requires Member States to designate or request natural gas undertakings which own storage or LNG facilities to designate one or more storage and LNG system operators for a period of time to be determined by Member States, having regard to considerations of efficiency and economic balance.[231]

Access to networks: In terms of the third-party access regime, the provisions are identical to that in the previous Directive. Member States are required to ensure implementation of a third-party access

228 Recital 9 of Directive 2009/73/EC.
229 Article 9(1) of Directive 2009/73/EC.
230 Article 14 of Directive 2009/73/EC.
231 Article 13 of Directive 2009/73/EC.

regime to distribution networks and storage facilities in a non-discriminatory manner.[232]

According to the Directive, in the case of a major new gas infrastructure the respective national regulatory authority has the competence to exempt this infrastructure from the general rules of third-party access under conditions stated in Article 36, e.g., the investment must increase competition in the gas supply market and enhance security of supply.[233]

Access to storage: Directive 2009/73/EC introduced a clear roadmap regarding access to storage facilities. According to the Directive, storage system operators must operate independently to facilitate the third-party access to storage systems needed for a technically and economically sufficient gas supply to consumers. Storage undertakings should be separate corporate entities in order to be able to make the necessary decisions for their facilities' maintenance, operation and development. The Directive also requires Member States to create and publish a non-discriminatory, clear framework which determines the appropriate regulatory regime applicable to storage facilities in order to increase transparency concerning the storage capacity offered to third parties.

Eligible customers: The provisions regarding eligible customers are identical to those in the previous Directive. According to Directive 2009/73/EC, Member States must ensure that the eligible customer is able to switch easily to a new supplier.[234]

Regulatory authority: Directive 2009/73/EC requires each Member State to designate a single national regulatory authority at national level, ensure its independence and ensure that it exercises its powers impartially and transparently.[235]

Assessment: The Commission actively supervised the application of Directive 2009/73/EC by Member States. The Commission initiated several infringement procedures against Member States which failed to transpose Directive 2009/73/EC into their national laws. These infringement proceedings incentivised Member States to put in place the national legislation fully transposing the Directive.

232 Article 32–35 of Directive 2009/73/EC.
233 Article 36 of Directive 2009/73/EC.
234 Article 3(3) of Directive 2009/73/EC.
235 Article 39 of Directive 2009/73/EC.

Despite the attempts of the Commission, Directive 2009/73/EC has not been successful in liberalising the natural gas market. Continuous increase in prices, high market concentration, low rates of customers switching suppliers indicates that Directive 2009/73/EC was actually not sufficient to create a liberalised and fully competitive natural gas market.[236]

B. Regulations Concerning Natural Gas

1. Regulation 1775/2005

Regulation 1775/2005[237] was adopted in 2005; it set out the conditions for access to natural gas transmission networks within the EU.

The Regulation aimed at establishing rules on non-discriminatory and fair access conditions to the natural gas transmission networks by also considering the features of national and regional markets and by setting harmonised principles for access to network for cross-border gas exchange. These rules were to ensure that the internal natural gas market functions properly. The Regulation contained harmonised principles for tariffs, or the methodologies underlying their calculation, for access to the network, for capacity allocation and congestion management, rules on TPA services, transparency requirements and principles for balancing rules and imbalance charges and facilitating capacity trading.[238]

According to the Regulation, the access tariffs were to be transparent[239] and to be applied in a non-discriminatory manner. Tariffs, or the methodologies used to calculate them, were to facilitate efficient gas trade and competition while at the same time avoiding cross-subsidies between network users, providing incentives for investment and maintaining or creating interoperability for transmission networks.[240] Moreover, the Regulation stated that tariffs for network access should

236 Yu, 2010, p. 22.

237 Regulation (EC) No 1775/2005 of the European Parliament and of the Council of 28 September 2005 on conditions for access to the natural gas transmission networks, OJ L 289, 3.11.2005, pp. 1–13.

238 Article 1 of the Regulation 1775/2005.

239 Article 3(1) of the Regulation 1775/2005.

240 Article 3(1) of the Regulation 1775/2005.

neither restrict market liquidity nor distort trade across borders of different transmission systems.[241]

The Regulation required transmission system operators to offer both long and short-term services to all network users without any discrimination.[242] In addition, these services were to be provided in a consistent manner without interruption.

The transmission system operators were required to make public detailed information concerning

- the services they offer,
- the relevant conditions applied,
- the technical data necessary for network users to gain effective network access[243], and
- the technical, contracted and available capacities on a numerical basis for all relevant points, including entry and exit points, on a regular and rolling basis and in a user-friendly, standardised manner.[244]

If the transmission system operator brought an application which required that a piece of information be kept secret, or should not be published, the competent authority would examine the matter and adjudicate upon the application by assessing it having regard to the trade secret concept and competition in the market.

2. Regulation 715/2009

Along with Directive 2009/73/EC, Regulation 715/2009[245] entered into effect. The purpose of Regulation 715/2009 included enabling the proper functioning of the internal natural gas market and ensuring the implementation of non-discriminatory rules regarding access conditions to LNG facilities and also to the storage facilities, thereby elimi-

241 Article 3(2) of the Regulation 1775/2005.
242 Article 4(1) of the Regulation 1775/2005.
243 Article 6(1) of the Regulation 1775/2005.
244 Article 6(3) of the Regulation 1775/2005.
245 Regulation (EC) No 715/2009 of the European Parliament and of the Council of 13 July 2009 on conditions for access to the natural gas transmission networks and repealing Regulation (EC) No 1775/2005, OJ L 211, 14.8.2009, pp. 36–54.

nating discrimination with respect to the access conditions upon entrance to such markets where natural gas transmission systems exist.

The Regulation envisaged the establishment of the European Network of Transmission System Operators for Gas (ENTSO-G) for ensuring the optimum management of all transmission system networks in the EU. It abolished Regulation 1775/2005 and introduced the following provisions on transparency in the EU's natural gas markets[246]:

- Transmission system operators should present detailed information about their services to the public.
- Transmission system operators and national authorities should publish reasonable and sufficiently detailed information about tariff preparation methodology and structure in order to create transparent, objective and non-discriminatory tariffs and facilitate the effective use of the gas network.
- Each system operator must give numerical information for the services about technical, contracted and current capacities related to all relevant points, including standard entry and exit points.
- Information about transmission points should be made public and be approved by competent authorities after negotiating with network users.
- Transmission system operators should disclose requested information in accordance with the Regulation constantly, clearly and in an easily accessible and non-discriminatory manner.

Furthermore, Regulation 715/2009 specifies the details for cross-border capacity allocation and congestion management. According to the Regulation, transmission system operators are responsible for promoting the development of energy exchanges and the coordinated allocation of cross-border capacity through non-discriminatory market-based solutions.[247] It can be stated that the difference between Regulation 1775/2005 and Regulation 715/2009 is that the latter adapts the regulatory regime to the new market conditions and pushes the progress further than the first regime did.[248]

246 Article 18 of the Regulation 715/2009.

247 Article 12(2) of the Regulation 715/2009.

248 Talus, 2011, p. 90.

III. Electricity

A. Directives concerning Electricity

1. Directive 90/547/EEC

Directive 90/547/EEC[249], the so-called Electricity Transit Directive, entered into force with the aim of creating an internal electricity market in order to accomplish the objective of establishing the European Common Market.[250] The main goal of the Directive was to eliminate obstacles to electricity transmission which were not related to the nature of the technology used and do not result from the nature of the networks themselves. The Directive claimed that such obstacles could be diminished or even eliminated by making the transit of electricity through transmission networks mandatory and introducing an appropriate system for monitoring compliance with this obligation. Moreover, the Directive established a basis for third-party access by defining transit of electricity through transmission grids as requiring the grid of origin or final destination be situated within the Community and the transport operation to involve crossing at least one intra-Community frontier.[251]

The undertakings responsible for networks monopolise the network on which they operate. Such a situation renders these undertakings relatively more powerful with respect to the undertakings operating in the area of electricity supply as well as import and export. Hence, they can impose their prices and conditions on electricity supply undertakings. Unreasonable conditions and prices determined by undertakings which own transmission networks cause prices to increase, reduce the speed and effectiveness of electricity exchange and inhibit the effective and efficient use of networks.

249 Council Directive 90/547/EEC of 29 October 1990 on the transit of electricity through transmission grids, OJ L 313, 13.11.1990, pp. 30–33.

250 The European Council has recognised the need for a single internal market in energy and that the achievement of the internal market more specifically in the electricity sector will help the further development of the Community's energy objectives.

251 Mitchell, 1999, p. 772; Article 2 of Directive 90/547/EEC.

The Electricity Transit Directive required Member States to take the measures necessary to facilitate the transit of electricity between high-voltage grids.[252] According to it, contracts concerning electricity transit between transmission grids must be negotiated between the grid operators and the undertakings responsible for importing and exporting electricity in Member States.[253] It required that the undertakings which were responsible for large networks in Member States and provided transmission into and from their countries should not stipulate unfair conditions to importers or exporters requesting access to transmission networks, that they must not make use of the weak position of the requesting party and that they not ought to reduce electricity exchange effectivity by blocking transmission. For this purpose, the Directive established the general standards for the conditions of transmission. According to the Directive, the conditions set on electricity transit contracts must be non-discriminatory and fair for all parties concerned; they should not endanger security of supply and service quality and should load electricity on current systems as effectively as possible by especially using reserve production capacities.[254] If networks operators violated the conditions of transmission, the Directive gave the Commission the authority to implement the procedures provided for by EC law.[255]

2. Directive 96/92/EC

Directive 96/92/EC[256], which provided common rules for establishing an electricity internal market, was adopted by the Council of Ministers on 19 December 1996 and enacted on 19 February 1997. A two-year

252 Article 1 of Directive 90/547/EEC.
253 Article 3 of Directive 90/547/EEC.
254 Article 3 of Directive 90/547/EEC.
255 Article 4 of Directive 90/547/EEC.
256 Directive 96/92/EC of the European Parliament and of the Council of 19 December 1996 concerning common rules for the internal market in electricity, OJ L 27, 30.1.1997, pp. 20–29.

period[257] was determined for Member States to make their national laws compatible with the Directive.

The Directive aimed at the gradually and partially opening of Member States' electricity markets. It established the necessary preconditions for the liberalisation of the electricity sector within the EU and the abandoning of the idea of national sovereignty over electricity.[258] It outlined common principles and rules for electricity production, transmission, distribution and supply. Moreover, it liberalised the generation sector and included rules on system operations such as the structure and operation of the electricity market, entrance to the market authorisation and tendering procedures for the construction of new generating capacity[259].

The gradual creation of the internal electricity market required by Directive 96/92/EC was based on three main pillars[260]:

- Upstream competition: Measures to introduce competition in production and supply and the creation of a non-discriminatory and transparent procedure for granting production licences;
- Unbundling: The unbundling of vertically integrated undertakings in terms of the management and accounting of the production, transmission and distribution activities; and
- Access to networks: The establishment of third-party access regime to the networks.

According to the Directive, Member States were to prevent such abuse of dominant positions and violations of competition which might have had negative results on consumers; for this purpose, they had to create effective control and transparency mechanisms. Within this scope, the

257 Belgium and Ireland were given one extra year to make their legislations compatible with 96/92/EC Directive, while Greece was given two extra years. See: Explanatory Memorandum of Directive 96/92/EU.

258 Jakovac, 2012, p. 317.

259 *"Member States were given two options. Under the first, authorisation, developers of new generation basically had to do no more than comply with national planning law for any industrial facility. No specific electricity sector planning procedures to determine need were required. Under the second, tendering, an official authority would determine generating capacity need and allocate the construction of this plant through an open non-discriminatory process."* Thomas, 2006, p. 789.

260 Johnston, 1999, p. 125; Hancher & Vlam, 2004, p. 31.

Directive required that Member States consider the provisions of the TFEU, especially those relating to competition.[261]

Unbundling: The Directive did not fully prohibit vertical integration. Thus it was possible for vertically integrated electricity undertakings to still own transmission or distribution assets.[262] However, the Directive required either Member States or undertakings owning the transmission system to designate a transmission system operator (TSO) to be responsible for operating the transmission lines, carrying out their maintenance and, if necessary, constructing a transmission line in a specific area and connecting this line to other systems.[263] According to the Directive, unless the TSO was already independent from generation and distribution activities, the transmission activity should be unbundled at least in terms of its management from other activities of the vertically integrated electricity undertaking.[264] In this framework, the undertakings possessing a vertically integrated structure were also required to keep their accounting records concerning production, transmission and distribution separately. Hence, "accounting unbundling" was brought within the realm of the aforementioned activities. Moreover, if such undertakings had activities outside of the electricity market, they were required to keep consolidated accounting records.[265]

In order for the system operators to fulfil their responsibilities while operating in transmission, production and distribution activities, compliance with the "Chinese Wall" provision (information barriers)[266] was required. This clause states that the use of commercially sensitive information by a vertically integrated undertaking which has been obtained in the course of carrying out its transmission and distribution activities is prohibited.[267] Moreover, such a prohibition would be especially effective when considering access to the system. Member States were to ensure that there is no flow of information between gen-

---

261 Article 22 of Directive 96/92/EC.
262 Mäntysaari, 2015, p. 101.
263 Article 7(1) of Directive 96/92/EC.
264 Article 7(6) of Directive 96/92/EC.
265 Article 14(3) of Directive 96/92/EC.
266 Cameron, 2002, pp. 182–183.
267 Articles 9 and 12 of Directive 96/92/EC.

eration and distribution activities of vertically integrated electricity undertakings and their single buyer activities. The only exception was if the information was deemed necessary to fulfil the single buyer responsibilities.[268]

System operator: Member States were required to designate system operators (TSOs and DSOs) being responsible for operating, maintaining and developing the transmission or distribution system in a given area in order to guarantee security of supply.[269] The Directive has forbidden system operators to discriminate between system users or classes of system users, particularly in favour of its subsidiaries or shareholders.

The Directive also stated that the system operators must be independent from other activities not relating to the transmission system. These provisions aimed at opening the market and avoiding discrimination of possible competitors by vertically integrated undertakings, because if a network company is not effectively separated from its competitive activities (generation and supply), effective competition simply would not emerge.[270]

Access to networks: Directive 96/92/EC required that the TSOs and DSOs grant non-discriminatory access to networks. It introduced three different methods for providing access to the networks. These methods were negotiated third-party access[271], regulated third-party access[272] and single buyer[273] methods. No matter which system a Member State adopted, the access was to be provided in accordance with objective, transparent and non-discriminatory criteria.[274]

268 Article 15(2) of Directive 96/92/EC.

269 Articles 7 and 10 of Directive 96/92/EC.

270 Jones, 2016, p. 10.

271 Under the concept of negotiated third-party access, consumers and buyers must be able to negotiate access to the network with the system operator. Article 17(1) of Directive 96/92/EC.

272 Under the concept of regulated third-party access, the prices for access to the network are regulated and not subject to negotiation, and they must be available publicly. Article 17(4) of Directive 96/92/EC.

273 Under the concept of single buyer, Member State was required to appoint a legal person to be the single buyer of power within the territory governed by the relevant system operator. Article 18(1) of Directive 96/92/EC.

274 Mitchell, 1999, p. 778.

Retail competition and eligible customers: Directive 96/92/EC introduced the concept of eligible customers. According to this concept, customers have the legal capacity to contract certain volumes of electricity from any supplier.[275] In terms of retail competition, the Directive made an attempt to increase such competition by giving eligible customers (mainly distribution companies and large consumers) a right to choose the supplier.

Directive 96/92/EC adopted a gradual approach in order to open the electricity markets to a competition-centric environment. Article 19 foresaw a six-year period encompassing three stages and specified the percentage share of the electricity market which should be opened for competition.[276] In all three stages, Member States were expected to open their markets at least to minimum thresholds.[277] Opening the electricity markets for competition is proportional to the number of consumers having the chance to choose their suppliers. These thresholds represented a minimum requirement of a market opening of 26% of all final consumers in 1999, 28% of all final consumers in 2000 and 33% of all final consumers in 2003.[278]

Directive 96/92/EC stated that a supply agreement between a Member State supplier and a consumer existing in another Member State cannot be rejected if the consumer in question has the status of an eligible consumer in both States. Furthermore, if a commercial transaction was to be rejected because the said consumer was an eligible customer solely in one of the two States, the Commission could oblige the refusing party to execute the requested electricity supply at the request of the Member State where the eligible customer was located.[279]

---

275 Roggenkamp & Boisseleau, 2005, p. 7.

276 The proportion of the market opened varied from country to country according to the percentage of power going to large users but was expected to average about 30% by 2003.

277 Member States were required to allow consumers using more than 40 GWh per year to choose their supplier as of when the Directive entered into force. Competition was extended to those annually consuming 20 GWh electricity three years after the entry into force of this Directive and subsequently to consumers using more than 9 GWh per year in 2003.

278 Roggenkamp & Boisseleau, 2005, p. 7.

279 Article 19 of Directive 96/92/EC.

Assessment: Directive 96/92/EC was criticised for allowing countries too many ways of avoiding complying with the spirit of the reforms[280] and for having left important points unaddressed:

- The Directive required only a minimal level of harmonisation.[281]
- It did not require a wholesale market to be set up.
- It did not provide for effective regulation and did not require the establishment of an independent sector regulator. There was not necessarily any impartial supervision to ensure the rules were being followed.
- It relied on other treaties for enforcing its objectives instead of including enforcement provisions within the Directive's own text.[282]
- Member States were merely required to ensure there was a dispute resolution procedure.
- The unbundling requirements could not ensure non-discriminatory access to the network. Moreover, the negotiated third-party access regime provided the incumbent undertakings a way to keep out their competitors.
- Competition was significantly limited in Member States which did not go beyond the distinguishing provisions of the Directive and discrimination was present in the markets.
- Retail competition remained limited. Only a few thousand consumers were able to choose their suppliers by 2003, even in the largest countries.
- The Directive created unequal market opening which has affected consumer choice.

The Commission came to the conclusion that, in order to complete the creation of an internal electricity market, provisions on unbundling, non-discriminatory access to the networks, retail competition and eligible customers were to be strengthened.

---

280 Thomas, 2006, pp. 791–792; Jakovac, 2012, pp. 318–319; European Commission, First benchmarking report on the implementation of the internal electricity and gas market, 2001.

281 Hancher & Vlam, 2004, p. 31.

282 Mitchell, 1999, p. 785.

3. Directive 2003/54/EC

In order to eliminate the shortcomings and also the criticised aspects of Directive 96/92/EC, Directive 2003/54/EC[283] was adopted on 26 June 2003. Directive 2003/54/EC did not essentially change the structure established by Directive 96/92/EC; however, it simplified some of the complex provisions[284] and introduced further detailed provisions, such as the monitoring of security of supply, the unbundling of distribution system operators, the establishing of a combined operator, the tracking of electricity import and the procedures of control. Directive 2003/54/EC aimed at achieving a genuine internal electricity market in the EU

- through the adoption of rules on cross-border tariff setting and congestion management,
- through the adoption of measures creating a non-discriminatory access for the transmission of electricity between Member States and
- by monitoring issues concerning security of supply.

Unbundling: Directive 2003/54/EC introduced rules regarding the legal unbundling[285] of undertakings engaged in transmission and distribution activities. According to the Directive, when the transmission or distribution system operator constituted a part of the vertically integrated undertaking, it was to be independent at least in terms of its legal form, organisation and decision-making with respect to the other activities not related to transmission or distribution (i.e., separate legal entity formed within the holding structure). In order to realise legal unbundling, Articles 10 and 15 introduced minimum standards.[286]

283 Directive 2003/54/EC of the European Parliament and of the Council of 26 June 2003 concerning common rules for the internal market in electricity and repealing Directive 96/92/EC, OJ L 176, 15.7.2003, pp. 37–56.

284 Hancher & Vlam, 2004, p. 32.

285 For further information, see: Chapter 7(I)

286 For example, Article 10 of Directive 2003/54/EC envisaged that in order to enable the independence of the transmission system operator, if this operator also operates under a corporate entity executing other electricity market activities, the persons who are in the board of directors of the transmission system undertaking cannot participate in production, distribution and electricity supply activities di-

The Directive further required a complete separation of the accounts for different operations within a vertically integrated undertaking.[287]

Article 17 with the heading "Combined Operator" was also one of the provisions introduced for the first time by Directive 2003/54/EC. Although this article highlighted the necessity of legal unbundling by referring to Articles 10 and 15, it envisaged that activities not related to transmission and distribution can be executed by a single undertaking meeting the conditions of Paragraphs (a)–(d) of Article 17.

System operator: The Directive required the designation of transmission and distribution system operators by Member States.[288] In order to ensure efficient and non-discriminatory network access, the distribution and transmission systems were to be managed by legally separate entities where vertically integrated undertakings existed. The transmission and distribution system operators were to have effective decision-making rights with respect to assets necessary to maintain, operate and develop networks when the assets in question were owned and operated by vertically integrated undertakings. The independence of transmission and distribution system operators was to be guaranteed especially with regard to generation and supply interests.[289]

Access to networks: Another point distinguishing Directive 2003/54/EC from the first Electricity Directive is Article 20 which regulated third-party access to the network. Directive 2003/54/EC envisaged the implementation of only one access model: regulated TPA. Negotiated TPA and single buyer systems were abolished because they created more competition issues than they resolved, mainly because of the structural lack of transparency.[290] Member States were required to ensure the implementation of a third-party access regime in accordance with objective, transparent and non-discriminatory criteria based on published tariffs, applicable to all eligible customers, and applied.[291]

rectly or indirectly. A similar provision concerning distribution system operator is included in Article 15.

287 Article 19 of Directive 2003/54/EC.
288 Articles 8 and 13 of Directive 2003/54/EC.
289 Recital 8 of Directive 2003/54/EC.
290 Hauteclocque & Talus, 2011, p. 2.
291 Article 20 of Directive 2003/54/EC.

Retail competition and eligible customers: According to Directive 2003/54/EC, by 1 July 2004 all consumers except for the household users should be considered as eligible customers[292] and by 1 July 2007 all consumers should assume the status of eligible customers.[293] As stated by *Roggenkamp & Boisseleau*, Directive 2003/54/EC introduced an important next step regarding the liberalisation process as it disposed of the market opening barriers of the previous Directive and included provisions on full market opening in all Member States.[294]

Regulatory authority: Another important Article of Directive 2003/54/EC was Article 23 titled "Regulatory Authorities". Directive 96/92/EC did not include an article concerning regulatory authorities.[295] Directive 2003/54/EC recognised the necessity of an *ex ante* regime in order to accelerate the liberalisation process and required Member States to establish sector-specific regulators.[296] According to the Directive, Member States had the obligation to designate one or more competent bodies as having the function of regulatory authorities. These authorities were responsible for ensuring non-discrimination, effective competition and the efficient functioning of the market and were to be wholly independent from the interests of the electricity industry.[297] They had to monitor[298]:

- the rules on the management and allocation of interconnection capacity,
- the terms, conditions and tariffs for access,
- the publication of appropriate information by transmission and distribution system operators concerning interconnectors, grid usage and capacity allocation to interested parties,

292 According to Paragraph 12 of Article 2 ("Definitions") in Directive 2003/54/EC, eligible customers are the consumers who have the liberty of choosing their suppliers. This definition was not included in Electricity Directive 96/92/EC and the consumers were defined in a general sense in Paragraph 7 of Article 2.

293 Article 21 of Directive 2003/54/EC.

294 Roggenkamp & Boisseleau, 2005, p. 7.

295 Although they are not regulated under a distinct title in Directive 96/92/EC, provisions on regulatory authorities are included in Article 20(3), (4) and 22.

296 Roggenkamp & Boisseleau, 2005, p. 12.

297 Article 23(1) of Directive 2003/54/EC.

298 Ibid.

- the effective unbundling of accounts, and
- the level of transparency and competition.

Assessment: As mentioned above, the Commission conducted an energy sector inquiry[299] in the electricity and gas markets in order to identify the main problems and find solutions. In the final report of the energy sector inquiry, it identified several deficiencies in the process leading to competitive electricity markets. These shortcomings can be summarised as follows:

- The level of concentration in the EU electricity market was high, and the undertakings that used to be monopolies before the liberalisation process continued to affect prices in the electricity market.
- The liquidity ratio was low in the EU electricity markets. Looking at the reasons for this, the wholesale sector was not so transparent, since the undertakings in these markets operate in both the production and retail sector. Vertical integration of generation and retail within the same group reduced the need to trade on wholesale markets.[300] Illiquid wholesale markets also raised significant barriers for new entry into both generation and retail market segments.[301] Moreover, unbundling between transmission, distribution and supply activities in the electricity market was not sufficient.
- Remaining obstacles regarding the cross-border trade of electricity between Member States prevented the establishment of the EU internal energy market.
- Transparency was not fully established, and monopolies that existed before liberalisation in Member States continued to benefit from this situation. Moreover, the lack of transparency in the electricity market was suspected to leading to unfavourable conditions for the new entrants and/or potential new entrants.

299 European Commission, Inquiry pursuant to Article 17 of Regulation (EC) No 1/2003 into the European gas and electricity sectors (Final Report) (SEC (2006) 1724), 2006.

300 Energy Sector Inquiry, 2006, p. 151.

301 European Commission, Energy sector competition inquiry – final report – frequently asked questions and graphics, 2007.

- Since the EU electricity market was not sufficiently transparent, the industry and consumers did not trust price formation mechanisms in wholesale markets.
- Since retail-sales agreements were long-term for the industrial users and local distribution firms, competition was generally limited at the level of retail sales.

Directive 2003/54/EC was enacted in order to eliminate shortcomings of Directive 96/92/EC in the areas on access to networks, unbundling and retail competition. However, it was not effective of breaking up vertically integrated incumbents and introducing competition in wholesale electricity markets. These deficiencies led the Commission to propose a new Directive.

4. Directive 2009/72/EC

Taking into consideration that Directive 2003/54/EC was insufficient for the full liberalisation of the electricity market in the EU, Directive 2009/72/EC[302] was adopted on 13 June 2009. It aims at liberalising the European electricity market, thereby stimulating competitiveness and also protecting the consumers. It establishes common rules for electricity generation, transmission, distribution and supply. It also encompasses provisions on the organisation and operation of the electricity sector as well as on opening the market.

Unbundling and system operator: One of the most important novelties of the Directive is its provisions concerning unbundling mechanisms. Directive 2009/72/EC introduces three new unbundling mechanisms: ownership unbundling, independent transmission operator (ITO) and independent system operator (ISO).[303] According to the Article 9(1), each undertaking which owns a transmission system acts as a transmission system operator.[304] However, Member States may decide not to apply Article 9(1) and designate an independent system operator.

302 Directive 2009/72/EC of the European Parliament and of the Council of 13 July 2009 concerning common rules for the internal market in electricity and repealing Directive 2003/54/EC, OJ L 211/55, 14.8.2009.

303 For further information, see: Chapter 7(I)

304 Article 9 of Directive 2009/72/EC.

Access to networks: One of the main goals of Directive 2009/72/EC is to ensure non-discriminatory network access.[305] Member States must implement a system of third-party access to the transmission and distribution networks.[306]

Retail and wholesale competition and eligible customers: While Directive 2003/54/EC gave all customers the right to choose their suppliers, Directive 2009/72/EC gave large non-household customers a right to enter into contracts simultaneously with several suppliers to secure their electricity requirements. Such customers are thus protected against exclusivity clauses.[307]

The Directive required Member States to ensure all customers to be regarded as "eligible customers" who may freely choose their own suppliers as of 1 July 2007[308] regardless of whether the supplier is a local one or is established in another Member State of the EU.[309] Member States must ensure that their administrative procedures do not discriminate against supply undertakings already registered in another Member State.[310]

Regulatory authority: Directive 2009/72/EC ensures very effective regulatory supervision of independent national energy regulators.[311] It stipulates that each Member State must appoint a single regulatory authority at the national level. Member States are responsible for ensuring the independence of these regulatory authorities as well as the objective and transparent use of their competences.[312]

One of the main goals of Directive 2009/72/EC is the development of a fully functioning internal electricity market through a network connected across the Community. Therefore, regulatory authorities should focus on regulatory issues of cross-border interconnections and regional markets in close cooperation with the Agency for the Cooper-

305 Recital 4 of Directive 2009/72/EC.
306 Article 32(1) of Directive 2009/72/EC.
307 Recital 20 and Article 41(3) of Directive 2009/72/EC; Mäntysaari, 2015, p. 106.
308 Article 33(1) of Directive 2009/72/EC.
309 Article 3(4) of Directive 2009/72/EC.
310 Ibid.
311 Jakovac, 2012, p. 328.
312 Article 4(4) of Directive 2009/72/EC.

ation of Energy Regulators[313] (ACER).[314] According to the Directive 2009/72/EC, regulatory authorities and transmission system operators should cooperate with the ACER to ensure the compatibility of regulatory frameworks between the regions with the aim of creating a competitive internal market in electricity. One of the tasks of the ACER is to make appropriate recommendations if binding rules on such cooperation are required.[315]

Assessment: The Commission has been actively supervising the application of Directive 2009/72/EC by Member States. It has initiated several infringement procedures against Member States which failed to transpose Directive 2009/72/EC into their national laws. These infringement procedures urged Member States to put in place the national legislation fully transposing the Directive. In 2017, the Commission sent formal notices to Hungary, Estonia and the Netherlands requesting them to ensure the correct implementation and application of the Electricity Directive (Directive 2009/72/EC).

The Commission conducted an *ex post* evaluation on the effectiveness of Directive 2009/72/EC. Overall and within the scope of the two evaluations carried out, the evaluations' findings support the view that the objectives of Directive 2009/72/EC, namely to promote competition and remove obstacles to cross-border competition in electricity markets, have been met.[316] Member States actively enforce the legislation and this resulted in significant positive outcomes for the electricity market, e.g. markets which are in general less concentrated and

313 The ACER has been established by Regulation 713/2009. Regulation (EC) No 713/2009 of the European Parliament and of the Council of 13 July 2009 establishing an Agency for the Cooperation of Energy Regulators, OJ L 211, 14.8.2009, pp. 1–14. The ACER's main tasks are: complement and coordinate the work of national regulatory authorities; participate in the creation of European network rules; take, under certain conditions, binding individual decisions on terms and conditions for access and operational security for cross border infrastructure; give advice on various energy-related issues to the European institutions; and monitor and report developments at the energy markets.

314 Recital 59 of Directive 2009/72/EC.

315 Article 6 of Directive 2009/72/EC.

316 Evaluation Report, http://eur-lex.europa.eu/legal-content/EN/TXT/?uri=SWD:2016:0412:FIN (accessed: 1 June 2019).

more integrated than in 2009.[317] Concerning consumers, the set of provisions on consumer rights introduced by Directive 2009/72/EC have clearly had a positive impact on the position of the consumer in energy markets.[318]

The strengthened unbundling requirements increased the competitiveness of energy markets and helped to reduce market foreclosure. The new provisions aiming at expanding cross-border electricity cooperation and trade through removing barriers to cross-border trade and enhancing cooperation between transmission system operators and regulators contributed to the increased liquidity of electricity markets and the development of cross-border trade, resulting in more competitive wholesale markets.[319]

However, the impact of the norms set out in Directive 2009/72/EC remains limited in a number of fields, both at the wholesale and the retail level. The Commission's *ex post* evaluation demonstrates there is room for improvement on the market design framework.[320] According to the evaluation, the level of competition in retail markets could be significantly improved. Electricity prices still vary widely from one Member State to another due to relatively high transportation cost (transmission losses) and transmission bottlenecks between countries.[321] Electricity prices have risen steadily for households as a result of significant increases in network charges, surcharge for renewable energy, taxes and levies, and increases in natural gas prices. As a part of the 2016 Clean Energy Package, the Commission proposed a new Directive on common rules for the internal market in electricity on 30 November 2016.[322] The proposed Directive would require Member States to take measures necessary to ensure a more competitive, customer-centred, flexible and non-discriminatory EU electricity market

317 Explanatory Memorandum, Proposal for a Regulation of the European Parliament and of the Council on the Internal Market for Electricity, p. 11.

318 Ibid, p. 12.

319 Evaluation Report, http://eur-lex.europa.eu/legal-content/EN/TXT/?uri=SWD:2016:0412:FIN (accessed: 1 June 2019).

320 Explanatory Memorandum, Proposal for a Regulation of the European Parliament and of the Council on the Internal Market for Electricity, p. 11.

321 OECD, 2011, p. 48.

322 Proposal for a Directive of the European Parliament and of the Council on common rules for the internal market in electricity, COM/2016/0864 final.

with market-based supply prices. According to the proposed Directive, Member States have to ensure that there are no undue barriers for market entry or market exit of electricity generators or electricity suppliers.[323] The proposed Directive also focuses on strengthening existing costumer rights and introducing new ones. According to it, customers should be able to freely choose their supplier or aggregator[324] and to switch their supplier without any fee, except in cases where a fixed-term contract that offers demonstrable advantages to the customer is terminated prematurely.[325] The proposed Directive will recast[326] Directive 2009/72/EC.

B. Regulations concerning Electricity

1. Regulation 1228/2003

Regulation 1228/2003[327] was adopted in 2003. It contained the norms governing the cross-border electricity trade, which were established in order to increase competition in the internal electricity market. The Regulation aimed at encouraging cross-border electricity exchange, establishing a compensation mechanism for the cross-border electricity flow and determining the cross-border transmission prices and the corresponding principles with respect to the allocation of the current interconnection capacity between the national transmission systems. According to the Regulation, the transmission system operators were to establish information exchange and coordination mechanisms in order to ensure the network security within the context of constraint management. Furthermore, the Regulation required that the market participants who wish to use the allocated capacity should inform the

323 Erbach, 2019, p. 5.

324 Aggregator means a market participant that combines multiple customer loads or generated electricity for sale, for purchase or auction in any organised energy market.

325 Ibid., p. 6.

326 "Recasting" means bringing a legislative act and all the amendments made to it together in a single new act. The new legislative act passes through the full legislative process and repeals all the acts being recast.

327 Regulation (EC) No 1228/2003 of the European Parliament and of the Council of 26 June 2003 on conditions for access to the network for cross-border exchanges in electricity, OJ L 176, 15.7.2003, pp. 1–10.

transmission system operator in advance within a certain period of time.

The provisions concerning the pricing of cross-border electricity exchanges, the allocation of sufficient interconnection capacity and the facilitation of the access to the system were laid out in the Regulation. The Regulation envisaged the implementation of general rules specifying issues such as pricing, making transparent the prices of access to the networks, capacity allocation and the adoption of the related methodologies. It thus aimed at harmonising different pricing systems which would otherwise harm competition. It required that the regulatory authorities in Member States implement properly the general rules specified above in Article 6 and, as and when necessary, collaborate with each other or with the Commission.[328]

2. Regulation 714/2009

Regulation 714/2009[329] abolished Regulation 1228/2003 and aims at increasing the competition in the internal market by specifying the fair rules regarding the cross-border electricity market and by establishing a transparent wholesale market operating with a high-level security of supply. As an addendum, the Regulation also includes several provisions on harmonisation mechanisms with respect to the cross-border markets in the electricity sector and envisages the establishment of a European Network of Transmission System Operators for Electricity (ENTSOE). Such an establishment enables all transmission system operators to collaborate at the level of the EU. It can be observed that this network is designed for contributing to the functioning of the internal electricity market in an integrated way and for encouraging cross-border trade.

328 Article 9 of the Regulation 1228/2003.

329 Regulation (EC) No 714/2009 of the European Parliament and of the Council of 13 July 2009 on conditions for access to the network for cross-border exchanges in electricity and repealing Regulation (EC) No 1228/2003, OJ L 211, 14.8.2009, pp. 15–35.

There are two important goals of the regulation[330]:

- setting fair rules for cross-border electricity trade, thus enhancing competition within the internal market in electricity, taking into account the particular characteristics of national and regional markets, and
- facilitating the emergence of a well-functioning and transparent wholesale market with a high level of security of electricity supply.

The new Clean Energy Package includes recasting the Electricity Market Regulation[331] which sets out stricter and harmonised rules concerning capacity mechanisms:

- It introduces principles for the development of a European resource adequacy assessment to arrive at a common European methodology to determine the need for a capacity remuneration mechanism (CRM).
- It clarifies the circumstances for the introduction of CRM.
- It clarifies market-compatible design principles for CRM.

The new Regulation will specify basic principles with regard to tarification and capacity allocation. Furthermore, it will reconcile the EU objectives of security of supply and emission reduction. The new Regulation will also include provisions on enhanced regional coordination which will improve market functioning and thereby competitiveness of the electricity markets.[332]

330 Article 1 of Regulation 714/2009.

331 Proposal for a Regulation of the European Parliament and of the Council on the internal market for electricity (recast), COM/2016/0861 final/2.

332 European Commission, Commission welcomes political agreement on conclusion of the Clean Energy for All Europeans package, 2018.

IV. Renewable Energy

A. Directive 2001/77/EC

Directive 2001/77/EC[333] aimed at increasing the generation of electricity from renewable energy sources. Through the Directive, the use of the renewable energy resources, the protection of the environment and sustainable development were encouraged. New employment opportunities ought to have been created within the EU, social cohesion would be reinforced, a major contribution to the energy supply security would be made and the objectives of the Kyoto Protocol would be achieved in an unprecedented, rapid fashion.

The Directive established a target for the EU regarding electricity generated from renewable sources. According to this target, EU15[334] had to increase the share of electricity generated by renewable energy to 22% in 2010 (compared with 14% in 2000).[335] In accordance with this objective, each Member State had to provide the specific reference values as well as the national values. Hence, it ought to have been possible to fulfil both the obligations pertaining to the Kyoto Protocol and the main objectives of the EU. In the course of realising the said aims and objectives, Member States were required to implement regulations.

The Directive introduced a "guarantee of origin" system. The guarantee of origin is a certificate stating that electricity is generated from renewable energy resources. Member States had to ensure that their electric energy would be generated from renewable energy resources.

The Directive also required Member States to evaluate their existing legislative and regulatory framework with regard to authorisation procedures. It aimed at reducing the regulatory and non-regulatory barriers related to the increase in electricity generation from renewable

333 Directive 2001/77/EC of the European Parliament and of the Council of 27 September 2001 on the promotion of electricity produced from renewable energy sources in the internal electricity market, OJ L 283, 27.10.2001, pp. 33–40.

334 Austria, Belgium, Denmark, Finland, France, Germany, Greece, Ireland, Italy, Luxembourg, Netherlands, Portugal, Spain, Sweden, United Kingdom.

335 With the participation of ten new members to the Union in 2004, this objective was decreased to 21%.

energy sources and at ensuring that the rules are objective, transparent and non-discriminatory.[336]

According to the Directive, Member States were expected to take the necessary measures to ensure that transmission and distribution system operators in their territory guarantee the transmission and distribution of electricity produced from renewable energy sources.[337] Moreover, Member States were responsible for prioritising the access of the energy produced from these resources to the network.

Member States had to implement the regulations required by this Directive by 27 October 2003. They had to inform the Commission regularly about their activities, and the Commission was to present an assessment report on the Directive to the EU Parliament and the Council every five years. However, since no binding objective was set, only some Member States achieved the objective and the others remained far behind it. After the adoption of Directive 2001/77/EC, because the objectives regarding renewable energy use had not been met by Member States, the EU decided to change its approach to renewable energy policy. The Commission filed 61 infringement proceedings against Member States for not implementing the necessary laws within the scope of Directive 2001/77/EC.[338]

B. Directive 2003/30/EC

Directive 2003/30/EC[339] aimed, in essence, at ensuring that obligations concerning climate change would be fulfilled, protecting the environment and providing energy supply security by decreasing the use of gasoline and diesel oil in transportation and encouraging biofuels[340] and other renewable fuels[341]. In this context, as it was the case in Di-

336 Article 6 of Directive 2001/77/EC.

337 Article 7 of Directive 2001/77/EC.

338 Ahner, 2011, p. 95.

339 Directive 2003/30/EC of the European Parliament and of the Council of 8 May 2003 on the promotion of the use of biofuels or other renewable fuels for transport, OJ L 123, 17.5.2003, pp. 42–46.

340 Liquid or gas fuels such as biogas, bio methanol, bioethanol and biodiesel produced from biomass.

341 This refers to fuels obtained from renewable energy resources except for biofuels and used in transportation.

rective 2001/77/EC, some reference values were determined, and Member States were expected to establish national objectives concerning the use of biofuel and other renewable fuels. The reference values for these objectives were determined to be 2% for 2005 (the share within the totality of the fuels such as gasoline and diesel by 31 December 2005) and 5.75% for 2010 (the share within the totality of the fuels such as gasoline and diesel by 31 December 2010).

Member States had to submit to the Commission reports before 1st June every year. These reports included the measures taken for the development of biofuel and other renewable fuels used in transportation. They should also contain the information pertaining to sales amount and market shares in related periods. Finally, the assessment report to be published by the EU Commission based on these reports had to be submitted to the EU Council and Parliament every two years, the first of which was published before 31 December 2006. The report was to be prepared with reference to the progress made in the use of biofuels and other renewable fuels in Member States.[342]

C. Directive 2009/28/EC

With the introduction of 20–20–20 objectives[343], Directive 2003/30/EC was also revised. Directive 2009/28/EC[344], the so-called Renewable Energy Directive, was enacted on 25 June 2009. It establishes a general framework for encouraging the generation of energy obtained from renewable energy resources. It enforces compulsory national renewable energy targets and promotes cooperation amongst Member States to help them meet their renewable energy targets, such as statistical transfers of renewable energy amounts between Member States[345] and cooperation on joint projects relating to the production

342 Article 4(2) of Directive 2003/30/EC.

343 The 2020 package is a set of binding laws to ensure that the EU meets its climate and energy targets for the year 2020. The package sets three key targets: 20% cut in greenhouse gas emissions (from 1990 levels), 20% of EU energy from renewables and 20% improvement in energy efficiency. https://ec.europa.eu/clima/policies/strategies/2020_en (accessed: 1 June 2019).

344 This Directive encourages the use of the energy obtained from renewable energy resources and replaces 2001/77/EC and 2003/30/EC Directives.

345 Article 6 of Directive 2009/28/EC.

of electricity, heating or cooling from renewable energy sources[346]. Moreover, it sets out rules on administrative procedures and access to the network.

According to the Renewable Energy Directive, each Member State will determine an objective showing the share of renewable energy in the gross final energy consumption by 2020. This objective should be compatible with the 20–20–20 common objective of the Community for 2020. Moreover, the share of renewable energy resources in the transportation sector should be at least 10% within the final energy consumption of the sector. The Directive is part of the energy and climate change legislation providing a legal framework for Community objectives concerning greenhouse gas emissions. The difference between the Renewable Energy Directive and Directive 2001/77/EC is the former's introduction of binding objectives for Member States. As per the binding provisions, infringement procedures may be filed against a Member State, if it fails to fulfil the objectives specified for it.

The Renewable Energy Directive contemplates the implementation of four stages by Member States in order to achieve the 2020 objectives. The first stage envisages that the share of energy generated by using renewable energy resources should increase to 20% by the 2011–2012 period; in the following stages this has to be 30% by the 2013–2014 period, 45% by the 2015–2016 period and, finally, 65% by 2017–2018.[347] These rates are determined to be an indicative trajectory. In other words, as distinct from 2020 objectives, these objectives are not binding.

One of the important regulations of the Renewable Energy Directive concerns national renewable energy actions plans.[348] According to this regulation, each Member State should create and implement its own national renewable energy action plan. In this plan, information about the objectives on the share of energy generated from renewable resources used in transportation, electricity and heating/cooling should be included.

Another important change brought by the Renewable Energy Directive involves *cooperation mechanisms*. The Directive develops three

346 Article 7 of Directive 2009/28/EC.

347 Ahner, 2011, p. 99.

348 Article 4 of 2009/28/EC.

cooperation mechanisms: statistical transfers between Member States[349], joint projects between Member States[350] and joint projects between Member States and third countries.[351] One of the reasons for establishing cooperation mechanisms between Member States is to understand whether renewable energy is cheap and where the potential for the deployment of renewable energy is highest.[352] Hence, the purpose is to enable Member States to achieve their national objectives at lower costs.[353]

The rule for submitting reports on renewable energy resources every two years by Member States is set out in Directive 2009/28/EC. Thus far, the Commission prepared a report in 2015 covering the whole EU and based on these reports.[354] According to this report, all Member States are progressing towards meeting the objectives concerning renewable energy resources, but some Member States should take additional measures. The Commission launched consultation studies for introducing a new Renewable Energy Directive. The new package is expected to reinforce the 2030 objectives[355] of the EU defined in October 2014.[356]

349 Article 6 of 2009/28/EC.
350 Articles 7 and 8 of 2009/28/EC.
351 Articles 9 and 10 of 2009/28/EC.
352 Ahner, 2011, p. 100.
353 Johnston & Block, 2012, p. 310.
354 Report from the Commission to the European Parliament, the Council, the European Economic and Social Committee and the Committee of the Regions – Renewable Energy Progress Report, Brussels, 15.6.2015, COM (2015) 293 final.
355 European Council, Council Conclusions 23 and 24 October 2014.
356 European Commission, Renewable Energy Package, 2015.

Part 3 Competition Law and Sector Specific Regulations

§ 5. Relations between Competition Law and Sector-Specific Regulations

> *"Regulation and competition are rhetorical friends and deadly enemies: over the doorway of every regulatory agency ... should be carved: Competition Not Admitted". (Stigler, 1975, p. 183)*

The correlation between competition law and sector-specific regulations has become a very controversial issue, particularly in respect of the interface between these two legal instruments in liberalised network industries.[357] In order to better understand the complex interdependence and substitution processes between competition law and sector-specific regulations, they should be examined in a separate manner since they are quite distinctive although they pursue similar objectives.[358] There are different approaches in literature regarding the application of both legal instruments. According to the widely accepted conventional approach, competition law and sector-specific regulations are legal instruments that are not conflicting, and they are considered complementary to each other as they are applicable in different settings. Even though the primary goal of both instruments is to address weaknesses within the market system, there are markets in which competition law will lead to satisfactory results, and other markets which need sector-specific regulations in order to attain secondary goals, e.g. the efficiency goal.[359]

Competition law exists to protect competition in a free market.[360] It, however, cannot create competition. Competition law consists of le-

---

357 Colangelo, 2013, p. 1.
358 Dunne, 2015, p. 6.
359 Kirchner, 2004, pp. 308–309.
360 Jones & Sufrin, 2016, p. 2.

gal norms and measures which are designed to forbid certain types of behaviours of market actors and, generally speaking, aim at preventing the illegitimate acquisition of market power and, where market power is already accumulated, controlling its exercise. These legal norms function as constraints for market players when they determine strategies on how to maintain or improve their position in a market.[361] However, there are limits to the effectiveness of competition law. Under certain circumstances, competition may not be feasible for technological or market reasons. These circumstances are often referred to as market failures.[362]

Governments implement regulations in order to address the market failures.[363] According to conventional wisdom, the most traditional and persistent rationale for regulation is the existence of a "natural monopoly".[364] Natural monopolies should be regulated to ensure that the market power of the monopoly is not abused, consumers are protected and the goal of allocative efficiency[365] is attained.[366]

A free-market model does not oblige a state to abstain entirely from market intervention. Particularly, the existence of market failures – or market absences – requires a state to intervene, for example through competition law or regulations.[367] In the narrow sense, regulation, thus, can be described as a state intervention into the operation of markets. Regulation comprises state activity to remedy market failures or defects.

According to *Jordana & Levi-Faur*, there are five notions that are used in the literature to capture the relationship between competition and regulation[368]:

---

361 Kirchner, 2004, p. 310.

362 Ibid., p. 308.

363 "Market failure" can be defined as a situation in which a market does not operate as it should. http://dictionary.cambridge.org/ (accessed: 1 June 2019).

364 Breyer, 1982, p. 15; Sidak & Spulber, 1998, p. 20.

365 Allocative efficiency is a state of the economy in which resources are allocated among all the possible goods and services that could be produced so that consumers get the products they want most at the price they are willing to pay for. Mabry & Ulrich, 1989, p. 40; Dabbah, 2004, p. 6.

366 Crampton, 2002, p. 4; Kirchner, 2004, p. 308.

367 Crampton, 2002, p. 7.

368 Jordana & Levi-Faur, 2004, pp. 6–7.

- Regulation of competition: National competition authorities have broader responsibilities which include sector-specific responsibilities. These broader responsibilities also imply that competition authorities can adopt a reactive approach to anticompetitive measures.
- Regulation for competition: It is a proactive implementation of regulation aiming to introduce competition into a formerly monopolistic market structure. Even though the responsibilities of regulatory authorities are confined to a sector or industry, they have much more influence over market actors than competition authorities. While regulatory authorities are proactively involved in market design and market control, competition authorities only react once a market abuse has already occurred or is in the making.[369] Regulatory authorities use their regulatory controls to restructure monopoly markets and to create competitive segments.[370]
- Deregulation: Deregulation can be defined as a transition from a regulatory regime to a competition policy regime leading to a reduction of economic, political and social restrictions on the behaviour of social actors.[371]
- Reregulation: Reregulation is often used to indicate that regulatory reforms and liberalisation in general lead to new sets of regulation instead of deregulation.
- Meta-regulation of competition: Meta-regulation of competition means that not only the actions of individuals and corporations get directly regulated but also the process of regulation itself becomes regulated.

I. The General Notion of Competition and Competition Law

A. The Concept of Competition

There is no official definition of competition. According to classical economists, such as Adam Smith, competition refers to a process of rivalry between participants in the market who endeavour to compete

369 Ibid., p. 6.
370 Dunne, 2015, p. 148.
371 Kirchner, 2004, p. 309.

by altering and transforming prices in response to the market conditions, thereby eliminating excessive profits along with unsatisfied demand.[372] This definition is considered as the most neutral and non-controversial approach.[373] It can be argued that the idea of competition characteristically is not an end in itself, or a culmination of different states of beings, but rather a dynamic process, while competition policy is a curative tool when that process fails to work.[374] Smith's definition has been developed by John Maurice Clark, a prominent early 20th century economist:

> *"Competition is rivalry in selling goods, in which each selling unit normally seeks maximum net revenue, under conditions such that the price or prices each seller can charge are effectively limited by the free option of the buyer to buy from a rival seller or sellers of what we think of as 'the same' product, necessitating an effort by each seller to equal or exceed the attractiveness of the others' offerings to a sufficient number of sellers to accomplish the end in view."*[375]

Besides the definitions provided by the economists, a leading competition lawyer, Daniel G. Goyder, defined the concept of competition in the following manner:

> *"Competition is basically the relationship between a number of undertakings which sell goods or services of the same kind at the same time to an identifiable group of customers. Each undertaking having made a commercial decision to place its goods and services on the market, utilising its production and distribution facilities, will by that act necessarily bring itself into a relationship of potential contention and rivalry with the other undertakings in the same geographical market whose limits may be a single shopping precinct, a city [....] or even the whole world."*[376]

The question that could well be asked is why competition is desirable. What makes competition desirable is the idea that competition leads necessarily to an effective allocation of particular resources and subsequently serves the consumer interests. Moreover, the rivalry is seen as

372 Cook et al., 2004, p. 5.
373 Dabbah, 2004, p. 2.
374 Joekes & Evans, 2008, p. 2; Stucke, 2012, p. 33.
375 Clark, 1940, p. 243.
376 Goyder, Goyder & Albors-Llorens, 2009, p. 8.

a significant driving force behind innovativeness and development within undertakings and industries.[377]

The process of competition may lead to various desirable outcomes.[378] Competition between undertakings can benefit consumers, workers, entrepreneurs, small businesses and the economy more generally.[379] Generally, benefits that are expected to be derived from competition are:

- the effective allocation of resources in a free market,
- the formation of supply and demand in the market without any intervention or limitation,
- the promotion of research and development activities and fund reservation, sustenance of the presence of small- and medium-sized undertakings in the market[380],
- greater product variety,
- offering goods and services with higher quality and lower price, and
- the creation of a structure which stipulates maximum consumer benefits in this process as a result.[381]

B. The Concept of Competition Law

1. Introduction

Modern competition law was implemented by several States, e.g., the USA and Canada, dating back hundreds of years, initially with the aim of addressing the issues regarding the trade limitations as applied by

377 Bengtsson, 1998, p. 1.
378 Dabbah, 2004, p. 6.
379 Council of Economic Advisers, 2016, p. 1.
380 *"Small businesses and entrepreneurs can benefit, for example, when upstream firms compete against each other for the opportunity to supply a product to a downstream small business or entrepreneur. If an entrepreneur sells its products to downstream firms rather than to end-users, it would benefit from there being a greater number of downstream firms to which it can sell products—the greater the number of downstream firms, the better the ability to negotiate a good price for the products it sells."* Council of Economic Advisers, 2016, p. 2.
381 Stucke, 2013, pp. 166–167.

private sector companies.[382] As mentioned above, competition law can be defined as applying a body of legal rules and standards to deal with market imperfections as well as to protect and develop competition in the current free market economy.[383] In other words, competition law emerges as a set of rules which control numerous actions and behaviours which might cause restriction and distortion of competition. Essentially, competition law focuses on anticompetitive behaviours, and its goal is *"ensuring an effective competitive process"*.[384]

Competition law attempts to ensure that the undertakings operating in a free market economy do not behave in a particular manner which prevents the optimal performance of the market and consequently restricts or distorts competition.[385] Thus, it is enforced to address three primary situations:

- anticompetitive agreements, whereby two or more undertakings are in agreement amongst themselves to limit the parameters of production, fix prices, share markets or customers, or rig bids[386] as and when tendering with respect to government contracts;
- abusive or exclusionary behaviour, where one undertaking is so powerful that it can act without considering its rivals or can act with an aim to exclude its rivals; and
- domain of mergers, whereby the pertinent firms which aim to merge are reviewed in order to ensure that any deals undertaken by them are not likely to reduce competition significantly.[387]

2. Competition Law in the EU

Although modern competition laws were introduced in North America as far back as the 19th century, it took more than 50 years for them

382 Papadopoulos, 2010, p. 1.
383 Jones & Sufrin, 2016, p. 1; Dabbah, 2004, p. 5.
384 Stucke, 2012, p. 29.
385 Jones & Sufrin, 2016, p. 1.
386 Bid rigging (or collusive tendering) occurs when businesses that would otherwise be expected to compete secretly conspire to raise prices or lower the quality of goods or services for purchasers who wish to acquire products or services through a bidding process. OECD, 2009, p. 1.
387 Joekes & Evans, 2008, pp. 6–7.

to be adopted in Europe.[388] The founding fathers of the EU enacted European-wide competition rules with the Treaty of Paris in 1951[389] and the Treaty of Rome, signed in 1957, which laid the formal basis for today's EU competition policy. EU competition law is enforced in a special context designed to eliminate barriers between countries and enhance the creation of a single market.

The Preamble as well as Articles 2 and 3 of the Treaty of Rome defined the basic goals of the EU. EU's primary objectives include creating an internal market to promote economic integration and to increase competition.[390] Within the framework of the free movement of goods and services[391], it is aimed at both uniting Member States and creating a single market by gradually converging their economies. In this context, competition law plays a substantial role.

Article 3(1)(g) of the EC Treaty set out the activities to be performed in order to reach the Community's goals, referred to as the formation of *"a system ensuring that competition in the internal market is not distorted"*. This objective is no longer set out explicitly in Article 3 TFEU but subsumed into the term "internal market" under Protocol No 27.[392] According to the Protocol, the contracting parties agreed that the EU must act within the framework of Treaty provisions, including Article 352 TFEU[393] if required, taking into consideration that the internal market set forth in Article 3 of the EU Treaty includes a system in which competition is intact. The Court of Justice (the CJ) accepts that this Protocol has the same effect as Article 3(1)(g) of the EC Treaty.[394]

---

388 Geradin et al., 2012, p. 14.

389 In Europe, cartels were seen favourably as engines of industrial development driving the economic growth of Europe, especially in Germany. Indeed, cartels were respected economic institutions, and economy by cartel was the rule in Europe prior to 1945.

390 Ilzkovitz et al., 2007, p. 1.

391 The Treaty of Rome, signed in 1951, created fundamental freedoms – free movement of goods, capital, labour and services. It aimed at abolishing all barriers erected by Member States.

392 European Parliament, Competition policy, http://www.europarl.europa.eu/ (accessed: 1 June 2019).

393 Ex-Article 308.

394 In its TeliaSonera decision, the CJ for the first time referred to the Protocol No 27. The CJ noted that *"Article 3(3) TEU states that the European Union is to establish*

Likewise, in order to achieve the goals set out in Article 3 TFEU, Article 119 TFEU states that the activities of the Member States and the Union include the implementation of an economic policy based on the coordination of the economic policies of Member States and its execution according to the principle of an open market economy in which free competition is present. In this respect, competition policy is a must for accomplishing the EU's basic goals.

It is obvious that competition rules are significant for the EU's progression to create a single market. As stated in Article 3(1)(b) TFEU, the establishment of a single market is inextricably bound to competition and competition is an indispensable part of the internal market. Hence, differently from the past, the TFEU ensures the necessity to include the rules of material law for supporting competition in the establishment of a common internal market. According to the Commission, the complementarity between these two policies is also clearly shown by the EU's objective of creating an internal market. While the internal market is a *conditio sine qua non* for the development of an effective and competitive industry, competition law is an essential tool to achieve, and to maintain, the goal of establishing an internal market through the enforcement of rules which ensure that the regulatory barriers to trade which have been removed are not replaced by new restrictions, having the same effect, by private or other public market players. Therefore, competition rules are considered necessary for a fully functioning single internal market.[395]

The principal legal norms at the level of primary law regarding the protection of competition are set out in Articles 101 to 109 TFEU. Due to the general supremacy of EU legislation, Member States have been required to bring their national competition laws in line with the principles of EU competition law. Pursuant to Regulation 1/2003, the implementation of the EU's general competition rules with regards to a

---

an internal market, which, in accordance with Protocol No 27 on the internal market and competition, annexed to the Treaty of Lisbon (reference omitted), is to include a system ensuring that competition is not distorted." Case C-52/09, *Konkurrensverket v TeliaSonera Sverige AB*, [2011] ECR I-00527, para. 20. See: Jones & Sufrin, 2016, p. 1.

395 European Commission, 25th Report on Competition Policy, 1995; Kekelekis, 2006, p. 5.

specific case is central among Member States' obligations.[396] The Commission focuses only on gross competition breaches. However, national courts and competition authorities cannot take measures conflicting with Commission decisions.[397] National authorities are obliged to implement EU competition rules, which at the same are time based on national competition law.

EU competition law *per se* prohibits competition-restricting agreements and abuse of dominant position. Unlike American competition law, EU competition law does not forbid dominance and monopolisation.[398] It only prohibits the exploitation of this position.[399] Thus, efforts have been made to prevent undertakings which hold a dominant position in certain markets or with high market shares from misusing their power and exploiting consumers or other competitive undertakings, or aiming to erase them from the market.[400]

EU competition law principally applies to all sectors of the economy and to all undertakings carrying out economic activities without making any distinction between private and public sectors. However, individual and group exemptions can be granted with regards to agreements and decisions which might restrict competition. Exemptions are possible if an agreement or a decision contributes to improving the production or distribution of goods and the acceleration of technical or economic advancement or if it benefits the welfare of the consumers, provided always that it does not substantially damage competition.[401]

---

396 Regulation 1/2003 made important steps towards decentralisation in the enforcement of the competition rules of the EU. Dabbah, 2004, p. 12.

397 Article 16 of Regulation 1/2003. The Commission is divided into several departments, and DG COMP (Directorate-General for Competition) deals with competition law and policy. Within DG COMP are various sectoral units which deal with mergers, antitrust and state aid.

398 The CJ stated that *"as Article 85(1) is based on an assessment of the effects of an agreement from two angles of economic evaluation [i.e., the effects on trade between Member States and the effects on competition, ed. note], it cannot be interpreted as introducing any kind of advance judgment [...]. Therefore, an agreement whereby a producer entrusts the sale of his product in a given area to a sole distributor cannot automatically fall under the prohibition in Article 85(1)."* Case 56/65, *Société Technique Minière v Maschinenbau Ulm GmbH*, [1966] ECR 235.

399 Bellamy & Child, 1987, pp. 389–390.

400 Peeperkorn & Mehta, 1999, p. 3 et seq.

401 Article 101(3) TFEU.

II. The General Notion of Regulation

A. The Concept of Regulation

In modern democratic societies, every state has the primary responsibility to promote economic and social development. Promoting economic development involves ensuring the effective, fair allocation and distribution of resources and fostering economic stability. As mentioned above, ensuring effective, fair allocation and distribution of resources only takes place in a free competitive market; thus, states are obliged to take measures for the introduction and maintenance of competition in markets, create the legal framework and undertake the monitoring. These functions of states lead to the formation of economic regulation. Modern economies and societies require the implementation of effective regulations in order to support the parameters of growth, investment, innovation and market openness.[402]

According to *Girdis*, regulation simply means government control of an undertaking's activities.[403] During the process of regulation, governments impose direct and indirect controls on the actions of state-owned and non-state-owned undertakings in a particular sector. Regulation is typically conducted through rules which are set by 2Tlaws, decrees and guidelines.[404] The term may thus encompass a wide range of instruments, varying from primary laws to secondary regulations, subordinate rules,

402 OECD, 2010, p. 7.

403 The term "regulation" has been defined in a number of ways. The OECD defines regulation as *"any instrument by which governments, their subsidiary bodies, and supranational bodies (such as the EU or the WTO) set requirements on citizens and businesses that have legal force"*. Selznick defines regulation as *"sustained and focused control exercised by a public agency over activities that are valued by the community"* (Selznick 1985, p. 363). In a more detailed way, Black defines regulation as *"the sustained and focused attempt to alter the behaviour of others according to defined standards and purposes with the intention of producing a broadly identified outcome or outcomes, which may involve mechanisms of standard setting, information-gathering and behaviour modification"* (Black, 2005, p. 11). Regulation was considered mainly as a law- and state-centred process of legislative action combined with administrative enforcement ("command-and-control"). Parker & Braithwaite, 2005, p. 127.

404 Girdis, 2001, p. 1.

administrative formalities and decisions that give effect to higher-level regulations (for example, the allocation of permits) and standards.[405]

Traditionally governments regulate for different reasons. A number of these reasons are grouped together under the term "market failure". Market failure can be defined as the inability of the market to deliver the goods or services efficiently to the consumers[406] due to reasons such as the abuse of monopoly power, public goods and externalities.[407] In such situations, the use of regulation may be appropriate and efficient as the uncontrolled marketplace will fail to produce results in accordance with the public interest.[408]

The reasons and motives behind regulation can be distinguished as follows:

- natural monopolies
- externalities
- windfall profits
- continuity and availability of service
- public goods and moral hazard
- information inadequacies
- anticompetitive behaviour and predatory pricing
- scarcity and rationing
- unequal bargaining power

It should, however, be taken into consideration that, with respect to any sector or industry, the case for regulating is likely to be based not on a single rationale but on a combination of rationales which may include market failures, human rights or social solidarity. Another point to be taken into account in considering whether there is a need to regulate is that regulation and all its failings should be compared with the market and all pertinent market failures. Conclusively, any analysis concerning the need to regulate will be skewed if it is assumed that regulatory techniques will operate perfectly.[409] It is important to clearly define and consider the circumstances when regulation is required.

405 OECD, 2010, p. 9.
406 Crampton, 2002, p. 4.
407 Cook et al., 2004, p. 9.
408 Baldwin et al., 2012, p. 15.
409 Ibid., pp. 15–22.

In other words, it is vital to decide at what point competition occurs and thus has to restrict regulation.[410]

To decide whether a system of regulation is good, acceptable or in need of reform, it is necessary to be clear about the benchmarks that are relevant in such an evaluation. According to *Baldwin, Cave & Lodge*, in order to decide whether the regulatory action is legitimate, one or more of five key tests can be applied:

- Is the action or regime supported by legislative authority?
- Is there an appropriate scheme of accountability?
- Are procedures fair, accessible and open?
- Is the regulator acting with sufficient expertise?
- Is the action or regime efficient?

These five tests constitute a set of benchmarks for assessing the regulatory regimes. These are the rationales which are employed and thus are relevant to real-life debates on regulation and its reform.[411]

Furthermore, an important issue remains to be addressed. As mentioned above, governments regulate various market failures. However, in

410 Ibid., p. 25.

411 Ibid., p. 32. There are several governmental statements on the criteria for good regulation. According to The Better Regulation Commission, any policy intervention and its enforcement should meet the following five principles: proportionality, accountability, consistency, transparency and targeting (Better Regulation Task Force, 2003, p. 1). According to the Department of the Taoiseach, there are six principles of good regulation: necessity, effectiveness, proportionality, transparency, accountability and consistency (Department of the Taoiseach, 2004, p. 2.). The World Bank has a different approach regarding good regulation. According to it, the principles of good regulation are: simplify and deregulate in competitive markets, focus on enhancing property rights, expand the use of technology, reduce court involvement in business matters and make reform a continuous process (World Bank, 2004, p. 92). OECD established principles of "good regulation" in its study named "OECD Recommendation on Improving the Quality of Government Regulation" as follows: (i) serve clearly identified policy goals and be effective in achieving those goals; (ii) have a sound legal and empirical basis; (iii) produce benefits that justify costs, considering the distribution of effects across society and taking economic, environmental and social effects into account; (iv) minimise costs and market distortions; (v) promote innovation through market incentives and goal-based approaches; (vi) be clear, simple and practical for users; (vii) be consistent with other regulations and policies; and (viii) be compatible as far as possible with competition, trade and investment-facilitating principles at domestic and international levels (OECD, 2005, p. 3).

doing this, the governments sometimes overregulate or require too strict arrangements. According to *Girdis*, the fundamental requirement for successful regulatory reform is to break away from the "overregulation" habit.[412] Overregulation might hinder competition in the market and cause higher prices as the market players are affected by excessive administrative burden caused by overregulation. Inefficient or excessive regulation would raise cost of production without any corresponding benefits, and ultimately it would be the consumers who have to bear these costs.[413]

Overregulation is often associated with the "over-stringent" and the "over-prescriptive" regulation which results in the reduction of possibilities with respect to innovation and research.[414] Similar to overregulation, over-stringent regulation might also produce a perverse effect which leads to "under-regulation". If a prescription is over-precise, it will be difficult to apply it in practice, because only a few complex situations will be covered by the exact wording of the provisions at issue. Likewise, over-formalism and punitive enforcement regimes may reduce the possibilities for cooperative relationships and healthy regulatory communications and can produce self-defeating outcomes (e.g., interventions in the banking sector are designed to increase stability levels but, in fact, lead to destabilising runs in the sector). There has, indeed, been a diagnosed tendency for regulatory activities to have countervailing effects. This may happen when regulatees are induced to move activities to less regulated areas (or, as in the example of transparency regulation, make their activities even less

412 For instance, if there is lack of competition in the electricity sector, regulations are likely to be implemented in every activity from production to sale. Moreover, they may be applied to transmission and distribution activities in the natural gas sector. Girdis, 2001, p. 1.

413 In the doctrine, it has been argued that overregulation might lead to underregulation because the "*threat of draconian regulatory requirements gives industries powerful incentives to fight regulation wherever they can, and gives agencies a powerful incentive not to promulgate or enforce them*". Sunstein, 1991, p. 630.

414 One of the most common criticisms concerning overregulation was towards "best available technology" standards in environmental regulation (the technology approved by legislators or regulators for meeting output standards for a particular process, such as pollution abatement). Sunstein, 1990; https://prospect.org/article/remaking-regulation (accessed: 1 September 2019); Shapiro & McGarity, 1991, pp. 730–752.

transparent) or when regulators move too quickly to "new" risks and consumers are afflicted with fears and anxieties that lead them to stick to older, and riskier, goods.[415]

B. The Concept of Sector-Specific Regulations

The examples of the state intervention in the market via regulations are generally encountered in the sectors dominated by the network industries. In the first half of the 20th century, infrastructure services were provided by stated-owned undertakings in most of the developed and developing countries. However, especially since the 1980s many governments have increasingly withdrawn from running network industries and have begun to assume a regulatory and monitoring role in order to ensure privatisation and competition. With the beginning of the privatisation movement, regulations increased at the sectoral level. They are either implemented by the government itself or by special sector-specific regulators established by the government.[416] Such independent regulatory authorities are mostly established as a public authority or a government agency.

While independent regulatory authorities impose rules in their areas of competency within their scope of regulatory authorisation, they also supervise and monitor the behaviours of market players to see whether they comply with the regulatory rules. They may impose remedies if they determine any behaviour is contradictory to these rules. Moreover, these authorities also have the competence to settle disputes related to their regulatory areas.

Sector-specific regulations refer to explicit market intervention by the regulatory authorities "before the fact"; in other words they establish conditions within the industry to ensure that the relevant markets function optimally.[417] These regulations attempt to eliminate market failures and provide efficiency in the spheres of production and distribution. The means of regulation are likely to display differences based on the market failures which may emerge temporarily or permanently depending on the structure of the market. In actual monopolistic mar-

415 Baldwin et al., 2012, p. 70.
416 Cook et al., 2004, p. 8.
417 Granville & Irvine, 2015, p. 1.

kets, wherein market failures are permanent, it is essential to implement the sector-specific regulations in order to eliminate them.

Generally, the primary reason as to why the network industries functioning in such sectors as electricity, natural gas pipelines, railways, telecommunication, mail, irrigation and sewage require regulation is that they are natural monopolies having very high fixed costs.[418]

III. Differences between Competition Law and Sector-Specific Regulations

A. Structural Differences

At the outset, it can be said that competition law and sector-specific regulations have similar objectives, such as the promotion of effective competition in the market. However, when examined in detail, it can be observed that the aforementioned two instruments do not resemble each other and, moreover, sometimes tend to achieve opposite aims.[419] These two instruments exhibit differences in terms of scope, implementation procedures and effects in the market.

Theoretically, the most significant difference between competition law and sector-specific regulations is based on the assumption that competition law properly functions under normal market conditions and operational decisions should be made by undertakings in the market. Therefore, competition law is concerned with the distribution and decentralisation of public and private powers. However, sector-specific regulations are implemented based on the assumption that the markets require the direct or the indirect supervision of the state.[420] While sector-specific regulations aim at introducing competition in the non-competitive markets, competition law aims at protecting existing competition.

Regarding the scope of application, competition law can be generally implemented in all markets unless the sector is exempted. Once

418 Klein, 1996, p. 3.

419 It is stated that incoherencies between these two regulation types are more than their commonalities (AAI, 2005).

420 Papadopoulos, 2010, p. 26.

enacted, competition law provides an economy-wide residual mechanism for market supervision.[421] In contrast, sector-specific regulations are implemented in order to address the specific individual problems in certain markets. At this juncture, it can be stated that, for instance, a regulation implemented in the energy markets incurs no effect on the structure and functioning of other sectors such as telecommunications. Another consequence of the general/specific separation is that, whilst the regulators have extensive knowledge of the sectors for which they are responsible, the competition authorities are professionals in realms of competition law and policies.[422]

Furthermore, sector-specific regulations are implemented *ex ante*.[423] In other words, they offer a framework in order to prevent the market failures even prior to their emergence. Competition law is implemented *ex post*, after the emergence of a competition-related problem or following the occurrence of a competition-disruptive behaviour, with exception of merger control.[424] Competition law retrospectively assesses whether certain behaviours of the undertakings are competition-restricting. The feature of most sector-specific regulations is that obligations are imposed *ex ante* on a limited number of undertakings.[425] In cases where *ex ante* regulations pose the risk of damaging the course of the market, preventing the emergence of new goods and services and causing high-cost failures, *ex post* control by competition authorities is preferred. However, under the conditions in which similar problems are repeated and continuously valid basic rules are needed, *ex ante* control by sector-specific regulatory authorities is preferred.[426] While competition

---

421 Dunne, 2015, p. 43.

422 Ibid., p. 43. Laffont & Tirole, 2000, p. 277. "*Regulators often have expertise superior to that of their antitrust counterparts, although the use of specialised courts and antitrust officials tends to reduce the informational wedge between the two. This wedge has three origins: Regulatory oversight is industry specific; antitrust enforcement is not. Regulators have long-term relationships with regulated firms; antitrust enforcers […] do not. Last, regulators have larger professional staffs as well as continued procedures of data collection.*"

423 However, sector-specific regulators might make *ex post* interventions in conflict resolutions. DG Energy and Transport, 2004.

424 Laffont & Tirole, 2000, p. 277.

425 O'Donoghue & Padilla, 2006, p. 47.

426 OECD 2005, pp. 5–6.

law dictates to the undertakings in the market what they should not do, sector-specific regulations tell the undertakings what to do.[427]

Sector-specific regulations potentially offer a much broader range of instruments and can impose a much broader spectrum of remedies on bottleneck incumbents than competition law, e.g., price regulation, access regulation, unbundling.[428] In contrast, competition law consists of a set of prohibitions of certain kinds of private conduct that restrict competition in the market or exploit dominant power.[429] Sector-specific regulations give public authorities competences to adopt measures designed to alter market conditions, to regulate behaviours of market players or prohibit otherwise lawful conduct in order to increase competition in the market, to control market power and to cure market failures. Public authorities may also need to deal with technical issues such as interconnection.[430] While competition law is only about preventing illegal interference with the market, sector-specific regulations give power to alter an existing situation.[431]

These discrepancies concerning the type of remedies they impose on undertakings result from the different institutional competencies and from human and technical resources. Remedies imposed by competition law to a large extent address a specific conduct or behaviour; generally they are structural remedies[432] which do not require future extensive

427 Dube, 2008, p. 1. Hellwig, 2008, p. 10. "*Competition policy consists, by and large, of a set of rules and measures which are designed to forbid certain types of behaviour. Competition policy is not designed to tell market participants what they should do. Cartel agreements are forbidden. Abuses of dominance are forbidden. Mergers that create or strengthen a dominant position, or, under the new Regulation, mergers that create a significant impediment to effective competition are forbidden. In none of these legal provisions is there any notion that the competition authority should tell companies what to do. Sometimes, the competition authorities do so anyway, e.g., when they approve a merger subject to certain obligations on the parties in question. However, these instances are taken to be the exception, sometimes even running counter to the very spirit of competition policy.*"

428 Jaag & Trinkner, 2009, p. 16.

429 Lang, 2007, p. 2.

430 Ibid.

431 Graells, 2015, p. 95.

432 Structural remedies are measures adopted by a competition authority which require some form of structural change on the part of the party or parties to whom the measures are directed, such as the divestment of assets. Structural remedies are to be

monitoring of the conduct of the undertaking.[433] On the contrary, regulatory remedies are very often detailed behavioural remedies, for example wholesale and resale pricing levels, or conditions for providing certain services.

Even though, in some situations, competition authorities might need to determine whether a given price is discriminatory, predatory or excessive, they have no authority to define what a non-discriminatory price should be or to determine the highest legitimate price or the lowest lawful price. Moreover, competition authorities have no power to regulate the conduct of undertakings even with the view for promoting effective competition, opening up the markets to new entrants, preventing excessive profits, increasing investment incentives or any other presumably desirable economic objective. Likewise, competition authorities cannot determine the terms and conditions of services offered by undertakings. They can only assess whether these terms and conditions are lawful or not.[434]

Unlike competition law, sector-specific regulations have a provisional function. They aim at facilitating the transformation of the sector from a monopoly to a competitive market. Once this aim is fulfilled, there might be no need for sector-specific regulation. Competition law, however, has a permanent nature based on general competition policy principles. The application of competition law is not limited to a certain time-period, and it does not end with the fulfilment of certain goals.[435]

It is arguable which characteristics of competition law and regulations are more preferable. According to *Carlton & Picker*[436], the relative advantages and the disadvantages of both mechanisms become known in time. Although sector-specific regulations have resulted in cross-subsidies and favours to special interests, they have successfully

---

distinguished from behavioural remedies, which are designed to regulate the future conduct of the relevant party or parties (for example, by regulating the prices which a party may charge) and which may require significant monitoring by the competition authority concerned. https://uk.practicallaw.thomsonreuters.com/ (accessed: 1 June 2019)

433 Buigues, 2006, p. 9.

434 Lang, 2007, p. 3.

435 Hofmann, 2013, p. 203.

436 Carlton & Picker, 2007, p. 51.

determined prices and specific rules of how undertakings should deal with each other. Competition law is clearly successful in promoting competition and avoiding the favouring of special interests; however, it is insufficient for the purpose of formulating specific rules for particular industries.

Sector-specific regulations are likely to result in certain shortcomings. For instance, they be unsuccessful in achieving the desired objectives and may go beyond the boundaries necessary to accomplish the objectives. Furthermore, although they may serve as a coordination mechanism with respect to the undertakings, they may become redundant as a result of the rapidly developing technology-based sectors or in cases where liberalisation has begun and some companies are moving fast to adapt to the new situation.[437]

Sector-specific regulation should not be considered as an alternative to competition law. Despite the benefits of both instruments, there are limitations too. It is important to make the necessary evaluations in terms of the restrictions to be imposed on competition law for the benefit of the sector-specific regulation. Generally, at this juncture, it is unfair to argue that competition law and sector-specific regulations should not be implemented at the same time, or that they should exclude each other. Although certain market failures can be addressed by means of competition law, e.g. anticompetitive mergers, some can only be handled with the application of remedies through sector-specific regulations, such as regulating exploitative pricing practices. There are also other market failures which require the application of both legal instruments, such as natural monopolies.[438]

B. Institutional Differences

Alongside the operational differences that exist between sector-specific regulations and competition law, it can be stated that there are particular differences between the implementing authorities, which can be determined based on six criteria:

437 OECD, 2011, pp. 22–25.
438 Dunne, 2015, p. 41.

- general approach
- flow of information
- experience and practical application
- timing of the intervention
- type of enforcement
- type of remedies

Competition authorities are required to intervene and impose remedies on the abuse of dominant position, anticompetitive practices, cartels, monopolistic activities or mergers in any industry. This requires expertise and know-how related to each different market structure.[439] Competition authorities have three main functions:

- to remedy anticompetitive conduct, such as collusion, and to control the ability of the incumbent to restrict competition;
- to ensure that industry mergers do not significantly decrease competition;
- to protect consumers from anticompetitive practices.

The main functions of sector-specific regulators are:

- to issue licenses to undertakings when they are entering to the market;
- to monitor and regulate prices;
- to fix or approve tariffs;
- to monitor the market (e.g. against exercise of market power) and to ensure that undertakings comply with their obligations;
- to monitor the level of transparency;
- to arbitrate and resolve disputes over the tariff and non-tariff conditions on which infrastructure operators provide services.

Competition authorities only intervene in response to a complaint and gather information only when necessary to determine whether an enforcement action is required. Sector-specific regulators, however, intervene more often and require a flow of information at regular intervals from those they regulate in order to fulfil their functions.[440]

439 Buigues, 2006, p. 7.
440 OECD, 1998, p. 9.

Compared with sector-specific regulators, competition authorities seem better suited by their accumulated expertise, experience and basic institutional characteristics to protect competition from anticompetitive behaviour and mergers. They have important expertise helping to reduce excessive market power and to protect competition. Sector-specific regulators, on the contrary, have a comparative advantage in obtaining and analysing the cost data needed for economic regulation and for some aspects of access regulation.[441]

The fact remains that sector-specific regulations require fast decision-making procedures. Sector-specific regulators are better positioned to take relatively speedy decisions in network industries. Concerning sector-specific issues such as tariffs and pricing, competition authorities usually take more time to resolve the issue. Sector-specific regulators have a comparative advantage here – at least under the assumption that the industry or politicians do not seize control of them. Banking, telecommunications and energy markets may require prompt decision taking procedures in cases of crises. Competition authorities may not be as sensitive to crises as regulators.[442]

With respect to pertinent issues such as the identification of the related market, the prediction of the possibility of competition disruption in the market, the determination of market entry rules or the estimation of the market power of undertakings, the special know-how of the competition authorities is acknowledged. However, sector-specific regulators possess extensive knowledge of the technical specifications of the goods and services in their area of regulatory competency. Also, they are superior in collecting and analysing sector-specific information.[443] For example, the competition authorities are neither competent to solve issues regarding price regulation nor established for the aforementioned purpose. Sector-specific regulators are better equipped to know the structure of the market.

According to generally accepted perception, competition authorities are better suited to deal with the aforementioned issues such as the identification and sanctioning of competition-disruptive behaviours in the market or the prevention of mergers and takeovers which would

441 OECD, 1999, p. 1.
442 Ardiyok & Oguz, 2010.
443 OECD, 2005, p. 5.

result in a restriction of competition; thus, they facilitate the opening of regulated markets to competition.[444] While sector-specific regulators may have skills in these areas, it is usually the case that competition authorities have a greater breadth of experience in competition law oversight and are adept at applying the competition law to different products and services. Therefore, it can be stated that competition authorities are best suited to competition law oversight.[445] On the contrary, sector-specific regulators possess long-term and comprehensive knowledge pertaining to the technical specifications of the goods and services that they regulate. Moreover, sector-specific regulators have relative superiority in terms of the collection and analysis of necessary cost data for sector-specific regulations.[446] A pre-emptive course of action deems it preferable for the concerned authorities to relegate the regulatory functions with respect to sector-specific regulators. This makes it preferable to leave regulatory functions to sector-specific regulators.[447] However, occasionally it is preferred that the competition authorities be equipped with various exclusive authorities to enforce competition in the sector.[448]

Another difference between the two authorities is the timing and the frequency of intervention. As it has been previously mentioned, while sector-specific regulators adopt an *ex ante* structural approach, the competition authorities apply an *ex post* enforcement approach except for merger control. Sector-specific regulators thus frequently intervene and require an information flow among the regulated entities. Competition authorities, however, act upon complaints and only collect information if deemed necessary.[449]

---

444 OECD, 1998, p. 1.

445 OECD, 2005, p. 5.

446 For example, competition authority is disadvantaged compared to sector-specific regulators in terms of determining the basic principles for cost accounting and cost calculation, continuous collection of necessary information and intervention in time. Hellwig, 2008, p. 15.

447 OECD, 1998, p. 1.

448 For more information, see: Dabbah, 2011, pp. 118–119.

449 Fodorova et al., 2014, p. 9. OECD, 1998, p. 26. "*The type of information required is also different. Regulators need much more in the way of accounting information than is usually required in competition cases. Regulators may also need the power to specify accounting systems to ensure they have relevant, understandable information, especially if they wish to engage in comparison, or 'yardstick' regulation. In addition,*

There is also a difference in terms of remedies competition authorities and sector-specific regulators impose on undertakings. The difference stems from institutional competencies as well as human and technical resources. Remedies imposed by competition authorities to a large extent address specific conduct or behaviour, and generally they enforce some form of structural change that will not require future extensive monitoring of the conduct of the undertaking.[450] On the contrary, sector-specific regulators very often impose detailed behavioural remedies, e.g., wholesale and resale pricing levels or conditions mandating the provision of certain services, which requires continued monitoring.[451] Moreover, it can also be the case that sector-specific regulators may impose structural remedies for example on licensing.[452] In other words, competition authorities dictate the undertakings what specific course of action to or not to undertake, while regulators dictate what path to follow.[453]

IV. Allocation of Competencies between Competition Authorities and Sector-Specific Regulators

Since the early 1990s, a series of heavily regulated markets have undergone liberalisation processes, such as telecommunications, energy and transport. After the liberalisation, these markets often continued to be subject to both competition law and sector-specific regulations. This causes an overlap of jurisdictions which can be addressed through the allocation of competencies between competition authorities and sec-

---

with their wider set of objectives, regulators will typically need a greater variety of information than competition agencies. This is especially true in connection with ensuring that universal service obligations are met, and safety and environmental protection rules are followed."

450 In some areas, structural remedies are not possible for regulators due to natural monopolies.

451 Buigues, 2006, pp. 9–10.

452 OECD, 1999.

453 This difference can be attributed to the different characteristics of regulations. It is stated that regulation, granted the power to stop detectable illegal actions in competition law by the *OECD*, has the competency to change a legal case. OECD, 2011, p. 25.

tor-specific regulators. Such allocation can be categorised into two models: exclusive jurisdiction and concurrent jurisdiction.

A. Exclusive Jurisdiction

Under the first model, the enforcement of competition law and sector-specific regulations are either allocated exclusively to competition authorities or to sector-specific regulators. Both options have advantages and disadvantages. The first option is that the competition authorities have competence to enforce both competition law and sector-specific regulations, and they have exclusive authority to enforce competition law in the regulated markets. The main advantages of this option are:

- The enforcement of sector-specific regulations by competition authorities can reduce the risk of unnecessary distortion of competition which can occur due to excessive intervention by sector-specific regulators.
- The independence of competition authorities reduces the risk of regulatory capture in the regulated markets.
- Competition law would be enforced in a more consistent manner across all markets.
- It eliminates costly duplication of sectoral expertise.
- It ensures that regulation is applied in a way which minimises restrictions of competition, and it will have a maximum impact in the market with minimal intervention.[454]

The disadvantages of this model include:

- Competition authorities might lack technical expertise in the relevant sectors; thus, they would have to acquire a considerable number of new staffs, especially staffs with know-how in engineering.[455]
- There is a risk that competition authorities might become embroiled in overly detailed and complex regulatory issues which do not have a sufficient link to competition.[456]
- Competition authorities might lack a mechanism for resolving disputes between market players which can easily arise in the sectors.

454 ICN, 2004, p. 5.
455 OECD, 1998, p. 21.
456 Dabbah, 2011, p. 119.

- It might also cause the creation of very complex institutions, increasing bureaucracy, reducing their ability to take prompt action and leading to lengthy procedures.[457]

The second option is that sector-specific regulators can have full competence to enforce competition law and sector-specific regulations over an industry. One must acknowledge the existence of important advantages when the enforcement of competition law is allocated to sector-specific regulators in their sectors. The advantages of this option are:

- Such a model can enable sector-specific regulators to develop a comprehensive and wide-ranging approach on how to regulate the markets in the most adequate way.
- Sector-specific regulators could embrace competition and its function in a way that would lead to a decrease in regulation.

These advantages, however, are not sufficient to justify exclusive allocation of enforcement of competition law to the sector-specific regulators. On the contrary, the effect of these advantages can be considerably enhanced with competition authorities having an involvement in the enforcement of competition law in the regulated markets alongside sector-specific regulators.[458] Thus, this option might have serious shortcomings:

- A conflict may arise between the objective to protect competition and other objectives pursued by sector-specific regulators (e.g. financial markets stability).[459]
- It might increase the risk of regulatory capture.
- A question as to whether sector-specific regulators will cooperate among themselves in a structured and meaningful manner may rise, especially when cross-sectoral issues occurs and when competition law is applied by sector-specific regulators in different sectors. Enforcement of competition should be consistent across all sectors.[460]
- Sector-specific regulators may not be able to fulfil competition related tasks due to resource constraints.

457 ICN, 2004, p. 5.
458 Dabbah, 2011, p. 121.
459 ICN, 2004, p. 4.
460 Dube, 2008, p. 2.

- There is also the uncertainty over whether sector-specific regulators can be relied upon to execute their tasks effectively and explore the full extent of their remit. As sector-specific regulators are created by specific statute (the sectoral law), they may assume that they must adhere closely to their duties as set out in the statute. This can give rise to a potential problem with far-reaching consequences, because the statute may contain a wide range of duties and objectives. Sector-specific regulators may struggle to prioritise or even reconcile between their duties and objectives specified by their statute. Thus, they might ultimately become over-burdened and lose focus in executing their remit. There is also the risk of achieving consistency in decision-making and undermining the legitimacy of the relevant sector-specific regulator.[461]

This option is not considered viable due to the fact that this institutional set-up can cause a conflict which may arise between the objective to protect competition and other objectives pursued by sector-specific regulators. Objectives of sector-specific regulations might therefore override those pursued by competition law.

B. Concurrent Jurisdiction

Under the concept of concurrent jurisdiction, competition authorities and sector-specific regulators simultaneously have jurisdiction over regulated markets. While competition authorities handle the enforcement of competition law, regulatory powers lie with the sector-specific regulators.[462]

Concurrent jurisdiction between competition and sector-specific regulators may provide number of advantages:

- This model may maximise the advantages enjoyed by competition authorities and sector-specific regulators and at the same time addresses the different disadvantages from which they suffer.

461 Dabbah, 2011, p. 120.
462 Dunne, 2015, p. 265.

- While sector-specific regulators bring their deep knowledge of the sector they regulate, competition authorities bring the competition expertise that the sector-specific regulators may lack.[463]
- It may increase consistency of approach across different sectors, both regulated and unregulated.
- Economic and technical regulations, which necessitate sector-specific knowledge, may require ongoing monitoring and application of sector-specific regulations, and such a task can best be performed by sector-specific regulators. Furthermore, sector-specific regulators may be more suitable to handle frequent intervention and continuous assessment of undertakings' behaviours against standards set by sector-specific regulations. Enforcement of competition, however, can best be handled by competition authorities.[464]
- It may enable competition authorities to carry out a number of competition advocacy tasks[465].[466]

The disadvantages of this model include:

- One of the major concerns over this model is that it might lead to an overlap of jurisdiction and the unnecessary duplication of the work of the competition authorities and sector-specific regulators.
- It might lack adequate coordination mechanism between the competition authorities and sector-specific regulators.
- Another concern is that there might be fundamental differences in approaches. Inconsistency may occur, mainly due to the fact that sector-specific regulators may put greater emphasis on non-competition considerations, that sector-specific regulators may use public interest test or considerations to assess competition issues or that they may approach key issues differently from competition authorities.

463 Holland & Luoma, 2014, p. 96.

464 Dube, 2008, p. 2.

465 Competition advocacy refers to those activities conducted by the competition authority related to the promotion of a competitive environment for economic activities by means of non-enforcement mechanisms, mainly through its relationships with other governmental entities and by increasing public awareness of the benefits of competition. Advocacy Working Group, 2002, p. 25.

466 Dabbah, 2011, pp. 117–121.

- Furthermore, there is also the risk that undertakings may play the competition authorities and the sector-specific regulators against one another.

This model would require a form of cooperation between the two authorities in order to ensure the consistent application of both regulations and competition law in a sector.

C. Summary

Generally, it can be said that enforcement of competition law is relegated to competition authorities, whereas the functions of regulating and controlling the market are left to sector-specific regulators. However, this may change in practice from nation to nation. In Australia, New Zealand and Estonia, competition authorities also assume the function of sector-specific regulator; thus, both act as competition authority and sector-specific regulator. In the UK, a competition authority and sector-specific regulators implement the rules of competition law together.[467] Similarly, in the USA, competition authorities and sector-specific regulators together enforce some rules of competition law.[468] In the Netherlands, competition authorities are also regulatory authorities in the energy and the transportation sectors. It is stated that such an extreme example where the enforcement of competition law and regulatory functions are consolidated in one institution can be seen as ideal with respect to the nations where the sectors which require detailed and close regulation have grown to a certain scale. However, in other countries, the aforementioned two functions should be performed by two different expert institutions. Indeed, in various countries such as Germany, Belgium, Algeria, Chile, Czech Republic, Denmark, Finland, France, England, Ireland, Spain, Italy, Sweden, Hungary, Norway, Portugal, Romania, Switzerland and Turkey, the en-

467 Whish & Bailey, 2015, p. 990. According to *Bower*, *"Ofgem (Office of Gas and Electricity Markets) is not a prerequisite for monitoring competition issues in the gas and electricity industry nor does it have any real powers to promote or enforce it. The general principle that it is always better to combine responsibility with authority to act must apply, even in the case of competition in gas and electricity markets, and that means giving OFT and Competition Commission full jurisdiction – and thereby relieving Ofgem of its responsibility."* Bower, 2003, p. 5.

468 Chemtob, 2007, p. 5.

forcement of competition law and the regulation of sectors with market failures are basically performed by different institutions.

At this juncture, it can be said that the enforcement of competition law and the functions of sector-specific regulations should be performed by two different authorities. However, in sectors with permanent market failures, sector-specific regulators are generally granted the duty and authority to separate the competition-worthy parts of markets that are attempting to become liberalised through privatisations from the parts exhibiting permanent market failure. It is widely accepted that the duties of sector-specific regulators should include the introduction, protection, promotion and development of competition. In terms of protecting existing competition in markets, the function of competition authority outweighs. However, in terms of sustaining competition in monopolistic or competition-deficient markets, it is preferable to prioritise regulation. Moreover, in cases in which it is possible to eliminate the competitive concerns emerging in the network sectors which are the common areas of competition authorities and sector-specific regulators, it is disputable if the competition law rules should be enforced.[469] This raises the question of whether there is a conflict of duty and authority in terms of ensuring and protecting competition between institutions. This question is especially important in the first stages of the process of opening markets for competition in which regulation is slightly more intense than competition.

Compared with sector-specific regulators, competition authorities are deemed more appropriate in terms of protecting competition from

469 In the literature there are contributions to this discussion. *O'Donoghue & Padilla* mention that there can be certain general remarks related to the issue although they vary from case to case. *"First, the scope for the residual application of competition law in circumstances where there is also regulation of course depends on the level of detail of the regulatory regime. The more prescriptive and detailed the regulatory framework, the less likely that competition law has any residual role. Second, when there is a sector-specific remedy that protects a competitive market structure in a given industry, and which has been correctly enforced by a national regulator and that does not violate EC competition rules (i.e., there is an 'effective' regulatory remedy), a competition authority should not intervene. Finally, when there is a sector-specific regime designed to protect a competitive market structure, but that regime has not been applied by the regulator […], competition authorities should be free to launch proceedings on the basis of Article 82 EC."* O'Donoghue & Padilla, 2006, pp. 31–32.

anticompetitive behaviour and mergers due to their know-how, experiences and institutional structure. For the same reasons, sector-specific regulators are more appropriate for the economic regulation of undertakings based on their specialities and knowledge pertaining to sectoral issues.[470] However, the aforementioned distinction is not visible regarding certain cases, such as the access regulation. The access regulation serves a dual purpose, which is both to protect and support competition in certain cases in which access to a part of a vertically integrated incumbent company is important for the development of competition. Regarding the cases of abuse of a dominant position, competition authorities are more experienced than sector-specific regulators; therefore, they are relatively better suited to undertake enforcement of such duties. However, determining the conditions of access and ensuring their implementation are considered the duty of sector-specific regulators.[471]

§ 6. Application of Competition law in Regulated Sectors

In the EU, while sector-specific regulations are implemented through secondary sources, competition law is considered a primary source, being a part of the TFEU. The Commission is bound by the preferentiality rule and has to take this rule into consideration in the application of EU law.

The application of competition law and sector-specific regulations differs between Member States. Each Member State has flexibility in respect of the distribution of competencies between competition authorities and sector-specific regulators. As mentioned above, there are several options regarding the application of these two legal instruments.[472] According to the EU's approach, competition law can be applied in parallel with sector-specific regulations. Below, the EU's approach will be examined focusing on the recent practice of the European courts.

470 OECD, 1998, p. 8.
471 Ibid., p. 8.
472 Hofmann, 2013, p. 209.

I. Deutsche Telekom

Among the decisions made by the Commission regarding the application of competition law in the regulated sectors, one of the most discussed and analysed decision is the *Deutsche Telekom* judgment[473].[474] The Commission implemented the rules of competition law on margin squeeze[475] in a regulated sector for the first time in its *Deutsche Telekom* decision.[476]

Prior to the liberalisation of the telecommunication markets in Germany on 1 August 1996, Deutsche Telekom was the legal monopoly in the sale of land-line telecommunication services. On the one hand, Deutsche Telekom had the capability of the independent commercial decision-making regarding retail prices for ADSL. On the other hand, it was subject to partial price regulations by the German sector-specific regulator. Deutsche Telekom's wholesale access charges were approved in advance by the German sector-specific regulator, and retail prices for analogue and ISDN lines were regulated under a price cap system.

Following the complaints of the competitors, the Commission concluded in its 21 May 2003 dated decision that Deutsche Telekom was abusing its dominant position on the relevant markets for direct access to its fixed telephone network. Such abuse consisted in charging unfair prices for wholesale access services to competitors and retail access services in the local network; thus, Deutsche Telekom has infringed Article 102 TFEU.[477] This, in turn, forced its competitors to charge their customers higher prices as compared to those which Deutsche Telekom charged its end users.

---

473 Case COMP/C-1/37.451, 37.578, 37.579, *Deutsche Telekom AG*, Commission Decision of 21 May 2003.

474 Fodorova et al., 2014, p. 47.

475 *"The term 'margin squeeze' is used to characterise a situation in which a dominant undertaking charges a price for a product or service on the upstream market which, compared to the price it charges on the downstream market, does not allow even an equally efficient competitor to trade profitably in the downstream market on a lasting basis. An abuse under Article 102 TFEU in the form of a margin squeeze has already been the subject of several antitrust cases in other network industries, namely in the field of telecoms."* Koch & Gauer, 2011, p. 221.

476 Geradin & O'Donoghue, 2005, p. 26.

477 Case COMP/C-1/37.451, 37.578, 37.579, *Deutsche Telekom AG*, para. 199.

Deutsche Telekom brought an action before the General Court for annulment of the Commission's decision; it argued that the Commission erroneously found Deutsche Telekom had infringed Article 102 TFEU.[478] The primary grounds of Deutsche Telekom's argument were[479]:

- All of the charges at issue were set *ex ante* by the regulatory authority. As a result of this *ex ante* tariff regulation, Deutsche Telekom was not able to determine the charges. It had no freedom to take independent commercial decisions against which competition proceedings might be brought at the Community level.[480]
- The Commission's methodology to establish the margin squeeze was unlawful.[481]
- The Commission's calculations on margin squeeze contained errors.[482]
- The margin squeeze as identified does not constitute an abuse per se, and the Commission did not consider whether the margin squeeze had anticompetitive effects on the market.[483]

The Commission argued that, while Deutsche Telekom's wholesale price was regulated, the company had substantial leeway to determine its retail prices; furthermore, the subsequent approval by the national regulatory authority did not affect Deutsche Telekom's autonomy. Moreover, the Commission argued that Deutsche Telekom could have avoided the margin squeeze by increasing retail charges because it was entitled to apply to the regulatory authority at any time asking for adjustments to charges.[484]

Despite Deutsche Telekom's argument that it had not been left enough scope by the regulator to adjust its prices, the General Court upheld the Commission's decision that Deutsche Telekom abused its dominant position on the markets for direct access to its fixed telephone network by engaging in a margin squeeze. In its decision, the General

478 Case T-271/03, *Deutsche Telekom*, [2008] ECR II-477.
479 Alexiadis, 2008, p. 3.
480 Case T-271/03, *Deutsche Telekom*, para. 70.
481 Ibid., para. 153.
482 Ibid., para. 214.
483 Ibid., para. 225.
484 Case COMP/C-1/37.451, 37.578, 37.579, *Deutsche Telekom AG*, para. 164.

Court addressed the issue regarding the relationship between competition law and sector-specific regulations. It stated that *ex ante* pricing regulation does not absolve undertakings in a dominant position from responsibility under Article 102 TFEU.[485] Dominant undertakings that are subject to *ex ante* price regulation must ensure that their pricing does not infringe Article 102 TFEU and that they use any discretion permitted by the regulatory system to avoid abusive pricing. Moreover, the General Court expressed the opinion that an *ex ante* price regulation by a national regulatory authority will not necessarily protect the undertaking against a Commission investigation under EU competition law due to infringement of Article 102 TFEU by the margin squeeze, particularly if the authority in question had not explicitly the intention to apply Article 102 TFEU in approving the prices.[486] The General Court further noted that, even if the national regulatory authority is required to inspect whether the charges proposed by the dominant undertakings are compatible with Article 102 TFEU, this would not preclude the Commission from opening an infringement procedure against the undertaking under Article 102 TFEU.[487] Moreover, if a national law merely encourages or makes it easier for undertakings to engage in autonomous anticompetitive conduct, those undertakings remain subject to Articles 101 and 102 TFEU.[488] Furthermore, the General Court clarified that if the system of sector-specific regulation confers upon the dominant undertaking no margin of freedom in which to pursue an independent pricing policy, *ex post* competition rules will be deemed inapplicable.[489]

Deutsche Telekom appealed to the CJ against the General Court's decision; however, the CJ refused the claims of Deutsche Telekom and upheld the General Court's decision. The CJ stated that Deutsche Telekom had performed abusive practices such as margin squeeze even if the wholesale prices for local network access services were determined by national regulatory authorities. It concluded that Deutsche Telekom had sufficient scope to adjust its retail prices charged to the end users and the General Court was therefore entitled to hold that the

485 Case C-280/08P, *Deutsche Telekom AG v Commission*, [2010] ECR I-9555, para. 80.
486 Alexiadis, 2008, p. 4.
487 Case T-271/03, *Deutsche Telekom*, para. 120.
488 Ibid., para. 89.
489 Alexiadis, 2008, p. 9.

margin squeeze at issue was a practice attributable to Deutsche Telekom, notwithstanding the fact that the national regulatory authority set wholesale prices for local loop access services.[490]

The judgment of the CJ confirmed that competition law can be applied where sector-specific regulations do not preclude the undertakings they govern from engaging in autonomous conduct that prevents, restricts or distorts competition. [491] The presence of the regulation can be taken into account as a mitigating factor in the determination of the penalty to be imposed. Nevertheless, the CJ established that, even under the assumption that the regulator is obliged to consider whether the behaviour of the undertaking concerned is compatible with Article 102 TFEU, the Commission would not be precluded from finding that the undertaking was responsible for an infringement of Article 102 TFEU.

With respect to the qualification of an abuse of margin squeeze, the CJ has confirmed that this practice is one of the prohibited cases in EU legislation and that it is not necessary to prove that wholesale or retail prices have the qualification of abuse on their own. The CJ further established that margin squeeze is a stand-alone abuse, independent of excessive pricing of the input or predatory pricing downstream; the essence of a margin squeeze is the unfairness of the spread between the wholesale and retail prices.[492] And although it was accepted that the national regulatory authorities might have violated the EU legislation and an action could have been brought against Germany because of the non-fulfilment of obligations, unfair prices had been set by Deutsche Telekom itself in the exercise of its own commercial freedom.

The decision is deemed important due to what it says about the relationship between sector-specific regulations and competition law.[493] It noted that, even when a national regulatory authority has adopted a decision based on a sector-specific regulation, a national competition

490 European Commission, The Court of Justice upholds the €12.6 million fine imposed by the Commission on Deutsche Telekom for abuse of its dominant position in the fixed telephony markets in Germany, 2010.

491 Case C-280/08P, *Deutsche Telekom AG v Commission*, para. 4.

492 Jones & Sufrin, 2016, p. 416.

493 Vickers, 2009, p. 8.

authority or the Commission remains entitled to intervene if the outcome of this decision leads to failure to prevent infringements of competition law from occurring.[494]

The major difficulty with this case is that it placed the regulated undertakings in a dilemma. On the one hand, they must comply with any non-competition objectives sought by the national regulatory authority under *ex ante* sector-specific regulations; on the other hand, they have to respect the primacy of *ex post* competition rules, even in circumstances where the two regimes clearly overlap and pursue similar objectives.[495]

II. TeliaSonera

TeliaSonera is the incumbent land-line telephone network operator in Sweden and owns the local loop[496].[497] It is a former state-protected monopolist providing land-line telephone services with a network connecting all Swedish households, and it offered users fast broadband connections. In addition, it offered to other Internet service providers access to its own facilities. TeliaSonera offered access to the local loop to other operators in two ways.[498] On the one hand, TeliaSonera granted service providers access rights to the so-called local loop in return for payment. On the other hand, without being legally obliged to do so, TeliaSonera offered to operators an ADSL product intended for wholesale users (i.e., on the upstream market), which enabled these wholesale firms to supply high-speed broadband connection services to end users (i.e., on the downstream market).[499]

According to Konkurrensverket, the Swedish Competition Authority, TeliaSonera abused its dominant position between April 2000 and January 2003. It exercised a pricing policy under which the margin be-

494 Geradin & O'Donoghue, 2005, p. 57.
495 O'Donoghue, 2008, p. 13.
496 The local loop is the fixed copper wires that link a local telephone exchange to the homes of customers. https://uk.practicallaw.thomsonreuters.com (accessed: 1 June 2019).
497 Case C-52/09, *Konkurrensverket v TeliaSonera Sverige AB*, [2011] ECR I-00527.
498 Ibid., paras. 5–7.
499 Wurmnest, 2012, p. 723.

tween the wholesale prices of ADSL products and the retail prices of services offered to end users were either negative or insufficient to cover the specific costs of the ADSL input services which TeliaSonera itself had to incur in order to distribute those services to the end users concerned.[500] Consequently, the Konkurrensverket brought an action before the Stockholm District Court, which in turn referred a number of questions regarding the condition of margin squeeze to the CJ for a preliminary ruling.

The CJ addressed the relationship between the sector-specific regulations and competition law in its decision dated 17 February 2011 and reaffirmed that Article 102 TFEU can be applied if it is found that the national legislation does not preclude undertakings from engaging in autonomous conduct which prevents, restricts or distorts competition.[501] In addition, the CJ held that an identified margin squeeze can be considered attributable to a vertically integrated undertaking in a dominant position under Article 102 TFEU solely on the ground that a dominant undertaking has the scope to adjust its retail prices alone, especially if an undertaking has complete autonomy in its choice of conduct on the market.[502] The CJ noted that it is not necessary to prove that the wholesale or retail prices are abusive in order to establish an abuse. It is the exclusionary effect on the dominant undertaking's equally efficient actual or potential competitors which constitutes the abuse.[503] The CJ further clarified that margin squeeze is a stand-alone abuse, distinct from that of refusal to supply[504], and indispensability of the wholesale product is not a prerequisite for this kind of abusive practice.[505]

500 Case C-52/09, *Konkurrensverket v TeliaSonera Sverige AB*, para. 8.
501 Ibid., para. 50.
502 Ibid., para. 51–52.
503 Ibid., para. 39; Ezrachi, 2018, p. 235.
504 Case C-52/09, *Konkurrensverket v TeliaSonera Sverige AB*, para. 56.
505 The CJ's view can be considered in contradiction with the Commission's Guidance Paper on Article 102 TFEU, where margin squeeze is considered as a subcategory of refusal to supply. Ezrachi, 2018, p. 236; European Commission, Guidance on the Commission's enforcement priorities in applying Article 82 of the EC Treaty to abusive exclusionary conduct by dominant undertakings, 2009, paras. 75–84.

III. Telefónica

Telefónica is the sole operator of a nation-wide land-line telephone network in the Spanish market. Telefónica was a state-owned undertaking which held a legal monopoly in the retail provision of land-line telecommunications services before the telecommunications markets was fully liberalised in 1998.[506] Currently, Telefónica operates the largest nation-wide land-line phone network in Spain.

On 11 July 2003, Wanadoo España filed a complaint with the Commission alleging that Telefónica's subsidiaries charged high broadband access rates to its competitors and kept the access rate very low for its own retail broadband access services. Wanadoo España argued that Telefónica's competitors were not able to compete in the broadband retail market due to an insufficient margin between the wholesale prices and the retail prices.[507]

On 4 July 2007, the Commission concluded in its decision that Telefónica have abused its dominant position in the Spanish wholesale access market at the regional and national levels. The Commission established that, between September 2001 and December 2006, the margin between Telefónica's prices for wholesale access at the regional and national level and retail prices was not sufficient to cover costs which would have to be incurred by an operator as efficient as Telefónica to provide retail broadband access.[508]

It was stated that Telefónica continued the violation by not providing lower wholesale prices. Thus, the focus was whether an undertaking subject to the sector-specific regulation had the discretion to end/prevent the violation through its own initiative. The decision indicated that, since the regulatory authority could not determine the competition violation and was not successful in preventing it, the enforcement of competition law did not violate the principle of *ne bis in idem*. The Spanish national regulatory authority had imposed an *ex ante* price control based on incorrect forecasts provided by the dominant land-line operator.[509] The

506 Case COMP/38.784, *Wanadoo España v Telefónica*, Commission Decision of 4 July 2007; Case T-336/07, *Telefónica, SA v European Commission*, [2012] not reported.

507 Case COMP/38.784, *Wanadoo España v Telefónica*, para. 5.

508 Ibid., para. 7.

509 Alexiadis, 2012, p. 142.

Commission has subsequently stated that the duty of the regulatory authority to protect competition has a broader concept as compared to the Commission's application of competition law. The Commission concluded that although some of the wholesale prices were regulated, it did not alleviate Telefónica's responsibility.[510]

Telefónica appealed to the General Court against the Commission's decision with the support of the Spanish government and demanded the reversal of the decision. The General Court upheld the Commission's decision. In its decision, it stated that Telefónica had freedom to reduce the price of the national wholesale product, since that price was not subject to regulation.[511] The General Court further emphasised that Telefónica ought to have known that conformity with Spanish telecommunication laws and legislation would not protect it from an intervention by the Commission based on competition law.

Telefónica appealed to the CJ against the General Court's decision and claimed that the Commission had acted *ultra vires* in applying Article 102 TFEU to an area regulated *ex ante* by the telecommunication commission[512] and that this error in law was perpetuated by the General Court. In its decision of 10 July 2014, the CJ explored the relationship between *ex post* competition law and *ex ante* sectoral regulation and upheld the General Court's decision.[513] The CJ emphasised that the general application of Article 102 TFEU is not affected by the existence of an *ex ante* regulatory framework regarding the telecommunications markets and that the fact that an undertaking's conduct com-

510 European Commission, Antitrust: Commission welcomes Court judgment in Telefónica margin squeeze case, 2014.

511 *"Moreover, as regards the price of the regional wholesale product of Telefónica, the General Court is of the view that the prices determined by the Spanish Telecommunications Market Commission (CMT) were maximum prices and that, as a consequence, Telefónica was free to request a reduction of its prices. Finally, as regards the retail prices, Telefónica did not dispute that it was free to increase its prices at any moment."* European Commission, The General Court confirms the fine of more than €151 million imposed by the Commission on Telefónica for having abused its dominant position in the market for access to broadband Internet in Spain, 2012; Case T-336/07, *Telefónica and Telefónica de España v Commission*, [2012], ECLI:EU:T:2012:172.

512 Comision del Mercado de las Telecomunicaciones (CMT).

513 C-295/12 P, *Telefónica and Telefónica de España v Commission*, [2014] pub. electr. EU:C:2014:2062.

plies with a regulatory framework does not mean that such conduct complies with Article 102 TFEU.[514] It was reaffirmed by the CJ that the decision taken by the Commission on the basis of Article 102 TFEU is not subject to prior consideration of any intervention on the part of the national regulatory authorities and is therefore, in principle, independent of such intervention.[515] This meant that the Spanish national regulatory authority's *ex ante* review did not enable Telefónica to argue that the Commission's intervention was not foreseeable.[516]

In the *Telefónica* decision, the approach of the EU Courts regarding the relationship between competition law and sector-specific regulations has been confirmed once more. The General Court stated that the existence of *ex ante* regulation does not by any means exclude *ex post* competition law enforcement. Competition law can be applied even though dominant undertakings have been subject to *ex ante* regulation as long as they still have complete autonomy in their choice of conduct and engage in a conduct which prevents, distorts or restricts competition.[517]

The General Court (and subsequently the CJ) reaffirmed that margin squeeze constitutes an independent form of abuse distinct from that of refusal to supply.[518] The Commission's and the EU Courts' approach to consider margin squeeze an independent form of abuse has been criticised in the doctrine. *Faella & Pardolesi* argue that the abovementioned approach might lead to an intrusion into the commercial freedom of dominant undertakings, which could negatively affect their incentives to invest and innovate.[519] *Geradin* argues that it could also lead to fundamentally misguided Article 102 decisions when national regulatory authorities have not conducted proper analysis or when there is an important time lag between the moment this analysis was conducted and the moment at which the Commission's assessment of a dominant firm's conduct takes place, with the consequence that market

514 Ibid., para. 133.

515 Case T-336/07, *Telefónica and Telefónica de España v Commission*, para. 180; C-295/12 P, *Telefónica and Telefónica de España v Commission*, para. 161.

516 Vertessy, 2015, p. 45.

517 Akman, 2012.

518 C-295/12 P, *Telefónica and Telefónica de España v Commission*, para. 150.

519 Faella & Pardolesi, 2010, p. 271.

characteristics may have significantly changed.[520] According to *Jones & Sufrin*, *"margin squeeze is a separate form of abuse from refusal to supply and it is not necessary that the input is indispensable. A margin squeeze will infringe Article 102 only if it has anti-competitive effects, but the effect need not be concrete, and it is enough that competitors are potentially excluded. Anti-competitive effects are considered 'probable' if the input is indispensable or the margin is negative."*[521] As mentioned above, this is also in contradiction with the view of the Commission in the Guidance Paper.

IV. Orange Polska

Orange Polska[522] is an incumbent telecommunications provider in Poland established in December 1991 from a state monopolist.[523] It is a market leader on the Polish market of fixed-line telephony, Internet and data transmission. It provides wide range of services including calls, messaging, content, access to the Internet and TV, data transmission, radio communication, multimedia and related services provided on fixed line and mobile, land and satellite networks. As the owner of the only nationwide access network and supplier of two wholesale broadband access products (local unbundling and broadband access), Orange Polska had a monopoly in the market for wholesale network infrastructure access and in the market for wholesale broadband access.[524] Given that Orange Polska had significant market power in a number of markets[525], the Polish regulatory authority[526] obliged Orange Polska to

520 Geradin, 2011, p. 12.

521 Jones & Sufrin, 2016, p. 430.

522 Previously Telekomunikacja Polska, now Orange Polska SA ("Orange Polska").

523 COMP/39.525, *Telekomunikacja Polska*, Commission Decision of 22 June 2011.

524 Ibid., para. 647.

525 According to the Telecommunications Law implementing the EU regulatory framework, Polish Regulatory Authority had to analyse electronic communication markets on a regular basis. As a result of these market studies, it would designate undertakings with significant market power and establish the *ex ante* regulatory obligations to be imposed on such undertakings to ensure more effective competition and better rights for consumers. Ibid., para. 71.

526 Urząd Komunikacji Elektronicznej ("UKE").

provide certain services[527] on regulated conditions (not worse than those Orange Polska applied to its own company or to its subsidiaries) and to provide access to the local loop under clear, fair and non-discriminatory conditions based on the domestic regulation implementing the EU telecommunications framework.[528]

Suspecting that Orange Polska abused its dominant position in the Polish wholesale broadband services market and infringed Article 102 TFEU by refusing to give access to bitstream and to the unbundled local loop, the Commission carried out an unannounced inspection at the premises of Orange Polska on 23 September 2008. In the follow-up to the inspection, the Commission opened formal proceedings against the Polish telecom incumbent on 27 April 2009.[529]

Alternative operators wishing to provide broadband Internet access to end users can either use the network of the incumbent operator or build an alternative access network, which is mostly not an economically viable option. In this case, there was no alternative infrastructure which was substitutable to Orange Polska's local access network and would enable alternative operators to offer retail broadband services in Poland.[530] In other words, access to Orange Polska's wholesale broadband services was essential for alternative operators wishing to compete in the retail market and to provide retail services to end users in Poland. Other operators need to acquire wholesale broadband access products, namely wholesale broadband access and local loop unbundling, to use the incumbent's network.

The Commission gathered extensive evidence which showed that Orange Polska pursued a strategy aimed at restricting competition on the broadband markets in Poland by hindering, from August 2005 until at least October 2009, alternative operators from efficiently accessing the incumbent's network and using its wholesale broadband prod-

527 These services included the offer of wholesale broadband Internet access services to other electronic communication operators, on the basis of which these operators may construct their own retail broadband offers. COMP/39.525, *Telekomunikacja Polska*, para. 20.

528 Ibid., para. 69.

529 European Commission, Antitrust: Commission opens formal proceedings against telecoms incumbents Telekomunikacja Polska and Slovak Telekom, 2009.

530 COMP/39.525, *Telekomunikacja Polska*, para. 808.

ucts.[531] Orange Polska never applied a straightforward refusal to access but engaged in anticompetitive practices which prevented, or at least delayed, the entry of alternative operators into Polish broadband markets. Alternative operators were faced with numerous difficulties to obtain access to the network of the Polish telecom incumbent. The abusive discriminatory conduct of Orange Polska included the following elements[532]:

- proposing unreasonable access conditions with regard to wholesale broadband products in the contract, i.e., exclusion or modification of contractual clauses and extension of deadlines to the detriment of alternative operators;
- delaying the process of negotiating access conditions;
- refusing to provide reliable and accurate information on its network which was crucial for alternative operators to be able to make sound business decisions and operate efficiently;
- refusing alternative operators' requests in an unjustifiable manner;
- limiting access to subscriber lines by inter alia rejecting alternative operators' orders to activate subscriber lines on unreasonable grounds.

The Commission found that the proposed conditions created several operational difficulties, thereby placing rivals at a disadvantage. Although separately each of the conditions may not have been burdensome, the combined effect was onerous. In addition, these conditions did not meet the minimum standards set out under the applicable regulatory framework. They must at minimum ensure non-discriminatory, secure and reasonable access to Orange Polska's wholesale products for alternative operators.[533] Orange Polska's delaying tactics had prevented alternative operators from reaching the critical customer size rapidly and, thus, from climbing the investment ladder earlier.[534]

The above-mentioned practices prevented alternative operators from competing effectively in the market and constituted an abuse of

531 Ibid., para. 803.
532 Ibid.
533 O'Donoghue & Padilla, 2013.
534 Jones & Sufrin, 2016, p. 507.

dominant position in the Polish broadband market. In consequence, the European Commission imposed a fine of €127 554 194 on Orange Polska for abusing its dominant position in the Polish market. Orange Polska appealed the Commission's decision to the General Court. The General Court dismissed Orange Polska's appeal in its entirety stating that the Polish incumbent's practices had the *"capacity to adversely affect competition and consumers"*.[535] On appeal before the CJ, Orange Polska argued that the GC's reading of recital 902 was distorted. On 25 July 2018, the CJ dismissed Orange Polska's appeal in its entirety. The CJ's judgment clarified that the Commission does not have to take into account the actual or likely effects of an infringement when determining the amount of the fine.

A major difference from the previous cases was that, unlike the German and Spanish regulators, the Polish regulator took an action in 2009 and investigated Orange Polska's abusive behaviour almost two years before the Commission's decision.[536] As a result of this investigation, Orange Polska committed to respect the existing regulatory obligation. However, the Commission adopted the infringement decision regardless and imposed a fine on the Polish incumbent operator.[537]

The Commission reiterated that the existence of national sector-specific regulation does not preclude the application of EU competition rules.[538] In this case, even though the Polish national regulatory authority put a regulatory mechanism in place which imposed on Orange Polska the obligation to grant access to its network, competition was restricted due to Orange Polska's anticompetitive discriminatory practices. The Commission's intervention does not in any case relate to the specific infringements of sector-specific regulations but to Orange Polska's pattern of abusive behaviour over more than four years, which constitutes a breach of Article 102 TFEU. With its Orange Polska deci-

535 Case C-123/16 P, *Orange Polska vs European Commission*, [2018], EU:C:2018:590.

536 The above-mentioned dilatory tactics were clearly in breach of the Polish Regulatory Framework. Pisarkiewicz, 2018, p. 510.

537 According to the Commission, the regulator in Poland did not assess whether Orange Polska's behaviour was compatible with Article 102 TFEU, but even if it had done so, the CJ and the General Court established that *"the Commission cannot be bound by a decision taken by a national body pursuant to Article 102 TFEU."* COMP/39.525, *Telekomunikacja Polska*, para. 128.

538 Ibid., para. 126.

sion, the Commission went further in developing a concurrent approach to the relationship between competition law and regulation.[539]

539 Dunne, 2015, p. 219.

Part 4 Competition in the European Energy Markets

§ 7. Sector-Specific Rules for Energy Markets

Liberalisation in the energy markets implies the creation of a market which can support an effective competitive environment. In monopolistic markets, undertakings with a dominant position tend to abuse their position. Such an abuse may lead to numerous market failures, i.e., preventing the new competitors from easily entering into the market, manipulating access tariffs and violating consumer rights.[540]

In order to protect and promote competition in a market with complementary competitive and non-competitive regulated segments, policymakers can use a number of sector-specific "tools". These tools can be generally categorised into two groups: structural measures, which mainly focus on the incentives of undertakings to restrict or hinder competition, and behavioural measures, which mainly focus on controlling undertakings' ability to restrict competition. While access regulation, price regulation and quality regulation are considered behavioural measures, vertical ownership separation and divestment of assets are structural remedies.[541] Operational separation, being kind of hybrid, falls somewhere between these two categories.[542]

In the EU, the liberalisation of the energy markets has focused on key issues such as the structural separation of the competitive segments (energy production and supply activities) from the non-competitive regulated segments (operation of transmission and distribution networks and other essential infrastructures), non-discriminatory third-party access regime to networks and other essential infrastruc-

540 Cabau & Sandberg, 2016, p. 92.

541 OECD, 2001, p. 53.

542 Mulder et al., 2005, p. 22.

ture, gradual removal of exclusive supply rights and the establishment of independent regulatory authorities with effective powers.[543]

I. Unbundling

Network industries, such as electricity and natural gas, have a structure in which a non-competitive component of the industry is vertically integrated with a potentially competitive component. The basic problem that arises in this context is that the owner of the non-competitive component may have both the incentive and the ability to restrict competition in the competitive component by controlling the terms and conditions at which rival firms in the competitive component have access to the non-competitive component.[544]

The degree of unbundling varies from sector to sector.[545] In telecommunication, postal service and railways, the degree of unbundling is not the same as in the energy sector. This situation is explained by political resistance, technical properties of sectors, the potential magnitude of reconfiguration costs, the proportionality principle expressed by the fact that measures should be proportional to the objective of increasing competition, and public policy issues such as public and universal service obligations.[546] Electricity and natural gas are transferred to their place of consumption through grids and pipelines.[547] Since no alternative method of carrying electricity and natural gas is available, the natural monopoly feature of energy networks is more conspicuous than that of other networks.[548] Furthermore, in comparison to other sectors, as it is

543 Kroes, 2007, p. 1389.

544 OECD, 2001, p. 7.

545 Mulder et al., 2005, p. 23.

546 Ehlers, 2010, p. 120.

547 In the electricity and gas sectors, natural monopolies exist on both the national level and the regional level. On the national level, electricity is transported by a high-voltage grid called the transmission network, and natural gas is transported by the high-pressure grid. On the regional level, low-voltage grids for electricity and low-pressure grids for gas constitute distribution networks. The transmission network plays a crucial role in coordinating generation in order to achieve equilibrium between supply and demand in the most efficient way at every moment of time. Mulder, Shestalova, & Lijesen, 2005, p. 20.

548 Praduroux & Talus, 2008, p. 4; Midttun, 2001, p. 27.

simple in a technical sense and economically viable, a more comprehensive unbundling practice can easily be realised in the energy sector.[549]

Prior to liberalisation, European energy markets were characterised by the state-owned vertically integrated undertakings which were active in all market segments including generation/supply and distribution/transmission.[550] Due to the natural monopoly characteristic of both the electricity and gas networks[551], the main activities, such as production and supply, should be unbundled from transmission and distribution activities to enable and increase fair and equal market access in energy markets and to decrease non-competitive and discriminative behaviours against rivals.[552] This is the underlying objective of unbundling: separate the competitive[553] from the non-competitive[554] segment in order to prevent misuse through the control of the latter and prevent situations which may give rise to a conflict of interests and incentives.[555] In short, unbundling in energy markets means *"running*

549 Ehlers, 2010, p. 124.

550 Cabau & Sandberg, 2016, p. 91.

551 Electricity and gas are required to be transferred to the areas where they are consumed and distributed to the end customers. Such a course of action is implemented through pipelines and electricity grids. Once a network has been constructed, it would be extremely difficult to construct a competing network: sunk costs for construction are extremely high, environmental issues (including opposition from environmental groups) are present and demand risks are significant – all this together with the advantage of the established operator militates against a potential market entrant. This makes it virtually impossible to construct a competing network. The network infrastructure thus is considered an essential facility, which means that access to such infrastructure is vital for undertakings wishing to carry out business in the energy markets. Talus, 2011, p. 72.

552 Thomas, 2007, pp. 3–4.

553 The activities in the energy sector which are usually competitive: electricity generation, electricity "retailing" or "marketing" activities, electricity market trading activities, gas production, gas storage (in some countries), gas "retailing" and "marketing" activities. OECD, 2001, p. 8.

554 The activities in the energy sector which are usually non-competitive: high-voltage transmission of electricity, local electricity distribution, high-pressure transmission of gas and local gas distribution. Ibid.

555 *"This is the underlying objective of unbundling: separate the competitive from the non-competitive segment in order to prevent misuse through the control of the latter."* Praduroux & Talus, 2008, p. 4. The 1988 Communication from the EC on the IEM considered horizontal and/or vertical integration of the industry (in particu-

energy transmission and distribution networks independently from the production and supply side".[556]

As networks in energy markets are considered essential for undertakings operating in the upstream and downstream markets, the establishment of the competitive markets depends on the non-discriminative behaviours of the undertakings which control the networks. All kinds of unbundling — legal, operational, accounting, ownership unbundling — apply to energy suppliers that are transmitting electricity through a high-voltage or extra-high voltage system or gas through high-pressure pipeline networks and at the same time fulfil at least one other market function such as the supply of energy, the generation of electricity or the production of gas.[557]

As mentioned above, unbundling can be accomplished to different degrees. In general, more comprehensive unbundling models are required for the transmission networks as compared to the distribution networks. In terms of the transmission networks, unbundling requirements generally focus on the ownership unbundling which prohibits any production and supply undertaking from owning the majority share of a transmission system. The other two models are transmission system operator and independent system operator. In terms of the distribution networks, the unbundling requirements focus on the legal, accounting and functional/management segregation.[558]

Although the aforementioned unbundling models provide for different degrees of structural segregation of network activities from production and supply activities, it is expected that each of them is to be effective in resolving any conflict of interests between producers, suppliers and transmission system operators. In other words, they should remove the incentive for vertically integrated undertakings to discriminate against competitors regarding access to the network, access to commercially relevant information and investments in the network.[559]

---

lar, the integration of network businesses with production and supply businesses) to be one of the main obstacles to the creation of a true internal EU energy market. Guayo et al., 2010, p. 329.

556 Zafirova, 2007, p. 29.

557 Malmendier & Schendel, 2006, p. 366.

558 Rodríguez, 2014, p. 10.

559 European Commission, The Unbundling Regime, 2010, p. 4.

According to *Mulder et al.*, "*unbundling breaks links between the network company and commercial activities. The stronger the unbundling, the more links are broken. This provides more independence to the network, which affects performance of the network company itself, as well as performance in the other parts of the electricity supply chain.*"[560]

The unbundling of activities within a former vertically integrated company minimises distortions in a single European electricity or gas market by ensuring transparent and non-discriminatory terms of transmission access for third parties and curtailing the risks of cross-subsidisation[561] of the generation and supply activities of incumbents.[562] Other benefits expected from unbundling include increased transparency in the energy sector, the facilitation of the undertakings' access to accurate information, the elimination of market closure[563] risk, the encouragement of competition and an increased effect of sector-specific regulations through more effective market regulation.

A. Unbundling in Transmission

1. Ownership Unbundling

The most advanced and radical unbundling model is ownership unbundling. Under this method, the ownership of a transmission network has to be transferred to a completely independent undertaking, which would also exclusively operate this network.[564] In other words, former vertically integrated generation and supply undertakings are no longer allowed to exercise any direct or indirect control over the independent network operator. According to *Buschle*, the introduction of ownership unbundling was a reaction to one particular barrier to the

560 Mulder et al., 2005, p. 43.

561 Unbundling is considered as a proper tool used to prevent the cross-subsidy practices of a vertically integrated company, inclusive of its cost and profit-loss transfers among the different activities.

562 EFET, 2000, p. 1. Unbundling reduces the incentive of the provider of the non-competitive activity to restrict competition in the competitive activity. This is an important advantage because it lessens the regulatory burden, enhancing the quality of the regulation and the level of competition. OECD, 2001, p. 21.

563 Market closure is defined as a strategic conduct by one or more undertakings to prevent potential rivals from entering into downstream or upstream markets.

564 Pielow et al., 2009, p. 99.

opening of electricity and gas markets, namely the proprietary rights of incumbents – vertically integrated undertakings – over their networks.[565]

Article 9 of Directive 2009/72/EC and Directive 2009/73/EC set out rules regarding the ownership unbundling. The conditions specified in Article 9(1)(a)–(1)(d) have a cumulative structure.[566] Under Article 9(1)(a) each undertaking having the ownership of the transmission system should act as a TSO[567]. According to Article 9(1)(b)(i), a person who is entitled to exercise control over an undertaking performing generation or supply function, cannot exercise control[568] or exercise any right[569] over a transmission system operator/transmission system or vice versa[570].[571] Article 9(1)(c) and (d) provide for two additional requirements. According to Article 9(1)(c), the same person is not entitled to appoint members of bodies legally representing[572] a TSO or a transmission system and to exercise control, directly or indirectly, or any right over an undertaking performing generation or supply functions. Furthermore, Article 9(1)(d) prohibits the same person from being a member of the board of both a supplier and a TSO.

---

565 "*The experience made in the first decade of liberalizing the EU energy markets made the Commission conclude that the incumbent's position to use its dual control over the networks and the generation and supply business in a way affecting the internal market objectives must be countered by more radical structural separation.*" Buschle, 2013, pp. 50–51.

566 European Commission, The Unbundling Regime, 2010, p. 7.

567 The transmission system owner has certain responsibilities such as granting and managing third-party access on a non-discriminatory basis to system users, collecting access charges, congestion charges and payments under the inter-TSO compensation mechanism, and maintaining and developing the network system.

568 According to the Article 3(2) EC Merger Regulation, control is constituted by "rights, contracts or any other means which, either separately or in combination and having regard to the considerations of fact or law involved, confer the possibility of exercising decisive influence on an undertaking", in particular by: (a) ownership or the right to use all or part of the assets of an undertaking; (b) rights or contracts which confer decisive influence on the composition, voting or decisions of the organs of an undertaking.

569 The rights include, in particular: (a) the power to exercise voting rights; (b) the power to appoint members of the supervisory board, the administrative board or bodies legally representing the undertaking; or (c) the holding of a majority share.

570 Article 9(1)(b)(i) of Directive 2009/72/EC.

571 European Commission, The Unbundling Regime, 2010, p. 8.

572 E.g., the supervisory board or the administrative board.

The advantages of ownership unbundling of transmission and distribution activities from production and supply activities are widely acknowledged.[573] The Commission claims that ownership unbundling is the simplest and most effective way to achieve effective separation and align the interests of network companies with those of the "market".

A detailed analysis undertaken with respect to unbundling the energy sector concluded that ownership unbundling has a number of positive impacts on the market, in particular because it stimulates investment in interconnectors, reducing market concentration and bringing down prices.[574] According to *Kroes*, there is a direct correlation between ownership unbundling and investments in networks. Available data relating to Member States indicates that ownership unbundling is conducive to investments in networks and that therefore it would remove the distortion of investment incentives within vertically integrated undertakings having no incentive to develop the network in the overall interest of the market thus facilitating new entry at the generation or supply levels.[575] TSOs demonstrate a significant and constant increase in investment levels after ownership unbundling has taken place.[576]

573 OECD, 2006, p. 137: "*Ownership separation of transmission from generation is, in principle, preferable. Introducing an independent systems operator while leaving transmission and generation in the ownership of the Verbundunternehmen would entail separation of transmission asset ownership from transmission asset management, which may result in inefficiencies.*" European Commission, Energy Sector Inquiry, 2007, p. 12:"*Economic evidence shows that ownership unbundling is the most effective means to ensure choice for energy users and encourage investment.*" Kroes, 2007, p. 1388: "*[...] ownership unbundling of transmission networks is the simplest, most effective and most stable solution to improve competition in European energy markets and that in order to be equally effective an ISO must be 'deep' in the sense that the system operator must be in full control not only of network operations but also of investments, and must be accompanied by detailed regulation and close regulatory oversight.*"

574 European Commission, Accompanying the legislative package on the internal market for electricity and gas – Impact Assessment, 2007.

575 Ibid.

576 Kroes, 2007, p. 1417.

2. Independent System Operator (ISO)

The independent system operator (ISO) model[577] is introduced as an alternative to ownership unbundling and is considered as the "the second-best solution".[578] Under this unbundling model, the ultimate owner of the network which still carries out production or supply activities will have to legally and functionally unbundle the part of the company which owns the network. In other words, the technical and commercial operation of the assets is put into an independent company that is designated by Member State.[579]

According to Article 13(1) of the Electricity Directive and Article 14(1) of the Gas Directive, in cases in which the transmission system is owned by a vertically integrated undertaking, Member States can determine an independent system operator upon the request of the transmission system owner. Solely the undertakings which are approved in the sense that they fulfil the conditions determined by the Electricity and Gas Directives can be appointed as independent system operators by Member States.[580]

The duties of an ISO correspond to the duties of a TSO. Within the scope of the Electricity and Gas Directives and the Electricity and Gas Regulations, the aforementioned entity should act in accordance with any duties applicable to TSO. The Electricity and Gas Directives stated clearly that *"the independent system operator shall act as a transmission system operator"*.[581]

The ISO's duties can be stated as follows[582]:

- granting and managing third-party access (including the collection of access charges and congestion rents);

577 *"ISO regime may be applicable to both the electricity and gas sectors. According to the explanatory memorandum fundamental conflict of interest between the supply and production activities on the one hand and the network operation and development on the other hand applies equally to both sectors. This has also been suggested by others and it has even been suggested that ownership unbundling may be even more effective in the gas sector where the concentration levels are currently greater."* Praduroux & Talus, 2008, p. 9.

578 Pielow & Ehlers, 2008, p. 5.

579 Kroes, 2007, p. 1426.

580 Article 13(3) of Directive 2009/72/EC and Article 14(3) of Directive 2009/73/EC.

581 Article 13(4) of Directive 2009/72/EC and Article 14(4) of Directive 2009/73/EC.

582 Ibid.

- executing payments under the inter-transmission system operator compensation scheme;
- operating, maintaining and developing the transmission system;
- ensuring the long-term ability of the system to meet reasonable demand through investment planning.

According to Article 14 of the Electricity Directive and Article 15 of the Gas Directive, if an ISO has been appointed, the owner of the network which is still active in supply or production will have to legally and functionally unbundle the part of its company which owns the network.[583]

3. Independent Transmission Operator (ITO)

According to Article 9(8)(b) of the Electricity Directive and Gas Directive, Member States may appoint an independent transmission operator in cases in which a transmission system is owned by a vertically integrated company. With respect to the scope of this model, the supply company can have the ownership of the network and operate it. However, the network has to be administered by a subsidiary of the parent company which can make financial, technical and other kinds of decisions independently. Although the model allows the continuation of the vertically integrated structure, it puts forth strict rules in order to ensure the independence and autonomy as well as the administrative independence of the transmission firm.[584] It can also be ascertained that the operating activity of the network is not unbundled from the supply activity structurally and that the ownership of the network is still held by the parent company, which distinguishes this model fundamentally from the concept of ISO.[585]

Although the ITO model has principles similar to those of legal and functional unbundling, the provisions are enhanced. The ITO model includes stricter provisions in order to increase the independence of the transmission operator in terms of management and personnel. As it is stated in Article 17(1) of the Electricity and Gas Direc-

583 Kroes, 2007, p. 1417.
584 Cabau & Sandberg, 2016, p. 106.
585 Ibid.

tives, the ITO must be equipped with all human, technical, physical and financial resources necessary for fulfilling its obligations under the Electricity and Gas Directives and carrying out the activity of electricity or gas transmission. Article 17(1)(a) of the Electricity and Gas Directives envisages that a multitude of assets necessary for electricity and gas transmission activities, including the transmission system, should be clustered under the ownership of the transmission operator. Collectively realising all corporate duties, all personnel necessary for electricity and gas transmission activities should be employed by the transmission operator.[586] The condition of autonomy does not include activities that are not directly related to the electricity and gas transmission activity, such as cleaning or security.[587]

Another important condition of the ITO model of unbundling is the establishment of a supervisory body. As stated in Article 20 of the Electricity and Gas Directives, "*the transmission system operator shall have a Supervisory Body which shall be in charge of taking decisions which may have a significant impact on the value of the assets of the shareholders within the transmission system operator, in particular decisions regarding the approval of the annual and longer-term financial plans, the level of indebtedness of the transmission system operator and the amount of dividends distributed to shareholders.*"

The duties of ITOs encompass[588]:

- to ensure that the system is able to meet the reasonable demands in long-term with respect to the electricity transmission;
- to ensure that the operation, management and development of transmission systems are done under the economic conditions of secure, reliable and efficient measures with due regard to the environment;
- to manage electricity flows on the system, taking into account exchanges with other interconnected systems;
- to ensure that adequate means are adopted with regards to service obligations;

586 Article 17(1)(b) of Directive 2009/72/EC and Directive 2009/73/EC.

587 European Commission, The Unbundling Regime, 2010, p. 15.

588 Article 12 of Directive 2009/72/EC and Article 13 of Directive 2009/73/EC; Article 17(2) of Directive 2009/72/EC and Directive 2009/73/EC.

- to contribute to the security of supply through ensuring adequate transmission capacity and system reliability;
- to collect all the transmission system-related charges;
- to grant and manage third-party access on a non-discriminatory basis between system users or classes of system users;
- to operate, maintain and develop a secure, efficient and economic transmission system;
- to undertake investment planning, ensuring the long-term capability of the system to meet reasonable demand and to guarantee security of supply;
- to provide any other system operator with which its system is interconnected with sufficient information to ensure the secure and efficient operation, coordinated development and interoperability of the interconnected systems;
- to provide the system users with the information required by them for an efficient access to the system; and
- to ensure non-discrimination between the system users.

B. Unbundling in Distribution

The regime for the unbundling of distribution system operators (DSOs) is determined by Article 26 of the Electricity and Gas Directives. In cases in which the DSO is part of a vertically integrated undertaking, the following unbundling regimes should be applied[589]:

- accounting unbundling,
- functional unbundling, and
- legal unbundling.

1. Accounting Unbundling

With reference to the weakest form of separation, the accounting unbundling primarily aims at preventing distortion of competition through cross-subsidies between network system operations and supply operations. To this aim it requires vertically integrated undertakings to keep separate accounts for each of their activities as they would be required to

589 European Commission, The Unbundling Regime, 2010, p. 23.

do if the activities in question were carried out by separate undertakings.[590] The main purpose of the accounting unbundling method is to prevent cross-subsidies, including cost and profit-loss transfers between network activities and activities open to competition, by making transparent the activities of vertically integrated companies.[591]

Accounting unbundling was the minimum requirement specified in Directive 96/92/EC. The main rules pertaining to accounting unbundling are laid out in Article 31 of the Electricity and Gas Directives. Accordingly, distinct balance sheets and income sheets should be prepared for network activities, and the accounting rules, asset and liabilities, income and expenditure, amortisation and profit for these activities should be stated clearly.

2. Functional Unbundling

Functional unbundling is relatively more intrusive than the accounting unbundling. It requires three levels of separation: management separation, independent decision-making powers and informational independence or confidentiality.[592]

First of all, the management personnel of the distribution system operator (DSO) must not participate in the corporate segments of the vertically integrated undertaking carrying out the day-to-day operation of the production, transmission, distribution or supply.[593] In other words, someone who is a director of a DSO cannot be a director of a production, supply or transmission undertaking and vice versa. Under the functional unbundling model, the network unit must have the necessary human resources and the necessary financial and infrastructural assets required for operating independently from other market activities within the vertically integrated structure.

Secondly, functional unbundling requires an independent decision-making power. The DSO must be able to independently take all decisions concerning the operation, maintenance and development of the network without involvement of other parts of the vertically integrated

590 Malmendier & Schendel, 2006, p. 379.

591 European Commission, The Unbundling Regime, 2010, p. 28.

592 Gao, 2010, p. 111.

593 Article 26 of Directive 2009/72/EC and Directive 2009/73/EC.

undertaking. The DSO must have all the necessary resources, including human, technical, financial and physical resources, in order to fulfil these tasks independently.[594]

Thirdly, the DSO is required to put a compliance programme in place which includes measures to ensure that discriminatory conduct is precluded[595] and that the network activities as a whole, as well as individual employees and the management of the DSO, comply with the principle of non-discrimination.[596]

The rules on functional unbundling are further strengthened by requiring the DSO to preserve the confidentiality of commercially sensitive information obtained in the course of carrying out its activities.[597] By limiting the information exchange and communication through the "Chinese Wall" created between network activities and commercial activities, it is possible to prevent production or supply undertakings from obtaining sensitive information and, hence, from discriminating against third parties.[598]

3. Legal Unbundling

Directive 2003/54/EC and Directive 2003/55/EC went one step further than the first Electricity and Gas Directives and introduced the concept of legal unbundling which is a more stringent unbundling than the separation of accounts. According to Electricity and Gas Directives, "*where the transmission system operator is part of a vertically integrated undertaking, it shall be independent at least in terms of its legal form, organisation and decision making from other activities not relating to transmission.*"[599] However, with respect to such an unbundling regime, it is not compulsory for vertically integrated undertakings to separate their ownership of assets in transmission systems.[600] In other words, a legally separated network company must be established, but it may re-

594 Article 26(2)(c) of Directive 2009/72/EC and Directive 2009/73/EC; European Commission, The Unbundling Regime, 2010, p. 24.
595 Article 26(2)(d) of Directive 2009/72/EC and Directive 2009/73/EC.
596 European Commission, The Unbundling Regime, 2010, p. 26.
597 Ibid., p. 27.
598 Ehlers, 2010, p. 20.
599 Article 10(1) of Directive 2003/54/EC and Article 9(1) Directive 2003/55/EC.
600 Ibid.

main a subsidiary of a vertically integrated energy company. In this case, however, the internal separation into departments is not considered sufficient, and it is required that network companies should be incorporated as legally independent subsidiaries. Nevertheless, the network company can be a subsidiary of the parent company which has energy production and supply activities. The purpose of such an unbundling is to prevent collaboration between unbundled departments and, hence, internal cross-subsidisation.[601]

However, combining regulated and unregulated companies under the same ownership constitutes a risk factor. According to *Thomas*, there would still be an incentive for the parent company of the grid owning company to treat its subsidiary active in power generation or retail better than companies with which it has no ownership connection.[602]

II. Third-Party Access

Third-party access (TPA) plays a key role as a regulatory tool in the liberalisation of European energy markets and the creation of an open and non-discriminatory energy infrastructure.[603] For competition to function in energy markets, network access must be non-discriminatory, transparent and fairly priced.[604]

According to the Commission, transmission and distribution segments have always constituted natural monopolies. Despite unbundling provisions, most of the time new entrants lack effective access to networks. Network owners or operators have mostly strong relations to energy producers and suppliers. They usually avoid granting access to third parties and favour their own affiliates.[605] Consequently, third party energy producers cannot reach their final customers and cannot trade, as there is no alternative to the existing energy network.[606] Although undertakings are allowed to construct a second transmission or distri-

601 Ehlers, 2010, p. 20.
602 Thomas, 2007, p. 4.
603 Palasthy, 2002, p. 1; Diathesopoulos, 2010, p. 5.
604 Recital 6 of Directive 2003/54/EC.
605 European Commission, Energy Sector Inquiry, 2007, p. 7.
606 Diathesopoulos, 2010, p. 5.

bution line, this is not considered economically viable due to high investment costs.[607]

In transmission and distribution sectors, market competitiveness depends substantially on the effective access of new entrants to the transmission and distribution infrastructures and, in the case of gas, to storage facilities.[608] In other words, one of the conditions of enabling an effective competitive environment in these sectors is requiring that the operators of transmission and distribution networks open their facilities to all electricity and gas suppliers.[609] Such a condition is defined as the "Third-Party Access Principle". The concept broadly refers to the possibility for electricity suppliers and/or customers to make use of electricity grids they do not own or control in order to sell or buy electricity.[610]

The rationale behind TPA is to allow producers, eligible customers, local distribution companies and other suppliers to have the right to be offered access to the gas or electricity networks by transmission and distribution undertakings.[611] This access is important to encourage competition on both the consumers' and the generators' side of electricity and gas markets. Although this requirement can be introduced by competition law, *ex post* rules of competition law have been deemed insufficient in practice.[612] For this reason, the rules and the conditions of access regime are determined by sector-specific regulations.[613]

TPA regarding electricity and gas markets is developed through sector-specific regulations at three different levels. Firstly, the main framework of TPA set out in the Electricity and Gas Directives includes the basic rules and principles. Secondly, the content of these rules is laid down in detail in Regulation 714/2009 and Regulation 715/2009. Thirdly, the most detailed regulations of TPA are network

---

607 Gräper et al., 2016, p. 27.

608 Vijver, 2012, p. 335.

609 *"For competition to function, network access must be non-discriminatory, transparent and fairly priced."* Recital (6) of Directive 2003/54/EC.

610 Palasthy, 2002, p. 1.

611 Salter, 1994, p. 86.

612 Vijver, 2012, p. 335.

613 European Commission, Questions and Answers on the third legislative package for an internal EU gas and electricity market, 2011.

codes and guidelines which are prepared based on the aforementioned Regulations.[614]

A. Types of Third-Party Access

The first Electricity and Gas Directives distinguished, *inter alia*, between the regulated access and the negotiated access.[615] Member States were able to choose either or both. However, the possibility to choose between negotiated access and regulated access was dropped in the second and third Directives. Regulated access is considered as a minimum TPA requirement for transmission and distribution networks.[616] Nevertheless, Member States may still choose between a negotiated or regulated system of access to storage and line pack facilities. In each case attention must be given to ensure that procedures operate in accordance with objective, transparent and non-discriminatory criteria.

1. Regulated Third-Party Access

The Electricity and Gas Directives envisage the implementation of regulated third-party access to all transmission and distribution networks including cross-border infrastructure and LNG facilities[617], which indicates that Member States must regulate and publish access tariffs. According to Article 32 of the Electricity Directive, "*Member States shall ensure the implementation of a system of third-party access to the transmission and distribution systems based on published tariffs, applicable to all eligible customers and applied objectively and without discrimination between system users.*" The regulated access enables the

614 Talus, 2013, p. 73.

615 "*As far as electricity is concerned, the first (1996) Directive offered a choice between three options. The first of these was the single-buyer model (included on French insistence), which was quickly recognised as not workable, and not adopted even in France. The second was the regulated access model. The third was negotiated access where, supposedly, the terms are freely negotiated but some pressure is exerted to push the recalcitrant network operator in the right direction if need be. As per Article 17(3) of the first electricity Directive, negotiated access did not require 'tariffs', but 'indicative prices'. However, it is not practical to consider that any transmission might be based on separate detailed negotiations.*" Talus, 2013, p. 71.

616 Gräper et al., 2016, p. 27.

617 Ibid., p. 43.

third party to use the network based on specified provisions and conditions. The aforementioned proposition is indicative of the fact that access terms and conditions should be examined *ex ante* by the national regulatory authorities.[618]

The Electricity and Gas Directives require all tariffs concerning access to electricity and gas transmission, distribution systems and LNG facilities to be published. These tariffs should be easily accessible, transparent and applicable to everyone without, once published, renegotiating at the individual level.[619] There are various applicable criteria in terms of the tariffs regarding transmission and distribution systems and LNG facilities.[620] Transmission and distribution tariffs must be non-discriminatory, cost-reflective[621], long-term and marginal. They should also avoid mingling network costs with costs associated with power generation. Demand-side management measures should be taken into account while determining these tariffs.[622] Together with this, another criteria is that an "*incentive, over both the short and long term, to increase efficiencies, foster market integration and security of supply and support the related research activities*" is given to transmission and distribution system operators.[623]

Within the network industries, inasmuch as the goods are transported through networks, access to networks is required and allocation of limited capacity in the network is vital in order to be competitive in these markets. The purpose of the regulated access is to allocate capacity without any form of discrimination and to enable the access of all

618 Börner, 2002, p. 28.

619 Gräper et al., 2016, p. 44.

620 Johnston & Block, 2012, p. 76.

621 "*Those tariffs or methodologies shall allow the necessary investments in the networks to be carried out in a manner allowing those investments to ensure the viability of the networks.*" Article 37 of Directive 2009/72/EC and Article 41 of the 2009/73/EC. And Article 13(1) of Regulation 715/2009 states: "*Tariffs, or the methodologies [...] take into account the need for system integrity and its improvement and reflect the actual costs incurred, insofar as such costs correspond to those of an efficient and structurally comparable network operator and are transparent, whilst including an appropriate return on investments, and, where appropriate, taking account of the benchmarking of tariffs by the regulatory authorities. Tariffs, or the methodologies used to calculate them, shall be applied in a non-discriminatory manner.*"

622 Recital 36 of Directive 2009/72/EC and Recital 32 of 2009/73/EC.

623 Article 37(8) of Directive 2009/72/EC and Article 41(8) of 2009/73/EC.

concerned parties to key infrastructures for participation in the electricity and gas markets.[624]

2. Access to Upstream Pipeline Networks

The access to upstream pipeline networks is regulated under Article 34 of the Gas Directive. Regardless of the location of the natural gas operators and customers meeting the required conditions, Member States are required to undertake the necessary measures with the aim of ensuring the access of the customers to the pipeline networks related to the natural gas production, including facilities providing secondary technical services for such access but, however, excluding the parts of such networks and facilities used for local gas production operations. The measures should be reported in accordance with the requirements of the Commission.[625]

The Directive requires Member States to put dispute-settlement arrangements in place and to establish an authority independent of the parties which has access to all relevant information in order to enable disputes relating to access to upstream pipeline networks to be settled expeditiously.[626] In cross-border disputes, the dispute resolution regulation of Member States having jurisdiction over the pipeline network related to the gas production to which access has been refused is valid. However, if in cases of cross-border disputes the related network includes more than one Member State, the respective Member States must consult each other to ensure consistent implementation of the provisions of the Directive.[627]

Considering the differences between the upstream and downstream sectors, it is reasonable to introduce such an exceptional regulation in terms of upstream pipeline networks.

---

624 Gräper et al., 2016, p. 55.
625 Article 34(1) of Directive 2009/73/EC.
626 Article 34(3) of Directive 2009/73/EC.
627 Article 34(4) of Directive 2009/73/EC.

3. Negotiated Third-Party Access

According to this method, the third party can enter into a contract with the network owner, and the provisions and terms are determined by them. However, they need to make a distinct contract by bargaining with the transmission and distribution system operators for access to transmission and distribution networks. In this case, the competition authority will check *ex post* whether the network owner has abused the powers arising from its control of the near monopoly.[628]

Article 33 of the Gas Directive, which has *lex specialis* status, regulates (alongside Article 32) access to natural gas storages. Article 33(3) states: *"In the case of negotiated access, Member States or, where Member States have so provided, the regulatory authorities shall take the necessary measures for natural gas undertakings and eligible customers either inside or outside the territory covered by the interconnected system to be able to negotiate access to storage facilities and line pack, when technically and/or economically necessary for providing efficient access to the system, as well as for the organisation of access to other ancillary services. The parties shall be obliged to negotiate access to storage, line pack and other ancillary services in good faith."*

In terms of the electricity markets, all transmission and distribution systems are subject to regulated third-party access. However, with respect to the gas market, the option of selecting between negotiated or regulated third-party access regarding gas storage and ancillary services is given to Member States.[629] According to the provision, Member States may, if they wish, select negotiated third-party access regarding gas storage and ancillary services. The reason for making a distinction in terms of access to gas storages is that gas storages do not necessarily constitute a natural monopoly.[630]

B. Refusal of Access

The transmission and distribution operators are allowed to refuse access to networks in case necessary capacity is lacking. The access can

628 Börner, 2002, p. 28.
629 Article 33 of Directive 2009/73/EC.
630 Gräper et al., 2016, p. 59.

be refused if duly substantiated justifications are provided.[631] Under the Electricity and Gas Directives, there are several situations when refusal of network access is possible[632]:

- Lack of capacity: A TSO may refuse access where it lacks the necessary network capacity.
- Public service obligations: If granting access would prevent undertakings from carrying out public service obligations[633] which are assigned to them, the access may be refused.
- Sudden crisis: A Member State may temporarily take the necessary safeguard measures in the event of a sudden crisis in the energy markets and where the physical safety or security of persons, apparatus or installations or system integrity is threatened.[634]
- Take-or-pay contracts: Natural gas undertakings may refuse access to the system on the basis of serious economic and financial difficulties with take-or-pay contracts.

With respect to storage facilities, refusal of access can be justified on the grounds of lack of capacity if the following two conditions are met[635]:

- Refusal should be objective and transparent. In other words, it must be conclusively proven by the storage operator that no capacity is available, by regularly disclosing the data on available capacity over a certain period of time, including historical data and distinguishing between firm and interruptible storage capacity. The data provided by the storage operator should demonstrate that the entire working capacity of the storage facility concerned is either contractually booked or physically used, i.e., no availability of firm or interruptible capacity.

631 Article 32 of Directive 2009/72/EC and Article 35 of Directive 2009/73/EC.

632 Dziadykiewicz, 2007, p. 119.

633 Such public service obligations may relate to security, including security of supply, regularity, quality and price of supplies, and to environmental protection, including energy efficiency, energy from renewable sources and climate protection. Article 3(2) of Directive 2009/72/EC and Article 3(2) of Directive 2009/73/EC.

634 Article 42 of Directive 2009/72/EC and Article 46 of Directive 2009/73/EC.

635 European Commission, Interpretative Note on Directive 2009/73/EC Concerning Common Rules for the Internal Market in Natural Gas, 2010, p. 14.

- Refusal should be non-discriminatory. The outcome of an access request to storage facility submitted to a storage system operator or a combined operator running a storage facility should be the same (i.e., refusal on the grounds of lack of capacity), no matter who submitted the request. Moreover, all concerned/interested parties must be informed in a non-discriminatory manner if there is a change in terms of available capacities. Thus, all interested/concerned parties should be able to submit their request under a non-discriminatory capacity allocation mechanism.

Natural gas undertakings could refuse access to the system under the following circumstances[636]:

- on the basis of lack of capacity;
- if the access to the system would prevent them from carrying out their public service obligations;
- on the basis of serious economic and financial difficulties with take-or-pay contracts.

Natural gas undertakings refusing access to their system must give duly substantiated reasons.

According to the Directive, in the event that access to the system is refused on the grounds of lack of capacity or a lack of connection, Member States may take measures to ensure that the refusing undertaking makes the necessary enhancements as far as it is economically viable to do so or if a potential customer is willing to pay for them.[637]

Refusal of access does not constitute an abuse *per se*. In the *Bronner* decision [638], the CJ analysed the case as a refusal of supply abuse. The CJ determined three conditions for considering a refusal of access an abuse within the scope of Article 102 TFEU [639]:

- The refusal of the service is likely to eliminate all competition in the relevant market on behalf of the person requesting the service.
- Such refusal is incapable of being objectively justified.

636 Article 35(1) of Directive 2009/73/EC.
637 Article 35(2) of Directive 2009/73/EC.
638 Case C-7/97, *Oscar Bronner v Mediaprint Re*, [1998] ECR I-7791.
639 Kotlowski, 2007, p. 106.

- The services as such are indispensable to carrying on the requesting party's business, inasmuch as there is no actual or potential substitute in existence for that service.

The CJ expressed that an undertaking in a dominant position is not *per se* obliged to grant access to its facilities, since this would refrain undertakings from investing in new infrastructures.[640] Thus, although these criteria can be useful when determining if a conduct infringes Article 102 TFEU, each case must be viewed separately.

C. Exemption of Third-Party Access

Non-discriminatory access to energy systems (networks, LNG and storage facilities) is a prerequisite for energy market liberalisation and is necessary for enabling new entries into the market.[641] As mentioned above, electricity and gas transmission system operators as well as operators of storage or LNG facilities are required to grant other market players non-discriminatory access to their infrastructure. The same service must be offered to different users under identical contractual conditions.

However, strict application of TPA has several disadvantages. Constructing a new electricity or gas network requires particularly high costs, and strict access provisions may decrease the incentive to finance new infrastructure projects as it reduces investor certainty as to its use.[642] The nature of some types of infrastructure, such as sub-sea interconnectors, gas storages and LNG facilities, are very expensive and risky.[643] In this case, market players might be faced with two issues: risk of underinvestment and risk of foreclosure. A balance must therefore be struck between TPA and the need for investments.[644]

The Electricity and Gas Directives allow national regulatory authorities (NRA) (with the permission of the Commission) to exempt

640 Fredriksson, 2001, p. 44.
641 Vedder et al., 2016, p. 287.
642 Vijver, 2012, p. 334.
643 Vedder et al., 2016, p. 289.
644 Vijver, 2012, p. 335.

new infrastructure from the TPA principle.[645] These exemptions are linked to strict conditions for both electricity and gas investments. However, it should be stated that the realisation of these conditions does not automatically mean that this exemption will be authorised.[646] In order to obtain the exemption, the following conditions must be met[647]:

- The investment must enhance competition in gas or electricity supply.
- The level of risk attached to the investment is such that the investment would not take place unless an exemption was granted.
- The infrastructure must be owned by a natural or legal person who is separate, at least in terms of its legal form, from the system operators.
- Charges must be levied on users of the infrastructure.
- The exemption must not be to the detriment of competition, the effective functioning of the internal market in electricity and gas or the efficient functioning of the regulated system to which the interconnector is linked.

The exemption request must be examined by the NRA of the related Member State, and, if conceded, the Commission will review the exemption decision of the NRA. The Commission is responsible for verifying that the conditions are met. If it comes to the conclusion that one or more conditions are not met, it may ask the national authorities to amend or withdraw their decisions.

645 In 2004, the Commission published an Interpretation Note regarding exemption from the provisions of the third-party access regime. This document clearly stated that the exemptions constitute exceptions to general rules, i.e., on a case-by-case basis they may be authorised.

646 Interpretation Note of DG Energy & Transport on Directives 2003/54–55 and Regulation 1228/03 in the electricity and gas internal market: Exemptions from certain provision of the third-party access regime, p. 4.

647 Article 17 of Regulation 714/2009 and Article 36 of Directive 2009/73/EC.

§ 8. An Overview of the EU Competition Rules

I. European Anti-Cartel Rules

A. Article 101 TFEU

Article 101 TFEU has a bifurcated structure. While Article 101(1)TFEU lays down the general prohibition rule, Article 101(3) TFEU sets out an exemption.

Article 101(1) TFEU constitutes a general prohibition against agreements between undertakings, decisions by associations of undertakings and concerted practices which may affect trade between Member States and have as their object or effect the prevention, restriction or distortion of competition within the internal market. According to *Ritter & Braun*, the main purpose of this rule is to guarantee that each undertaking independently can determine its business policy and market conduct within the EU.[648]

As a principle, Article 101(1) TFEU can be applied to:

- Horizontal relations: It refers to the concerted practices or agreements between two or more undertakings operating at the same level in a production or distribution chain.
- Vertical relations: It refers to the concerted practices or agreements between two or more undertakings operating at different levels in a production or distribution chain.

The CJ demands evidence of cooperation and coordination between undertakings which may cause restriction or distortion of competition in order to implement Article 101(1) TFEU. In general, it can be said that three main elements must exist together for the implementation of Article 101(1) TFEU: the presence of an agreement or decisions by associations of undertakings and concerted practices; the distortion of conditions of competition; the possibility that trade between Member States may be affected because of these two factors.

648 Ritter & Braun, 2004, p. 95.

There would be no infringement of Article 101(1) TFEU unless the agreement affects[649] trade[650] between Member States. In other words, the agreement must be capable of affecting trade between Member States.[651] Moreover, agreements and other arrangements are not prohibited unless they have as their object or effect the prevention, restriction or distortion of competition. Article 101 TFEU contains a non-exhaustive list of arrangements that may prevent, restrict or distort competition, which includes price-fixing arrangements, market share arrangements, export bans and resale price maintenance. The scope of the aforementioned list is extended regularly through judicial decisions.

Article 101(3) TFEU includes *"an exemption basis"* for agreements, decisions and concerted practices which contribute to improving the production or distribution of goods or to promoting technical or economic progress while allowing consumers a fair share of the resulting benefit. The prohibition specified by Article 101(1) TFEU may be declared inapplicable when the four criteria set out in Article 101(3) TFEU are fulfilled.[652] The exemption given in Article 101(3) TFEU is, however, only applicable to the activities specified in Article 101 TFEU. In other words, since an agreement that may be granted an exemption within the scope of Article 101(3) TFEU will only be considered exempt

649 *"The function of the notion 'may affect' is to define the nature of the required impact on trade between Member States. According to the standard test developed by the Court of Justice, the notion 'may affect' implies that it must be possible to foresee with a sufficient degree of probability on the basis of a set of objective factors of law or fact that the agreement or practice may have an influence, direct or indirect, actual or potential, on the pattern of trade between Member States."* European Commission, Guidelines on the effect on trade concept contained in Articles 81 and 82 of the Treaty, 2004, para. 23.

650 *"The concept of 'trade' is not limited to traditional exchanges of goods and services across borders. It is a wider concept, covering all cross-border economic activity including establishment. This interpretation is consistent with the fundamental objective of the Treaty to promote free movement of goods, services, persons and capital."* Ibid., para. 19.

651 Ibid., para. 14. The CJ has adopted a broad interpretation of the above stated requirement. In the *Béguelin* case, the CJ stated that in order to be subsumed within the prohibition imposed by Article 101 TFEU the agreement must affect trade between Member States and the free play of competition to an appreciable extent. Case C-22/71, *Béguelin Import v G.L. Import Export*, [1971] ECR 949, para. 16. See also: Case 56/65, *Société Technique Minière v Maschinenbau Ulm Gmbh*, [1966] ECR 235.

652 Jones & Sufrin, 2016, p. 114.

from Article 101 TFEU, it may nonetheless infringe upon Article 102 TFEU or other competition rules.

According to Article 101(3) TFEU, a practice which falls within the scope of Article 101(1) TFEU can be exempted from the prohibition if it fulfils two positive and two negative cumulative conditions:

- The agreement (decision and concerted practice) must contribute to improving the production or distribution of goods or to promoting technical or economic progress.
- Consumers must receive a fair share of the resulting benefits.
- Restrictions must be indispensable to the attainment of these objectives.
- The agreements must not afford undertakings the possibility of eliminating competition in respect of a substantial part of the products in question.

These conditions are not an alternative for one another, and they should all be met in each case. According to settled case law, the four conditions of Article 101(3) TFEU are cumulative, i.e., they must all be fulfilled for the exception to the rule becoming applicable.[653] If they are not, the application of the exception to the rule as stated in Article 101(3) TFEU must be refused.[654]

B. Article 102 TFEU

Article 102 constitutes another important antitrust rule and prohibits any abuse by one or more undertakings of a dominant position within the internal market or in a substantial part of it which may affect trade between Member States. Article 102 TFEU only covers the existing abuse of a dominant position. Viewed from this point, Article 102 TFEU basically plays a controlling role for monitoring the behaviours of rivals in the market in order to enable the effective functioning of competition. However, the main goal of this Article is to protect consumers and defend

653 See, e.g., Case C-238/05, *Asnef-Equifax*, [2006] ECR I-11125, para. 65; Case T-185/00, *Métropole télévision SA*, [2002] ECR II-3805, para. 86; Case T-17/93, *Matra*, [1994] ECR II-595, para. 85; Joined Cases 43/82 and 63/82, *VBVB and VBBB*, [1984] ECR 19, para. 61.

654 European Commission, Guidelines on the application of Article 81(3) of the Treaty, 2004, para. 42.

their interests from the possible results of abuse of a dominant position by undertakings.

In order for Article 102 TFEU to be implemented in any case, the following four main elements must be fulfilled together:

– a certain number of rivals;
– a dominant position;
– an abuse of a dominant position;
– trade between Member States is negatively affected by this situation.

Article 102 TFEU requires the pursuance of two steps. The first step is ascertaining whether the dominant position[655] exists. In order to identify the dominant position of an undertaking, the Commission and the CJ have established some criteria in their decisions. The most important indicator is the market share. According to the Commission, the higher the market share, and the longer the period of time over which it is held, the more likely it is to be a preliminary indication of dominance.[656] The second step is to identify whether the abuse[657] of a dominant position by

655 According to settled case law, dominance is a position of economic strength enjoyed by an undertaking which enables it to prevent effective competition being maintained on the relevant market by affording it the power to behave to an appreciable extent independently of its competitors, its customers and, ultimately, of the consumers. European Commission, DG Competition discussion paper on the application of Article 82 of the Treaty to exclusionary abuses, 2005. Case 6/72, *Continental Can*, [1973] ECR 215; C-27/76, *United Brands v Commission*, [1978] ECR 207; Case 85/76, *Hoffmann-La Roche v Commission*, [1979] ECR 461.

656 *"It is very likely that very high markets shares, which have been held for some time, indicate a dominant position. This would be the case where an undertaking holds 50 % or more of the market, provided that rivals hold a much smaller share of the market. In the case of lower market shares, dominance is more likely to be found in the market share range of 40 % to 50 % than below 40 %, although also undertakings with market shares below 40 % could be considered to be in a dominant position. However, undertakings with market shares of no more than 25 to %35 are not likely to enjoy a (single) dominant position on the market concerned."* European Commission, DG Competition discussion paper on the application of Article 82 of the Treaty to exclusionary abuses, 2005.

657 The CJ laid down the definition of abuse as following: *"The concept of abuse is an objective concept relating to the behaviour of an undertaking in a dominant position which is such as to influence the structure of a market where, as a result of the very presence of the undertaking in question, the degree of competition is weakened and*

an undertaking or undertakings occurred or not.[658] Holding a dominant position is not indicative of the fact that there is an infringement of Article 102 TFEU. The undertaking must abuse its dominant position.

Article 102 does not define the concept of abuse, but it provides four main examples. However, the CJ argues that these examples are not exhaustive and there may be other types of abuses.[659] Generally, the abuse of a dominant position can be divided in three groups[660]:

- Exploitative abuse: In this kind of abuse, the undertaking in a dominant position uses its market power advantage to obtain profit from consumers in a way that an undertaking not in the dominant position cannot obtain, or takes advantage of consumers in other ways. Product-binding agreements through excessive pricing practices are included in this scope.
- Exclusionary abuse: It is the abuse situation in which market power is used to damage the rival through uncompetitive behaviours such as refusal of deal and predatory pricing.[661]
- Structural abuse: This refers to the situation of influencing competition and eliminating rivals through company mergers.

---

which, through recourse to methods different from those which condition normal competition in products or services on the basis of the transactions of commercial operators, has the effect of hindering the maintenance of the degree of competition still existing in the market or the growth of that competition." Case 85/76, *Hoffmann-La Roche v Commission*, [1979] ECR 461, para. 91.

658 Bishop & Walker, 2010, p. 102.

659 *"It is in the light of these considerations that the condition imposed by Article 86 is to be interpreted whereby in order to come within the prohibition a dominant position must have been abused. The provision states a certain number of abusive practices which it prohibits. The list merely gives examples, not an exhaustive enumeration of the sort of abuses of a dominant position prohibited by the Treaty. As may further be seen from letters (c) and (d) of Article 86(2), the provision is not only aimed at practices which may cause damage to consumers directly, but also at those which are detrimental to them through their impact on an effective competition structure, such as is mentioned in Article 3(f) of the Treaty. Abuse may therefore occur if an undertaking in a dominant position strengthens such position in such a way that the degree of dominance reached substantially fetters competition, i.e. that only undertakings remain in the market whose behaviour depends on the dominant one."* Case 6/72, *Continental Can*, [1973] ECR 215. See: Case 85/76, *Hoffmann-La Roche v Commission*, [1979] ECR 461, para. 128–136.

660 Hofmann, 2013, p. 176.

661 See: Case 6/72, *Continental Can*, [1973] ECR 215, para. 26.

II. State Aid Rules

The basis of the EU's state aid policy is set out in Articles 107–109 TFEU. Article 107 ensures that aid granted by a Member State does not distort competition and does not affect trade within the EU. Article 108 deals with the procedural aspects of the state aid policy of the EU. Article 109 empowers the Council to make any appropriate regulations for the application of Articles 107 and 108.

Article 107 TFEU consists of three paragraphs. While the first paragraph provides the general prohibition rule, the second and third paragraphs specify exemptions in the scope of basic bans and define the aid compatible with the internal market.

Article 107(1) prohibits any aid granted by a Member State or through state resources in any form whatsoever which distorts or threatens to distort competition by favouring certain undertakings or the production of certain goods insofar as it affects trade between Member States and deems such an aid to be incompatible with the internal market. In order to apply Article 107(1), various criteria must be met. Although there is not a fully coherent approach in the CJ precedent decisions regarding how to apply these criteria, the CJ always uses the following four criteria[662]:

- an intervention through state or state resources;
- the possibility of this intervention to affect the trade between Member States;
- an advantage for the recipient;
- distortion of competition.

Article 107(2) provides three state aid categories which are compatible with the internal market and not forbidden:

- aid having a social character and granted to individual consumers without discrimination related to the origin of the products concerned;
- aid granted to compensate for the damage caused by natural disaster or other extraordinary events;

662 Quigley, 2015, p. 4.

- aid for empowering the economy in some regions after the reunification of Germany.

This means that if a state aid measure falls under one of these types, the Commission will have to approve the measure.

Article 107(3) covers state aid that may be deemed compatible with the internal market and hence may be permitted by the Commission. These are:

- aid to promote the economic development of poor areas in the EU;
- aid to facilitate the development of certain economic activities or of certain economic areas;
- aid to promote the execution of an important project of common European interest;
- aid to remedy a serious disturbance in the economy of a Member State;
- aid to promote culture and heritage conservation.

The Council may add other categories of aid which can be considered compatible.

As it is clear, not all state aid is forbidden; only the aid which is incompatible with the internal market is forbidden. On the one hand, the Treaty bans state aid which affects trade between Member States and distorts competition; on the other hand, it permits state aid granted for realising common interests.[663]

According to Article 108 TFEU, the Commission must be notified regarding any plans to grant new aid and the aid should not be put into effect without the Commission's authorization.[664] As per Article 108(2), if the Commission concludes that aid granted by a state or through state resources is not compatible with the internal market, or that such aid is being misused, it can decide that the aid should be abolished or altered by the state concerned within a period of time to be determined by the Commission. Article 108(3) establishes the stand-still clause regarding the issues of state aid. Pursuant to this provision, Member States should not grant any state aid without the approval of the Commission.

663 Buts et al., 2011, p. 400.
664 Recital 5 of Regulation 2015/1589.

Although it is not specified in the Treaty, there is a De Minimis Regulation[665] designed especially for the implementation of Articles 107 and 108 TFEU which envisage another "exceptional condition" similar to the implementation of the first paragraph of Article 101 TFEU. The second paragraph of Article 3 of this Regulation states that no notification is needed to be declared to the Commission for aids below the 200'000 Euro threshold. These exemptions justify the Commission giving permission to planned state aids in accordance with Article 108 TFEU. According to this article, Member States should inform the Commission before executing any programme. Moreover, this article grants the power of decision to the Commission to determine whether the suggested aid measure is in the scope of the exemption or should be abolished or modified by the Member State.[666] The decision of whether a state aid measure is compatible with the common market can be given in different ways:

- in the case where the aid meets the conditions within the Block Exemption Regulations[667] adopted by the Commission (these regulations can be executed directly by the national courts);
- following the proper procedure in the case where the aid is granted when the Commission decides on the compliance of an individual project or it approves a plan;
- in the case where compliance is declared by the Council.[668]

In order to exercise its authority, the Commission has developed special criteria depending on the size, location or sector of the company and the purpose of the aid. The Commission sets out the criteria it uses for deciding on whether a measure is in the scope of the exemption in order to ensure transparency, predictability and legal precision.[669]

665 Commission Regulation (EU) No 1407/2013 of 18 December 2013 on the application of Articles 107 and 108 of the Treaty on the Functioning of the European Union to de minimis aid, OJ L 352, 24.12.2013, pp. 1–8.

666 European Commission, Vademecum Community Rules on State Aid, p. 4.

667 Regulation (EU) No 330/2010 of 20 April 2010 on the application of Article 101(3) of the Treaty on the Functioning of the European Union to categories of vertical agreements and concerted practices, OJ L 102, 23.4.2010, pp. 1–7.

668 Faull & Nikpay, 2014, p. 1720.

669 European Commission, Vademecum Community Rules on State Aid, p. 4.

III. Merger Regulation

The Merger Regulation[670] is aimed at ensuring that mergers do not cause too much market concentration, which may lead to abusive behaviour. The Regulation provides a mechanism for the control of mergers and acquisitions at the European level. The purpose of the Merger Regulation is to enable competition authorities to regulate changes in the market structure by deciding whether two or more undertakings may merge, combine or consolidate their businesses into one.[671]

The Commission has almost exclusive jurisdiction to review concentrations having a Community dimension. However, Member State competition authorities are free to exercise their jurisdiction over concentrations which fall below the threshold determined in the Merger Regulation.[672] In other words, Member States cannot apply their national legislations on competition to any concentration that has a Community dimension.[673]

In this context, a "concentration" shall be deemed to arise where a change of control on a lasting basis result from[674]:

- the merger of two or more previously independent undertakings[675] (full-blown mergers);
- the acquisition of control: one or more persons already controlling at least one undertaking, or one or more undertakings acquire direct or indirect control of the whole or parts of one or more other

670 Council Regulation (EC) No 139/2004 of 20 January 2004 on the control of concentrations between undertakings, OJ L 24, 29.1.2004, pp. 1–22.

671 Jones & Sufrin, 2016, p. 1085.

672 The division of competence between the Commission and the NCAs is based on the application of the turnover thresholds set out in Article 1 and includes three corrective mechanisms. The first corrective mechanism is the so-called "two-thirds rule". The objective of this rule is to exclude from the Commission's jurisdiction certain cases which contain a clear national nexus to one Member State. European Commission, Report on the functioning of Regulation No 139/2004, 2009, para. 8.

673 Article 22(3) of Regulation 139/2004.

674 Article 3 of Regulation 139/2004. See also: Commission Consolidated Jurisdictional Notice under Council Regulation (EC) No 139/2004 on the control of concentrations, 2008/C 95/01.

675 Ibid.

undertakings whether by purchase of securities or assets, by contract or by any other means

Moreover, the creation of a joint venture, which functions as an autonomous economic entity on a lasting basis, would constitute a concentration (joint ventures that have all the functions of independent undertakings and are established on a permanent basis).[676]

All mergers having a community dimension[677] are subject to a merger control procedure.[678] According to Article 1, a concentration has a Community dimension where:

- the combined aggregate worldwide turnover of all the undertakings concerned is more than EUR 5000 million; and
- the aggregate Community-wide turnover of each of at least two of the undertakings concerned is more than EUR 250 million,

unless each of the undertakings concerned achieves more than two-thirds of its aggregate Community-wide turnover within one and the same Member State.[679] The rationale behind the concept of EU dimension is to be able to apply the Merger Control Regulation to significant structural changes the impact of which on the market goes beyond the national borders of any one Member State.[680]

Pursuant to the Regulation, the Commission must be notified of any merger with an EU dimension prior to its implementation. The Commission examines whether the merger subject to the review is compatible with the common market and issues a ban when the merger harms the effective competition environment.[681]

676 Article 3(4) of Regulation 139/2004.

677 *"The scope of application of this Regulation should be defined according to the geographical area of activity of the undertakings concerned and be limited by quantitative thresholds in order to cover those concentrations which have a Community dimension."* Recital 9 of the Regulation 139/2004.

678 However, the European Commission envisages a simplified procedure regarding some limitations to certain mergers which are required and defined directly for mergers. For more information, see: Commission Notice on a simplified procedure for treatment of certain concentrations under Council Regulation (EC) No 139/2004, OJ C 366, 14.12.2013, pp. 5–9.

679 ICN, 2012, p. 34.

680 Recital 8 of Regulation 139/2004.

681 Goyder, Goyder & Albors-Llorens, 2009, p. 391.

There is a two-stage investigation mechanism regarding the merger control procedure. During the first stage, the Commission examines the notified concentration and takes one of the following decisions:

- The concentration does not fall within the scope of the Merger Regulation.
- The concentration falls within the scope of the Merger Regulation but does not raise serious doubts as to its compatibility with the common market.
- The concentration falls within the scope of the Merger Regulation and there are doubts as to whether it is compatible with the common market.

As regards the first stage, the Commission has to take a decision within 25 working days following the receipt of a complete notification. It may be extended to 35 working days. Under this stage, the "obligatory suspension principle" must be applied and, hence, the notified concentrations that have a Community dimension are suspended until they have been declared compatible with the common market pursuant to a Commission decision.

Within the framework of the second stage, the Commission takes one of the following decisions:

- The concentration is compatible with the common market.[682]
- The concentration, following modifications, is compatible with the common market.
- The concentration is not compatible with the common market.

This decision is made according to criteria measuring the legality of the concentration.

The second stage must be completed in 90 working days. The period may be increased to 105 working days where the undertakings concerned

682 The decisions of the Commission made to identify whether the concentrations are compatible with the common market should include ancillary restraints (restraints such as competition-restricting obligations necessary for executing the mergers or directly related to mergers, license agreements, supply and purchase obligations) without the need for the Commission to examine these restraints one-by-one. Commission Notice on restrictions directly related and necessary to concentrations, published in the OJ C 56, 05.03.2005, pp. 24–31 and the section on "Important Notices Concerning Mergers" of this Guide.

offer commitments with a view to rendering the concentration compatible with the common market.[683] If the Commission finds that a concentration:

- has already been implemented and that concentration has been declared incompatible with the common market, or
- has been implemented in contravention of a modification,

it may require the undertakings concerned to dissolve the concentration and order any other appropriate measure to ensure that the undertakings concerned dissolve the concentration or take other restorative measures as required in its decision.[684] Furthermore, the Commission may take interim measures appropriate to restore or maintain conditions of effective competition where a concentration:

- has been implemented in contravention of Article 7 and a decision as to the compatibility of the concentration with the common market has not yet been taken;
- has been implemented in contravention of a condition attached to a decision under Article 6(1)(b) or Paragraph 2 of this Article;
- has already been implemented and is declared incompatible with the common market.[685]

§ 9. Decisional Practice (Jurisprudence) in Energy Markets

I. Article 101

A. Joint Selling: GFU

1. Subject Matter

The case[686] is related to the joint gas sales in Norway through a single seller, the so-called GFU (Gas Negotiation Committee). The Norwegian government established the GFU in 1987. The Committee consisted of

683 Article 10 of Regulation 139/2004.
684 Article 8(4) of Regulation 139/2004.
685 Article 8(5) of Regulation 139/2004.
686 Case COMP/36.072, *GFU – Norwegian Gas Negotiation Committee*, 2001.

Norway's largest gas producers, Statoil and Norsk Hydro. The principal task of the GFU was to negotiate all supply agreements on behalf of the gas producers in Norway with foreign buyers.[687] The GFU had power to set prices, volumes and other trading terms on behalf of 30 Norwegian gas producers.

Between late 1980s and 2001, Norwegian gas was sold after the GFU had agreed on all sales conditions with the buyers. GFU engaged in long-term agreements on behalf of Norwegian gas suppliers and European gas operators, and it negotiated all the terms of the sale, including the price on a field-neutral basis. In other words, during the negotiations neither the sellers nor the supplying gas field were known.[688] This joint selling scheme enabled fixing the amount and price of the natural gas exported from Norway to the EU. As a result, the European gas market suffered from significant rigidity and liquidity scarcity. [689]

The Commission had been investigating the case since 1996 and had warned Norwegian gas suppliers that joint gas sales through the GFU constituted a breach of the EU competition rules since it fixed the price and the quantities sold.[690]

2. Preliminary Assessment and Decision

In 2001, based on Article 101 TFEU, the Commission initiated formal proceedings against around 30 Norwegian gas companies operating under GFU scheme, claiming that the scheme infringed upon the EU competition rules. Subsequently, during the hearing, the Norwegian gas producers along with the Norwegian government argued that EU competition rules are not applicable to this case because the scheme had been abolished by Royal Decree in June 2001.[691] Besides, Norwegian gas producers argued that the Norwegian government forced them to sell gas

687 Park, 2013, p. 279.

688 Uchelen & Roggenkamp, 2004, p. 455.

689 Although individual gas producers in Norway could de jure independently and bilaterally enter into agreements with buyers, the GFU's negotiating authority was in practice exclusive. Waloszyk, 2014, p. 63; Talus, 2013, p. 120.

690 European Commission, Commission objects to GFU joint gas sales in Norway, 2001.

691 European Commission, Commission successfully settles GFU case with Norwegian gas producers, 2002.

through the GFU scheme and the government admitted that it created the GFU.[692]

Following the hearing, the Norwegian gas producers and the Commission explored the basis for a settlement. Most of the gas companies were willing to undertake commitments in order to settle.[693] In subsequent negotiations between the Norwegian gas producers and the Commission, the following distinction was made[694]:

- the permanent members of the GFU (Norsk Hydro and Statoil),
- the six companies that sold Norwegian gas under contracts of sale negotiated by the GFU (ExxonMobil, Shell, TotalFinaElf, Conoco, Fortum and Agip) and
- all other defendants in this case.

The first group comprised Statoil and Norsk Hydro, and the settlement consisted of two main elements[695]:

- terminating all joint marketing and sales activities unless these are compatible with EU competition rules, and
- reserving certain gas volumes (more than 15 billion cubic metres) for new customers in Europe.

Moreover, Norsk Hydro and Statoil committed to refrain from introducing territorial and any other type of sales restrictions in the associated contracts of sale even though this issue was not part of the GFU case.[696] The second group, which comprised the other six Norwegian gas companies that operated under the GFU scheme, committed to cease their joint marketing and sales activities. As regards the third group, the Commission decided not to pursue the case on the express assumption that they would not sell Norwegian gas jointly in the future.[697]

692 Kjolbye, 2016, p. 185.
693 Cameron, 2007, p. 306.
694 Lindroos et al., 2002, p. 50; Uchelen & Roggenkamp, 2004, p. 456.
695 European Commission, Commission successfully settles GFU case with Norwegian gas producers, 2002.
696 Uchelen & Roggenkamp, 2004, p. 456.
697 European Commission, Commission successfully settles GFU case with Norwegian gas producers, 2002.

The GFU case highlighted that, in order to successfully create a common gas market in Europe, competition must be introduced in the upstream sector. The case also demonstrated that competition issues between the EU and non-EU undertakings can be solved successfully. Moreover, the case established that the Commission is able to take into consideration the commercial interests of the concerned undertakings whilst ensuring that EU competition law is protected.[698]

B. Joint Marketing: DONG/DUC

1. Subject Matter

The case[699] is related to the joint marketing activities of three Danish gas producers and to anticompetitive restriction clauses set out in their gas supply contracts with the Danish incumbent gas supplier DONG (Dansk Olie og Naturgas A/S).[700] The Danish Underground Consortium (DUC) was a joint venture between Shell, AP Møller/Maersk and ChevronTexaco.[701] Together with DONG, they were the largest oil and natural gas suppliers in Denmark. DUC partners produced around 90% of the gas for sale at the Danish continental shelf and sold it under three supply agreements exclusively to DONG. The clauses set in these contracts were considered horizontal as well as vertical restraints on competition by the Commission.[702]

On June 2001, the Commission initiated antitrust proceedings against DONG and DUC due to "joint marketing of North Sea gas". The subject of the investigation consisted of the gas sales agreements in 1979, 1990 and 1993 between DONG and each of the DUC partners. According to these agreements, DUC partners sold DONG gas that could meet all of Denmark's gas demand, and they supplied additional volumes for Sweden and Germany.

698 Lindroos et al., 2002, p. 51.
699 European Commission, Commission and Danish competition authorities jointly open up Danish gas market, 2003.
700 European Commission, Application of competition rules to the gas sector, 2003.
701 DUC, which accounts for 90% of Danish gas production, is composed of Shell (46%), AP Møller (39%) and ChevronTexaco (15%).
702 Lowe, 2003, p. 5.

2. Preliminary Assessment and Decision

The Commission focused on joint marketing and the restrictive provisions of gas supply agreements concluded between DONG and DUC.[703] It established that these agreements contained horizontal (joint marketing) and vertical restraints (the reduction clause and restrictions on use).

Although the gas supply agreements were negotiated jointly by the DUC partners and DONG, they were entered into separately by each of the DUC partners and by DONG. The agreements contained clauses concerning DUC partners giving some priority rights to DONG over the sale of "additional" or newly discovered gas volumes. Furthermore, the agreements contained pricing formulas which varied according to the customers to whom DONG resold the gas. Additionally, the agreements contained a mechanism that became operational if the parties commenced sales in Denmark itself.[704]

The Commission first addressed horizontal restraints (joint marketing). It concluded that such joint marketing agreements reduce the possibilities of customers to choose between suppliers/producers and thus considerably restrict competition, which results in infringement of EU competition law.[705] During the investigation, it was claimed that DUC partners' joint marketing activities were in the scope of the Block Exemption Regulation. However, the Commission did not agree that the Block Exemption Regulation could be used, and it argued that the conditions for joint distribution exception were not present.[706] An exemption was not appropriate since joint marketing does not usually contribute to improve the production or distribution of goods within the meaning of Article 101(3) TFEU.[707]

The arguments of both sides were inconclusive. However, while reserving their legal position, DUC partners and DONG offered the following commitments which brought the investigation to a conclusion[708]:

---

703 Cameron, 2007, p. 308.
704 Ibid.
705 Lowe, 2003, p. 5.
706 Kjolbye, 2016, p. 209.
707 Cameron, 2007, p. 309.
708 Ibid.

- to discontinue joint marketing activities for un-contracted gas extracted from the Danish continental shelf;
- to market all new gas individually in the future;
- to carry out negotiations individually concerning existing contracts when prices were renegotiated;
- to offer for sale 7 billion cubic meters of gas to interested third parties.[709]

Secondly, the Commission conducted an investigation regarding vertical restraints based on the horizontal approach. The DONG/DUC case raised the following issues relating to vertical restraint[710]:

- Restraints imposed on DUC partners in their function as suppliers (reduction clause): The 1993 gas supply agreement between DUC partners and DONG included a necessary adjustment mechanism. According to this mechanism, if the DUC partners commenced sales of gas into Denmark, the DUC partners and DONG had to agree on adjustments to the gas supply agreements such as the take-or-pay obligations of DONG.[711] The Commission stated that such a clause would hinder entrance by the DUC partners into the downstream Danish gas markets.[712]
  DONG agreed to limit the scope of the clause by not invoking it for gas originating from sources other than the DUC gas fields. Moreover, DONG undertook to waive the clause once a new pipeline is commissioned linking the gas fields on the Danish continental shelf with other continental European countries.[713]
- Restraints imposed on DONG in its function as buyer/customer (restriction on use): According to supply agreements, DONG was required to report to the DUC partners the volumes of gas sold to

709 Kjolbye, 2016, p. 209.
710 Lowe, 2003, p. 6; Schnichels & Valli, 2003, p. 61.
711 The Commission stated that this case was similar to the reduction clause described in previous decisions. For more information regarding reduction clause, see: European Commission, Commission clears gas supply contracts between German gas wholesaler WINGAS and EDF-Trading, 2002; Cameron, 2007, p. 310.
712 Lowe, 2003, p. 6.

certain categories of consumers in order to benefit from special price formulas for these customers. The Commission considered this situation as a specific form of use restriction.[714] DONG was not free to sell the gas to whichever customer it chose without running the risk that it would lose the benefit of the specific price formula. The DUC partners and DONG committed to amend their supply contracts, and DONG undertook to refrain from buying the volumes dedicated by the DUC partners to new customers.

The settlement of the DONG/DUC case brought important clarifications regarding the application of EU competition law to the gas market. The case established that the joint marketing of gas by gas producers was no longer acceptable by the Commission in the context of an ongoing EU energy market liberalisation.[715] Moreover, it was also established that certain forms of vertical restraint such as reduction clauses and use restrictions which hinder competition are no longer acceptable in a liberalised gas environment. For this reason, the DONG/DUC case set an important example of how competition law contributes to the liberalisation of European energy markets.[716]

C. Market Sharing: E.ON/GDF

1. Subject Matter

The case[717] is related to the infringement of Article 101 TFEU from 1980 to 2005 through agreements/concerted practices. The parties agreed to only offer gas transported through their jointly owned pipeline, MEGAL, to customers in their respective territories and to monitor the implementation of the agreement.[718]

E.ON is a leading German energy company active in the production, transportation, distribution and supply of electricity and gas in

713 European Commission, Commission and Danish competition authorities jointly open up Danish gas market, 2003; Cameron, 2007, p. 310; Schnichels & Valli, 2003, p. 62.

714 Cameron, 2007, p. 311.

715 Schnichels & Valli, 2003, p. 63.

716 Cameron, 2007, p. 312.

717 Case COMP/39.401, *E.ON/GDF*, Commission Decision of 8 July 2009.

718 Ibid., para. 3.

Europe. It is the largest natural gas supplier in Germany. GDF Suez (Gaz de France Suez) is the leading gas supplier in France and it is active in both upstream and downstream segments of the electricity and gas sectors. On May 2006, the Commission carried out unannounced inspections at the premises of E.ON Ruhrgas[719] and GDF. The Commission suspected that E.ON and GDF breached the competition rules on restrictive business practices (Article 101).[720] Following the inspection, the Commission initiated antitrust proceedings against E.ON and GDF Suez alleging the infringement of Article 101 TFEU on July 2007. The Commission focused on a possible agreement or concerted practice between E.ON and GDF to keep out of each other's home market.[721]

2. Preliminary Assessment and Decision

In 1975, E.ON and GDF agreed to jointly build the MEGAL pipeline to bring Russian natural gas into both France and Germany. In the meantime, they decided not to enter each other's home markets through two side letters which prohibited Ruhrgas from transporting gas via the MEGAL pipeline to France and GDF from supplying customers in Germany with the gas transported through this pipeline.[722]

Until the expiry of the deadline for the transposition of Directive 98/30/EC into the domestic law in 2000, GDF had a legal monopoly on the import of gas into France. During the gradual liberalisation of the European gas markets, GDF lost its dominant position as an import monopoly; however, the parties continued to apply this market-sharing agreement (the 1975 side letters), and this helped them to maintain their market power. E.ON and GDF took measures to protect their powerful position in the German and French markets respectively.[723]

---

719 The company was formerly known as Ruhrgas AG. Until 2013, Ruhrgas was wholly owned by E.ON. On 2 May 2013, E.ON Ruhrgas was merged with E.ON Global Commodities SE.

720 European Commission, Antitrust: Commission opens formal proceedings against E.ON and Gaz de France concerning suspected market-sharing, 2007.

721 Ibid.

722 Case COMP/39.401, *E. ON/GDF*, Summary of Commission Decision of 8 July 2009, para. 3.

723 Battista et al., 2009, p. 38.

During the investigation, the Commission realised that the infringement in the German gas market began on 1 January 1980 when the MEGAL pipeline became fully operational. As for the French gas market, the Commission concluded that the infringement began on 10 August 2000 when GDF lost its dominant position concerning gas import to France. E.ON and GDF met regularly at various levels, discussed how to implement the agreement in the newly liberalised market and monitored each other's actions.[724] The agreement was not terminated until 30 September 2005.[725]

With the decision of 8 July 2009, the Commission concluded that E.ON and GDF infringed Article 101 TFEU, and both firms were fined.[726] The decision of the Commission stated that agreements regarding market sharing constituted the most serious infringements under Article 101 TFEU.[727] The Commission issued a fine, thus for the first time sanctioning an antitrust infringement in the energy sector. Additionally, it stated that the firms or persons harmed by the agreement could file actions for compensation in national courts. In the words of *Kroes*: "*This decision sends a strong signal to energy incumbents that the Commission will not tolerate any form of anticompetitive behaviour. Market sharing is one of the worst types of antitrust infringement. This agreement deprived customers of more price competition and more choice of supplier in two of the largest gas markets in the EU. The Commission has no alternative but to impose high fines.*"[728] Based on its investigation, the Commission concluded that these anticompetitive agreements were in force during a vast period of time and that such an infringement had an important impact on the market because it empowered the monopolies and delayed the effects of liberalisation.[729]

E.ON and GDF filed an appeal against the Commission's decision in 2009. In its 29 June 2012 decision, the General Court mostly upheld

724 European Commission, Antitrust: Commission fines E.ON and GDF Suez €553 million each for market-sharing in French and German gas markets. 2009.

725 Case COMP/39.401, *E. ON/GDF*, Summary of Commission Decision of 8 July 2009, para. 4.

726 Ibid., para. 13

727 Ibid., para. 364.

728 European Commission, Antitrust: Commission fines E.ON and GDF Suez €553 million each for market-sharing in French and German gas markets. 2009.

729 Battista et al., 2009, p. 39.

the Commission's decision. It found, however, that the Commission made errors in determining the duration of the infringement.[730] According to the General Court, the Commission made two errors: firstly, when the infringement on the German market started, and secondly, when the infringement on the French market ended. On the one hand, the Commission did not show that there was potential competition in the period from 1980 to 1998, which could have been affected by the MEGAL agreement, in the German gas market. The General Court therefore annulled the Commission's decision regarding the period from 1980 to 1998.[731] On the other hand, the Commission had failed to demonstrate, with regard to the French market, that the infringement continued following the MEGAL agreement of August 2004. Accordingly, the General Court annulled the Commission's decision on this point.[732] Taking into consideration the partial annulment of the Commission's decision, the General Court reduced the amount of the fine imposed on the two companies.[733]

In the E.ON/GDF case, the Commission and the General Court imposed fines for the first time for a substantive antitrust violation in the energy sector based on Article 101 TFEU, and it is the only case which did not result in a commitment since the energy sector inquiry.[734] In the absence of such a commitment, the Commission's decision could be appealed before the General Court by the parties concerned and it was the subject of an assessment as to its legality. The General Court considerably reduced the extraordinarily high fine imposed by the Commission.[735]

730 Case T-360/09, Judgment of the General Court of 29 June 2012, para. 125.
731 Hofmann, 2013, p. 32.
732 Case T-360/09, Judgment of the General Court of 29 June 2012, para. 246.
733 European Commission, The fines of €553 million imposed on GDF and E.ON for sharing the French and German markets for natural gas are reduced to €320 million for each company, 2013.
734 Hofmann, 2013, p. 329.
735 Ibid.

D. Non-Competing: EPEX Spot and Nord Pool Spot

1. Subject Matter

The case[736] is related to the single and continuous infringement of Article 101 TFEU pertaining to spot electricity trading services[737] from 21 June 2011 until 7 February 2012. The parties, EPEX Spot and Nord Pool Spot, engaged in a non-competition arrangement covering all their electricity spot trading services in the EEA and beyond.[738]

EPEX Spot is an exchange for power spot trading in Western European countries such as Germany, France, the United Kingdom, the Netherlands, Belgium, Austria, Luxembourg and Switzerland. It is a joint venture established through the merger of the spot activities of Powernext SA in France and the European Energy Exchange AG in Germany. Nord Pool Spot is an electricity market that is used by Nordic power producers and buyers for trading with one another and operates in Estonia, Latvia, Lithuania, Denmark, Sweden, Norway, Finland, Germany and the UK. It is currently owned by the Nordic and Baltic Transmission System Operators.

From 7 to 9 February 2012, the Commission carried out unannounced inspections at the premises of EPEX Spot (in France) and Nord Pool Spot (in Finland, Norway and Sweden).[739] On 22 March 2013, the Commission initiated proceedings against the parties alleging a non-competing agreement with a view to engaging in settlement discussions with them.[740]

2. Preliminary Assessment and Decision

The parties agreed not to compete with one another for their spot electricity trading services in the EEA, in particular by allocating territo-

736 Case AT 39.952, *EPEX Spot – Nord Pool Spot AS*, Commission Decision of 5 March 2014.

737 Spot trading means trading in the short run, such as within the same day or for the next day.

738 Case AT 39.952, *EPEX Spot – Nord Pool Spot AS*, para. 24.

739 European Commission, Antitrust: Commission confirms unannounced inspections in the electricity sector, 2012.

740 Case AT 39.952, *EPEX Spot – Nord Pool Spot AS*, para. 18.

ries between themselves.[741] According to the Commission, they aimed at restricting competition among each other, protecting their traditional strongholds and agreeing on expansion to new countries while maintaining the power balance between themselves.[742]

The non-competition arrangement was established in the context of legitimate cooperation between stakeholders. The parties decided to establish a joint approach on the technical systems to be used for cross-border trade.[743] The goal was to develop an optimal joint system platform for both day-ahead and intraday trading to meet customers' expectations.[744] However, the Commission found that the parties had used this initiative as a cover to enter into a non-competition arrangement.

Concerning territorial allocation, the aim of their anticompetitive agreement was to protect their traditional strongholds by not operating in each other's home markets.[745] The parties also agreed to share new markets. Countries south of Poland were reserved for EPEX Spot and countries north of Poland (including Poland) were reserved for Nord Pool Spot.[746] The infringement lasted for at least seven months from 21 June 2011 until 7 February 2012, ending when the Commission carried out unannounced inspections at the companies' premises.[747] The Commission concluded that the agreement established by EPEX Spot and Nord Pool Spot presented all the characteristics of an agreement and/or a concerted practice which is prohibited by Article 101 TFEU.[748] The Parties had participated in a single and continuous infringement of Article 101 TFEU. The Commission therefore imposed fines on the parties that committed the infringement.[749]

---

741 Ibid., para. 28.

742 Ibid., para. 24–25.

743 European Commission, Antitrust: Commission fines two power exchanges € 5.9 million in cartel settlement, 2014.

744 Nord Pool Spot, The Leading Power Market, 2013, p. 7.

745 Case AT 39.952, *EPEX Spot – Nord Pool Spot AS*, para. 30.

746 Ibid., para. 31.

747 European Commission, Antitrust: Commission fines two power exchanges € 5.9 million in cartel settlement, 2014.

748 Case AT 39.952, *EPEX Spot – Nord Pool Spot AS*, para. 43.

749 Ibid., para. 66.

Power exchanges are critical to the efficient functioning of electricity markets, as they increase liquidity. The Commission's decision highlighted that the EU competition law applies not only to energy suppliers, traders and purchasers but also to the power exchanges themselves. Thus the allocation of trading markets is considered an infringement of that law.[750] According to *Joaquín Almunia*, the decision is significant, because power exchanges are central to the efficient functioning of electricity markets; it is in the best interest of consumers and is also a good illustration of how EU competition policy helps to build and sustain the Single Market.[751] It can be also said that the Commission used EU competition law as a tool to lower energy prices by penalising the misconduct and collusive practices of EPEX Spot and Nord Pool Spot.[752]

II. Article 102

A. Exclusionary Abuses (Network Related Foreclosure)

1. Capacity Hoarding: RWE, ENI and ČEZ

a. RWE

1) Subject Matter

The case[753] is related to third-party access on a regional wholesale market in Germany and to an alleged abuse of a dominant position through raising rivals' costs and refusing new entrants access to the capacity on RWE's gas transport infrastructure.[754] RWE, a fully integrated German-based energy and utility company, is primarily active in the production and supply of electricity as well as in the production,

750 Ratliff & Grasso, 2014, p. 372.

751 European Commission, Statement by Vice-President Joaquín Almunia on antitrust decisions on power exchanges, 2014.

752 European Economic and Social Committee, Opinion of the European Economic and Social Committee on the Report on competition policy 2014, 2015, para. 2.7.

753 Case COMP/39.402, *RWE Gas Foreclosure*, Commission Decision of 18 March 2009.

754 Talus, 2011, p. 208.

transmission, import and storage of gas and in downstream gas distribution.

On 20 April 2007, the Commission initiated antitrust proceedings against RWE claiming that RWE refused third-party access to its natural gas transportation network, subsequently abused its dominant position by means of margin squeeze and, hence, infringed Article 102 TFEU. The antitrust proceedings against RWE were initiated based on the information obtained during the inspection[755] carried out in 2006, which gave rise to suspicions that RWE created obstacles to third-party access on the regional wholesale market in its core area in North Rhine-Westphalia.[756] The pertinent practices put forth by RWE which were believed to have infringed upon Article 101 TFEU included fixed prices for access to the gas network operated by RWE TSO, inflation of RWE TSO's costs, maintenance of an artificial network fragmentation and failure to release transportation capacity to allow customer switching. These practices created additional obstacles for RWE's competitors to access the regional bulk gas supply market, which resulted in preserving RWE's dominant position in the gas supply market, market foreclosure and the detriment of consumers.[757]

2) Relevant Markets and Dominant Position

In the preliminary assessment, the relevant markets were identified as the markets for the sale (supply) of gas and the markets relating to gas infrastructure, such as gas transport services.[758] The gas supply market was divided into two groups: wholesalers[759] and end customers[760].

755 European Commission, Competition: Commission has carried out inspections in the EU gas sector in five Member States, 2006.

756 European Commission, Antitrust: Commission initiates proceedings against RWE Group concerning suspected foreclosure of German gas supply markets, 2007.

757 European Commission, The Commission decided to initiate antitrust proceedings in case COMP/B1/39402, 2007.

758 Case COMP/39.402, *RWE Gas Foreclosure*, para. 12.

759 "Regionalferngasgesellschaften" (regional distributers) and "Stadtwerke" (smaller distributers).

760 Large industrial customers and smaller customers such as household and small commercial customers.

With regards to the gas transport market, the Commission defined two markets, a gas transmission market for services offered by TSOs, on the one hand, and the gas distribution market offered by DSOs, on the other hand. The reason behind this distinction was that competitive conditions in both segments differ significantly.[761]

Regarding the relevant geographic market, in the preliminary assessment it was concluded that the gas transmission market cannot be defined larger than grid-wide due to the fact that the construction of competing parallel gas networks is not economically viable in most cases. Therefore, competitive constraints from TSOs outside RWE's network remain negligible. Moreover, the gas downstream (supply) markets were also defined as grid-wide due to missing competitive constraints from suppliers outside RWE's gas network.[762]

According to the preliminary assessment, RWE might have held a dominant position in the gas transmission market within its grid area since 2003, on the one hand, and also in downstream supply markets within its grid, on the other hand. Concerning the transmission of gas, the Commission noted that the majority of customers had no other choice than RWE's network for their gas transmission needs as it was not possible to build new connections to other pipelines due to absence of economically viable conditions.[763] As regards the downstream (supply) markets, the Commission observed that third-party suppliers were not able to compete with RWE within its grid, because they were limited due to the small volumes of transport capacities available to them. It was therefore concluded in the preliminary assessment that RWE might have held a dominant position on the wholesale supply markets within its grid area.[764]

3) Preliminary Assessment and Decision

The Commission gathered evidence that RWE may have pursued a systematic strategy aimed at foreclosing potential third-party transport

761 Case COMP/39.402, *RWE Gas Foreclosure*, para. 13.
762 Ibid., para. 15.
763 Ibid., para. 18.
764 Ibid., para. 19.

customers and keeping transport capacities for itself, especially on important bottlenecks. Indeed, RWE booked almost the entire capacity on its transmission network on a long-term basis. Therefore, the opportunities for competitors to get access to RWE's transmission network were already reduced. In other words, demand for transmission capacities on RWE's network by third-party transport customers who sought to compete with RWE in the downstream gas distribution markets largely exceeded the offered capacities by RWE, which led to numerous rejections of transmission requests.

In the preliminary assessment, the Commission concluded that RWE failed to justify these rejections.[765] Furthermore, the Commission found that RWE prevented many competitors from gaining access to its network by understating its technically available capacity and managing the scarce transport capacities on its network. Consequently, only a small portion of the transport capacity on RWE's transmission grid was made available to new entrants, who thus were not able to compete in an effective manner on the downstream supply market.[766]

RWE was firstly accused of allocating the capacity for its own downstream supply businesses, especially in bottlenecks.[767] According to the estimates of the Commission, RWE deliberately prevented the access of rivals with respect to the gas network by the poor management of the capacity by RWE Transportnetz Gas GmbH, the subsidiary of RWE, and did not systematically leave free the distribution capacity.[768] RWE reserved the capacity for its own supply businesses for a long time through its own TSO and refused the capacity requests from other parties. According to the Commission, another reason for refusing these distribution demands was probably RWE's keeping its ready-to-use capacity values low. In fact, the capacity used by RWE on the bottlenecks was much lower than the estimated highest technical capacity. According to the Commission, this conduct of RWE indicated the intention to deliberately exclude potential third-party distribution clients (capacity hoarding). One of the reasons for refusing third-party

765 Ibid., para. 24–26.
766 Koch et al., 2009, p. 32.
767 Hauteclocque, 2016, p. 344.
768 Hofmann, 2013, p. 258.

requests was that RWE had not implemented an effective congestion management.[769]

The Commission's second concern was related to the possible abuse of the dominant position by a behaviour aiming at lowering the margins of RWE's downstream competitors in gas supply (margin squeeze). There were indeed indications that RWE might have squeezed the margins of its rivals by implementing its transmission tariffs at an artificially high level with very low tariffs within the downstream supply market.[770] It can be argued that RWE was likely to have kept its prices immensely high with the aim to decrease the margins of its rivals. Such behaviour had the effect of preventing RWE's competitors from competing effectively on the downstream gas supply markets, or limiting the ability of competitors or potential entrants to remain in or enter the market.[771] Indeed, its rivals could not compete in the gas transmission market as effectively as could RWE. Thus, it became difficult for new rivals to enter into the market.

On 18 March 2009, the Commission accepted the legally binding commitments suggested by RWE for solving concerns arising from the investigation.[772] RWE committed to divest its German high-pressure gas transmission network including assets, personnel and ancillary services necessary for a viable gas transport business. Moreover, it committed to sell this network to a purchaser who was independent from RWE and who did not give rise to *prima facie* competition concerns.[773]

In its RWE decision, the Commission concluded that the problem emerged from RWE's vertically integrated structure covering import, supply and network operation activities. The Commission took structural measures against RWE due to the possibility of market closure in the natural gas network, and, as a result, RWE agreed voluntarily to unbundle ownership of its natural gas transmission network. This commitment of RWE is considered an indication that ownership of the network does

769 Ibid.
770 Hauteclocque, 2016, p. 344.
771 Case COMP/39.402, *RWE Gas Foreclosure*, Commission Decision of 18 March 2009, para. 30.
772 Hofmann, 2013, p. 259.
773 Case COMP/39.402, *RWE Gas Foreclosure*, para. 38; European Commission, Antitrust: Commission market tests commitments proposed by RWE concerning German gas market, 2008.

not constitute a requirement for natural gas commerce.[774] As understood from the RWE decision, the Commission aimed at eliminating the disruptions in the liberalised energy market by accepting the legal commitments suggested by the party under investigation.

b. ENI

1) Subject Matter

The case[775] is related to capacity hoarding and strategic underinvestment in the transmission system, leading to the foreclosure of competitors and harm for competition and customers in one or more supply markets in Italy. ENI is an Italian state-controlled company mainly operating at multiple levels of the production, transportation and supply chain in natural gas and oil markets. ENI (co-)owned and controlled the main gas import pipelines into Italy (TAG[776], TENP[777] and Transitgas[778] pipelines).[779] Although it is predominantly active in Italy, it has operations in more than 70 countries.

On 20 April 2007, based on the information it obtained during the inspection carried out in 2006[780], the Commission initiated an *ex-officio* investigation[781] concerning the Italian company ENI and claimed

774 Lohmann, 2009, pp. 103–104.

775 Case COMP/39.315, *ENI*, Commission Decision of 29 September 2010.

776 The Trans Austria Gasleitung (TAG) is a natural gas pipeline leading from the Slovak-Austrian border at Baumgarten an der March to Arnoldstein in the south, near the border with Italy.

777 The Trans Europa Naturgas Pipeline (TENP) is a natural gas pipeline which runs from the German-Netherlands border to the German-Swiss border. It carries North Sea natural gas from the Netherlands to Italy and Switzerland.

778 The Transitgas is a natural gas pipeline in Switzerland, which connects Trans Europa Naturgas Pipeline (TENP) from Wallbach at the German border and the Gaz de France gas grid from Rodersdorf/Oltingue at the French border.

779 Koch & Gauer, 2011, p. 216.

780 European Commission, Antitrust: Commission initiates proceedings against the ENI Group concerning suspected foreclosure of Italian gas supply markets, 2007.

781 The case aroused out of the inspection carried out in 2006 on ENI premises and premises of ENI subsidiaries in Italy, Austria and Germany. The European Commission carried out unannounced inspections at the premises of gas companies in five Member States on 16 May 2006. The countries concerned were Germany, Italy, France, Belgium and Austria. The Commission had reason to believe that

that ENI was hoarding capacity and deliberately limiting investments in capacity on its networks, which resulted in foreclosing competitors as well as harming customers and competition in one or more supply markets in Italy.[782] These practices created a bottleneck on import capacity and thus negatively impacted the security of gas supply in Italy.[783] The Commission suspected that ENI abused its dominant position within the scope of Article 102 TFEU by a systematic and constructive refusal to supply on its international pipelines transporting gas into Italy, specifically on the TENP (1), Transitgas (2) and TAG (3) pipelines.[784]

2) Relevant Markets and Dominant Position

Similar to the RWE Decision, in the preliminary assessment the Commission identified the relevant markets as the markets for the sale (supply) of gas and the markets relating to gas infrastructure, such as gas transport services. Within the gas transport market, the Commission made a clear distinction between high pressure transmission networks and low-pressure distribution networks, because competitive conditions in both markets differ significantly. As for the gas supply market, it was divided into two groups: wholesalers and end customers.

---

the companies concerned may have violated EU competition rules that prohibit restrictive business practices and/or abuse of a dominant market position. European Commission, Competition: Commission has carried out inspections in the EU gas sector in five Member States, 2006.

782 *"The legal base of this procedural step is Article 11(6) of Council Regulation No 1/2003 and article 2(1) of Commission Regulation No 773/2004. Article 11(6) of Regulation No 1/2003 provides that the initiation of proceedings relieves the competition authorities of the Member States of their authority to apply Articles 81 and 82 of the Treaty. Moreover, Article 16(1) of the same Regulation provides that national courts must avoid giving decisions which would conflict with a decision contemplated by the Commission in proceedings that it has initiated."* European Commission, 2007.

783 European Commission, Antitrust: Commission confirms sending Statement of Objections to ENI concerning the Italian gas market, 2009.

784 Case COMP/39.315, *ENI*, Summary of Commission Decision of 29 September 2010, para. 5.

The Commission considered all transport ways reaching Italy to meet the Italian bulk companies as important relevant markets in a geographical sense. It was concluded that, for the purpose of this case, all of the viable routes that could be used by a shipper/supplier to bring gas to the wholesale market in Italy constituted one relevant market.[785] According to the Commission, ENI had a dominant position both in the natural gas distribution market in the direction of Italy and in the subsequent supply market. The Commission also concluded that ENI was in the dominant position in terms of gas transmission, particularly in terms of the gas transportation to and within Italy.[786] Concerning the transmission of gas, the Commission concluded that ENI was in a dominant position on the market for the natural gas transport to Italy by means of its ability to effectively control and influence the usage of all viable international pipelines for shipping gas into Italy.[787] As regards the downstream (supply) markets, it was established that ENI held a dominant position on the wholesale supply market in Italy as a whole and particularly on the market for gas supply to fired power plants and on the market for gas supply to large industrial customers.[788]

3) Preliminary Assessment and Decision

The Commission put forth and presented three alternative justifications in accordance with its claim of abuse.[789] Firstly, the Commission gathered evidence that ENI might have implemented a systematic

785 Ibid., Commission Decision of 29 September 2010, para. 26.

786 *"Notably, ENI controls (or joint controls) all those viable network infrastructures and owns the transport companies holding significant capacity/use rights on those import pipelines including the LNG Terminal, existing at the date the Statement of Objections was issued."* Ibid., para. 29–31.

787 Ibid., para. 30.

788 Ibid., para. 33.

789 Based on an assessment of ENI's management and operation of the TENP/Transitgas and TAG pipelines, the Commission took the preliminary view that ENI may have foreclosed its competitors by refusing to grant them access to capacity available on its transport networks (capacity hoarding), by granting access in a less attractive manner (capacity degradation) and by strategically limiting investment. Ibid., para. 43.

strategy to restrict the access of distribution clients to infrastructure capacities (capacity hoarding). ENI implemented this by refusing to offer existing available capacity upon the demand of third parties. ENI showed the current capacity lower than it actually was. The investigation of the Commission showed that short- and long-term demands of third parties were much higher than the amount of capacity offered by ENI and that this caused the refusal of these demands of third parties by ENI without any justified reason. The Commission investigated whether ENI had the related transport capacity in its pipelines, and it requested that ENI presents detailed information about the 2001–2007 period. In the framework of this analysis, the Commission concluded that, although ENI had enough capacity, it hoarded it and did not make it available to third parties.[790]

Secondly, the Commission further gathered evidence indicating that ENI made it difficult to purchase capacity and offered it to sale under inappropriate conditions that might cause its degradation (capacity degradation). This led to the deliberate delay in sharing the capacity or to the sales of it for a short time. Additionally, it was determined that ENI followed a strategy of deliberately avoiding capacity expansions in order to ultimately limit third-party access to capacity.[791]

Thirdly, an additional justification can be found in the investment decisions of ENI on whether it was necessary to increase the current transport capacity on pipelines and in the systematic limitation of strategic plans (investment less than strategically necessary and needed). ENI deliberately avoided increasing its capacity. In this context, the capacity demands of third parties were not considered as "Open Season Procedure" and their joint financing offers were not taken into consideration concretely.[792]During its investigation, the Commission found evidence that the reason for not undertaking additional investment on transport capacity was not the low profitability rate but the will to continue the control by ENI of its transport capacity. It was found that opening additional capacity to third-party use would increase competition in the downstream market and that ENI worried that its margin in this market would be in danger.

790 Maier-Rigaud et al., 2011, p. 20.
791 Case COMP/39.315, *ENI*, para. 60.
792 Hofmann, 2013, p. 261.

The Commission took a decision on 29 September 2010 and made binding the commitments suggested by ENI to cope with the preliminary concerns of the Commission that ENI might have abused its dominant position in the gas transport market.[793] ENI committed to divesting its current shareholdings in the companies related to international gas transmission pipelines (TENP, Transitgas and TAG) to a suitable purchaser independent from and unconnected to ENI who does not raise *prima facie* competition concerns.[794]

According to the decision of the Commission on 29 September 2010, the commitments implemented by ENI were significant since they covered the structural divestiture of the international transport activities of ENI in Italy for gas import. The reason underlying the aforementioned decision was the will to solve the competition problems created in related pipelines which played a significant role in creating a single competitive European gas market.[795] It can be said that the commitments that are the subject of the decision opened up the way for making the downstream supply market more competitive. The Commission stated that ENI's avoidance of investment, when there was a clear demand, prevailed against the interests of the transmission company. ENI suggested some commitments including selling out its shares in transmission networks. With this decision, the Commission aimed at reviving proper incentives to manage and operate gas transport networks in Europe.[796] In order to achieve this aim, ENI committed to divestiture of its gas networks.

The Commission's ENI decision followed a line started with the RWE case. In both cases, the distortion of competition was caused by an internal conflict of interest resulting from vertical integration of an energy undertaking which owns and operates the electricity or gas transmission network while also supplying electricity or gas in its network area. This conflict of interest was addressed by the Commission through imposition of a structural remedy which required the vertically integrated entity to separate the ownership of the network from its

793 Maier-Rigaud et al., 2011, p. 18.

794 Case COMP/39.315, *ENI*, Summary of Commission Decision of 29 September 2010, para. 7.

795 Maier-Rigaud et al., 2011, p. 18.

796 Ibid., p. 23.

other activities. The ENI decision demonstrated that structural remedies are indeed a legitimate and proportionate means to address distortion of competition caused by anticompetitive conduct of vertically integrated undertakings.[797]

c. ČEZ

1) Subject Matter

The case[798] is related to the anticompetitive conduct of ČEZ within the Czech electricity market, particularly to the pre-emptive booking of capacities in the Czech electricity transmission network with the aim of hindering the entry of competitors into the market.[799] The state-owned undertaking ČEZ is the incumbent operator in the Czech electricity market. ČEZ is active in a number of areas of the electricity and lignite sectors in the Czech Republic (lignite mining and trading, electricity generation, distribution, trading and supply) and several other countries in Europe (Bulgaria, Germany, Hungary, Poland, Romania, Slovakia and Turkey).

On 24 November 2009, the Commission carried out an inspection without prior notice at the premises of the energy company ČEZ. The Commission had reason to believe that ČEZ had performed certain activities unilaterally or together with other market players which caused significant damage to competition and subsequently led to strengthening its dominant position within the Czech wholesale electricity market. The Commission was concerned that these activities would increase prices in the Czech wholesale electricity market and would cause the exclusion of rivals in the market.[800] In the follow-up to the inspection on 24 November 2009, the Commission initiated on 11 July 2011 antitrust proceedings to determine whether ČEZ was in a dominant position as regards electricity production in the Czech Republic

797 Ibid.
798 Case AT 39.727, *ČEZ*, Commission Decision of 10 April 2013.
799 Ibid., para. 1.
800 European Commission, Antitrust: Commission confirms inspections in Czech electricity sector, 2009.

and whether it infringed upon Article 102 TFEU by abusing its dominant position in the electricity market.[801]

2) Relevant Market and Dominant Position

According to the preliminary assessment of the Commission, the relevant product market was segregated into the electricity generation and wholesale supply markets. Such segregation included the electricity generated in and imported into the relevant geographic area through interconnectors.[802] Concerning the geographic market, the Czech electricity production and wholesale markets were considered national. This was based on the different structures of supply in the Czech Republic and in the neighbouring countries, the different fuel mix of the power plants in the Czech Republic and in neighbouring countries and the existence of congestion at interconnection points with neighbouring Member States.[803]

According to the preliminary assessment, the Commission provisionally concluded that ČEZ held a dominant position on the market for the electricity generation and wholesale supply in the Czech Republic during the relevant period (2007–2012).[804]

3) Preliminary Assessment and Decision

The Commission raised the concern that ČEZ might have abused its dominant position on the generation and wholesale supply of electricity markets in the Czech Republic. More specifically, ČEZ might have pursued a strategy aiming at preventing new market entry. As part of this strategy, in January 2007 ČEZ made a potentially pre-emptive reservation in the Czech electricity transmission system.[805] Thus the

801 European Commission, Antitrust: Commission opens formal proceedings against Czech electricity incumbent ČEZ, 2011.
802 Case AT 39.727, *ČEZ*, Commission Decision of 10 April 2013, para. 11.
803 Ibid., para. 12.
804 Ibid., para. 14.
805 Ibid., para. 22.

Commission concluded in the preliminary assessment that ČEZ might have reportedly abused its dominant position in the market by reserving in advance its capacity in the transmission network.

As a result of ČEZ's pre-emptive reservation, the available transmission capacity which could have otherwise been used by ČEZ's competitors was exhausted. Consequently, these competitors could have been denied access to the transmission network system, a condition indispensable for every large-scale electricity generator.[806] According to the Commission, due to the aforementioned reason the rivals were prevented from entering into the electricity wholesale and production market.[807] On 10 April 2013, the Commission declared that the commitments of ČEZ are legally binding. ČEZ agreed to divest its energy power plant (Pocerady, Chvaletice or Melnik III and Tisova) and, hence, liberate nearly 800–1000 m^3 of its production capacity.[808]

2. Long Term Capacity Booking: GDF Suez and E.ON

a. GDF Suez

1) Subject Matter

The case[809] is related to the anticompetitive practices conducted by GDF Suez in the French gas market, such as long-term reservation of transport capacity and a network of import agreements, but also underinvestment in import infrastructure capacity.[810] GDF Suez is the leading gas supplier in France which controls, via its subsidiary GRTgaz, the most important gas transmission networks in France. GDF Suez clearly enjoyed a dominant position in the gas import and supply markets in the two French balancing zones (North and South) of the GRTgaz transport network.

806 Ibid., para. 26.

807 European Commission, Antitrust: Commission opens formal proceedings against Czech electricity incumbent ČEZ, 2011.

808 Case AT 39.727, *ČEZ*, Summary of Commission Decision of 10 April 2013, para. 11; European Commission, Antitrust: Commission accepts commitments from ČEZ concerning the Czech electricity market and makes them legally binding, 2013.

809 Case COMP/39.316, *GDF Suez*, Commission decision of 3 December 2009.

810 European Commission, Antitrust: Commission opens formal proceedings against Gaz de France concerning suspected gas supply restrictions, 2008.

Suspecting that GDF Suez infringed upon EU competition rules, the Commission carried out an inspection without prior notice at the premises of GDF Suez on 16 May 2006. Based on this inspection, the Commission initiated, on 22 May 2008, formal antitrust proceedings against GDF Suez with the claim that it abused its dominant position in the French gas market and thus infringed Article 102 TFEU.[811] The Commission claimed that the actions of GDF Suez led to the foreclosure of the downstream natural gas supply market in France through long-term transport capacity reservations. It was concerned that this conduct largely closed off access to the French gas market to other potential gas suppliers.

2) Relevant Market and Dominant Position

In order to determine the relevant product market, the Commission distinguished the gas transmission market and the markets related to the infrastructure.[812] Then, within the gas supply market, the Commission made a distinction between the wholesale supply of gas to the shippers and the retail supply to final customers. In its preliminary assessment, the Commission further divided the product market into two submarkets, namely the supply via the transmission or the distribution network and supply by a particular type of customer (household, professional or industrial).[813] For the markets related to gas infrastructure, the Commission defined a market in terms of gas import capacity, including import capacity via gas pipelines and via LNG terminals. Concerning geographic markets, the Commission determined that each balancing zone of the transport network in France constituted a geographic market for gas supply because of the different conditions for transporting gas to and between those zones. Moreover, the zones differed with regard to market shares of suppliers.[814]

---

811 Ibid.

812 Case COMP/39.316, *GDF Suez*, Commission decision of 3 December 2009, para. 11; Hofmann, 2013, p. 286.

813 Ibid., para. 13.

814 Ibid., para. 16.

According to the preliminary assessment of the Commission, it has been provisionally concluded that GDF Suez held a dominant position on the gas import and supply markets in each of the balancing zones (North and South) of the GRTgaz transport network.[815]

3) Preliminary Assessment and Decision

On 22 June 2009, the Commission adopted a preliminary assessment concerning the alleged infringements carried out by GDF and its subsidiaries, GRT S.A. and Elengy S.A. (known jointly as "GDF Suez") in the French gas market. After its investigation, the Commission concluded that GDF Suez abused its dominant position in a way infringing Article 102 TFEU and foreclosed access to gas import capacities in France. This situation caused the restriction of competition in the supply market. It can be said that the foreclosure was the result of the long-term reservation of most of the import capacity of France.[816]

The Commission stated that with the import capacity of GDF, including the interconnection capacity between the Northern and Southern balancing zones of GRTgaz network in France, the gas infrastructure constituted an important component regarding access to this infrastructure and that import capacity was a requirement for supplying gas in the balancing zones of the GRTgaz network.[817] According to the findings of the Commission, GDF Suez reserved on a long-term basis an important percentage of the import capacity of GRTgaz network in each balancing zone. As a result of this long-term reservation, third-party shippers lacked the necessary access to this capacity under conditions which would allow them to exert effective competition on the downstream gas supply markets in these zones (long-term capacity booking).[818]

815 Ibid., para. 18.
816 Notice published pursuant to Article 27(4) of Council Regulation (EC) No 1/2003 in Case COMP/B-1/39.316 – Gaz de France (gas market foreclosure), OJ C 156, pp. 25–26, para. 2–3.
817 Case COMP/39.316, *GDF Suez*, para. 26.
818 Ibid., para. 30.

In its preliminary assessment, the Commission realised that there are further competition-related issues concerning a possible refusal by GDF Suez to supply import capacity at the Fos Cavaou LNG terminal.[819] Although there was a demand for reserving a significant amount of the capacity, GDF Suez did not perform a clear, open, transparent and non-discriminative process for allocating its capacity in the new Fos Cavaou terminal on a long-term basis. As a result, only one third-party supplier (Total) could obtain long-term capacities at the Fos Cavaou terminal.[820]

The Commission found that GDF Suez ignored the genuine proposals of third-party shippers to co-finance the construction of the Fos Cavaou terminal. Moreover, GDF Suez did not explore the possibility of increasing its reception capacity in order to facilitate third-party access to this infrastructure while the terminal was being built.[821] Furthermore, GDF Suez allocated a substantial proportion of total capacity at the Fos Cavaou terminal to its own gas trading division on a long-term basis.[822]

Finally, the Commission expressed concerns regarding GDF Suez's strategic limitation of investments in additional capacities at the Montoir de Bretagne liquid-gas terminal. It found that, even though GDF Suez knew that there was a demand for additional capacity and in spite of a study showing that extending capacity would have been profitable, GDF Suez refused to supply by means of a strategic limitation of investments in additional capacities (so-called strategic underinvestment). According to the Commission, GDF Suez's refusal might constitute an infringement of Article 102 TFEU.[823] In deciding not to extend the import capacities, GDF Suez had denied third parties' extra capacity requests at the Montoir de Bretagne liquid-gas terminal and also narrowed the

819 Ibid., para. 31.

820 *"On the contrary, the preliminary assessment showed that GDF Suez made third-party access to the Fos Cavaou terminal conditional on receiving nonmonetary strategic assets in return and that, as a result, no third-party (other than Total) obtained long-term capacity at the Fos Cavaou terminal."* Ibid., para. 32.

821 Ibid., para. 33.

822 Ibid., para. 34.

823 Monti, 2017, p. 32; Hofmann, 2013, p. 285; Case COMP/39.316, *GDF Suez*, para. 40.

access possibilities, which made the gas import into France even more difficult.[824]

On 3 December 2009, the Commission adopted a decision making the commitments of GDF Suez legally binding. As an urgent measure, GDF Suez committed to release a large share of its long-term gas import capacity reservations in France to third parties in order to enable third-party shippers to reinforce rapidly their position on the downstream gas supply markets in France, thus increasing the competitive pressure on GDF Suez in the short term.[825] Furthermore, GDF Suez committed to release significant firm long-term capacities at the Montoir de Bretagne and Fos Cavaou LNG terminals to third parties in the short term. In the long term, GDF Suez guaranteed to reduce its capacity reservations below 50% of total firm as of October 2014.[826]

According to *Kroes*, the commitments offered by GDF Suez enabled competitors to enter the French gas market. Consequently, consumers were offered a greater choice of gas suppliers and more competitive prices. The commitments assured to enable effective structural access to French gas import infrastructure and contributed to an integrated and competitive single European energy market, which could provide a secure supply of energy at affordable prices.[827]

b. E.ON

1) Subject Matter

The case[828] is related to the competition-restricting conduct of E.ON AG and its subsidiaries, E.ON Ruhrgas AG and E.ON Gastransport GmbH, in the German gas supply and transmission markets. E.ON is one of the

824 *"As a result, GDF Suez not only prevented another shipper that had submitted a firm capacity request in the open season procedure from reserving capacity on a long-term basis, but it also greatly restricted any possibility of third-party access to this infrastructure until 2023, thereby making it even more difficult for third parties to import gas into France."* Case COMP/39.316, *GDF Suez*, para. 38.

825 Ibid., para. 67.

826 Ibid., para. 47.

827 European Commission, Antitrust: Commission accepts commitments by GDF Suez to boost competition in French gas market, 2009.

828 Case COMP/39.317, *E.ON Gas*, Commission Decision of 4 May 2010.

largest European energy companies and performs production, transportation, distribution and supply of electricity and gas activities on a European level. It is the largest natural gas supplier in Germany, and it also operates the largest German gas transmission network.

On 22 December 2009, the Commission initiated antitrust proceedings with an abuse claim against E.ON. The proceedings concerned an abuse of a dominant position in the form of a refusal to supply. According to the Commission, this could have been achieved by way of long-term bookings on E.ON's gas transmission network, resulting in a foreclosure of competitors from access to that network. The suspected practice would have constituted an infringement of Article 102 TFEU.

2) Relevant Market and Dominant Position

In its assessment, the Commission made a distinction between the gas supply market and the gas transport market. According to the Commission, the distinction in terms of the gas transport market is dependent on whether the transport capacity is contracted as firm or interruptible capacity. A further distinction was made between the transport of the H-gas (high-calorific gas) and L-Gas (low-calorific gas).[829] The transport of these two different gases is made through different pipelines and different networks.

Within the gas supply market, a distinction can be made between the sale of gas to wholesalers (wholesale level) and to end customers (retail level). At the wholesale level, the Commission and the Bundeskartellamt generally make this distinction[830]:

- Supra-regional gas companies, which purchase (import) gas from producers (mostly abroad), supply, *inter alia*, regional wholesalers which have no access to gas production.
- Regional wholesalers sell gas to small local and regional distributors, i.e. mostly "Stadtwerke".

At the retail level, the Commission and the Bundeskartellamt made a distinction between supply of gas to large industrial customers and the

829 Ibid., para. 15.
830 Ibid., para. 16.

supply of gas to small customers (i.e. household and small commercial customers).[831]

The relevant geographic market was the respective gas transport network (E.ON Gastransport's L-Gas network or E.ON H-Gas network, including the NCG market area). The Commission concluded that E.ON held a dominant position in both the H- and L-gas transport markets as well as in the markets for the supply of wholesalers and the retail supply to industrial customers.

3) Preliminary Assessment and Decision

In its preliminary assessment dated on 22 December 2009, the Commission found that E.ON reserved significant parts of the available firm and freely allocable entry capacities at the entry points giving access to its gas transmission grid and that such an action caused foreclosure of competitors trying to transport and sell gas to customers connected to the E.ON grid.[832] Only little or no free capacity had been available to competitors wanting to transport gas into the network. As a result, E.ON had restricted competition in the downstream gas supply markets.[833] The Commission also held that E.ON's long-distance gas transmission network constitutes an essential facility. Access to it was objectively necessary to carry out business in the gas supply markets within E.ON's grid areas.[834] The evidence found by the Commission indicated that the capacity situation was not likely to improve in the next years and therefore competitors would not be able to compete freely and effectively. Indeed, based on current bookings it was clear that the capacity problem would remain at least until 2019.

On 4 May 2010, the Commission took a decision according to Article 9 of the European Union Directive 1/2003. In this decision, the

831 Ibid., para. 17.

832 "*The Commission came to the provisional conclusion that E.ON may have abused its dominant position on the markets for the supply of end customers in the form of a refusal to supply by way of long-term bookings on E.ON's gas transmission system, thereby violating Article 102 of the Treaty on the Functioning of the European Union ('TFEU').*" Ibid., para. 2.

833 Ibid., Summary of Commission Decision, para. 3.

834 Ibid., para. 32.

commitments of E.ON were declared to be legally binding. E.ON committed to release large capacity volumes at the entry points to its gas networks by October 2010. The capacities released at different entry points by October 2010 correspond to around 15% of the pipeline capacity and were to be published on the website of E.ON Gastransport. As of October 2015, E.ON further reduced its entry capacity bookings in its grid for low-calorific gas to 64% of the pipeline capacity and in the NetConnect Germany grid to 50%. The Commission expected the commitments to have a major structural impact by opening German gas market to new entrants, to the benefit of domestic and industrial gas consumers.[835]

In this case, the Commission did not impose a structural remedy, e.g. unbundling of the network. It believed that the reduction of E.ON's share of transport capacity into its transmission grid would lead to a permanent change in the structure of German gas transport markets. The Commission highlighted that commitments must relate directly to a specific, potentially abusive, behaviour and must constitute a necessary, adequate and proportionate remedy. The behaviour identified by the Commission in its preliminary assessment concerned capacity reservations by E.ON as a shipper of gas.[836] The Commission concluded that unbundling would therefore not have resolved the competition problem in this case, as E.ON's long-term reservations would still close off competitors even if the grid would have been sold to another operator.[837]

835 European Commission, Antitrust: E.ON's commitments open up German gas market to competitors, 2010. The European Commission has released the German energy firm E.ON from commitments to reduce long-term bookings on the German gas grid almost five years ahead of schedule since E.ON successfully implemented its commitments and competition on the market has increased significantly. European Commission, Antitrust: successful opening of German gas markets allows early termination of E.ON commitments, 2016.

836 European Commission, Antitrust: Commission's commitment decision opens German gas pipelines to competitors – frequently asked questions, 2010.

837 However, in September 2010 the E.ON Gastransport (now Open Grid Europe) has been fully unbundled from the parent company E.ON and set up as an independent transmission operator. In November 2011, E.ON informed the Commission of its planned divestment of Open Grid Europe, and the sale has been completed seven months later.

On 24 June 2016, E.ON requested to be released from the commitments. The Commission's assessment showed that E.ON was no longer dominant in the gas transport market due to the divestment of its grid and that it is not evident that E.ON could still have a dominant position in the relevant gas supply markets.[838] In July 2016, the Commission released E.ON from its commitments to reduce long-term bookings on the German gas grid almost five years ahead of schedule. The Commission concluded that competition on the market increased significantly as a result of successful implementation of the commitments by E.ON. The E.ON case set a good example of how the Commission's commitments decision can open up markets to competition quickly and effectively.[839] The commitments were deemed no longer necessary to ensure sufficient gas transport capacity for E.ON's competitors.

3. Summary

a. Refusal to Supply

Generally, any undertaking, whether it is in a dominant position or not, should have the right to choose its trading partners and to decide whether to supply them or not.[840] Contractual freedom is one of the most important features of all market economies.[841] Undertakings in a dominant position do not have an absolute duty to supply all those who request them to do so.[842] However, contractual freedom is sometimes limited by certain provisions, such as Article 102 TFEU. The Commission therefore was of the opinion that an intervention based

838 Case AT.39.767, *E.ON Gas*, Commission Decision of 26 July 2016, para. 12.

839 European Commission, Antitrust: successful opening of German gas markets allows early termination of E.ON commitments, 2016.

840 European Commission, Guidance on the Commission's enforcement priorities in applying Article 82 of the EC Treaty to abusive exclusionary conduct by dominant undertakings, 2009, para. 75; Opinion Advocate-General Jacobs in Case C-7/97, *Oscar Bronner GmbH v Mediaprint Zeitungs-und Zeitschriftenverlag*, [1998] ECR I-7791, para. 56: *"the right to choose one's trading partners and freely to dispose of one's property are generally recognised principles in the laws of the Member States [...] Incursions on those rights require careful justification."*

841 Hauteclocque, 2016, p. 335.

842 Jones & Sufrin, 2016, p. 496.

on EU competition rules requires a careful analysis where the application of Article 102 TFEU would lead to the imposition of a supply obligation on the dominant undertaking.[843]

According to the Commission, the existence of such an obligation may reduce the undertakings' incentives to invest and innovate and, thereby, possibly harm consumers. On the one hand, being aware of the fact that they may be obliged to supply against their will may lead dominant undertakings — or undertakings which anticipate that they may become dominant — not to invest, or to invest less, in the activity in question. On the other hand, competitors may be tempted to free ride on investments made by the dominant undertaking instead of investing themselves. Neither of these consequences would, in the long run, be in the interest of consumers.[844]

Although all of the above-mentioned abuse cases in the energy sector, which concern types of anticompetitive behaviour (capacity hoarding and degradation, strategic underinvestment, margin squeeze and long-term bookings), may seem quite different, the Commission considered all these practices as a similar type of the abuse of a dominant position under Article 102 TFEU, namely refusal to grant access to essential facilities, a prominent sub-category of the refusal-to-supply concept.[845] As a general principle, an objectively unjustifiable refusal to supply by an undertaking holding a dominant position on a market constitutes an infringement of Article 102 TFEU.[846]

The Commission defined an essential facility as a facility or infrastructure which is essential for reaching customers and/or enabling competitors to carry on their business, and which cannot be replicated by any reasonable means.[847] A facility is essential if its duplication is impossible or extremely difficult due to physical, geographical, legal or

843 European Commission, Guidance on the Commission's enforcement priorities in applying Article 82 of the EC Treaty to abusive exclusionary conduct by dominant undertakings, 2009, para. 75.

844 Ibid.

845 Koch & Gauer, 2011, p. 223.

846 London Economics, 1997, p. 138.

847 European Commission, Notice on the application of the Competition Rules to access agreements in the telecommunications sector, 1998, para. 68

economic constraints.[848] The essential-facility doctrine imposes on owners of essential facilities a duty to deal with competitors[849]; in other words, holders of an "essential facility" can be obliged under competition law to grant access to this facility. According to the Commission's case practice, a refusal to grant access to an essential facility might constitute an abuse within the scope of Article 102 TFEU under the following circumstances[850]:

- Access to a facility is indispensable and objectively necessary to be able to compete effectively on a downstream market.
- The refusal is likely to lead to the elimination of effective competition on the downstream market.
- The refusal is not objectively justified and likely to lead to consumer harm.

Taking into consideration these criteria, the Commission concluded in all above-mentioned cases that the incumbents' gas networks should be considered essential facilities, since access to these networks was crucial in order to supply gas to customers within the incumbents' grid areas.[851]

According to the Commission, gas networks should be considered essential facilities due to the fact that transport capacity on a transmission grid is an essential structured component for competing gas suppliers wishing to supply customers on the grids of the gas incumbents. In other words, gas suppliers would not be able to transport gas to their customers as they have no alternative than to use the gas networks' entry points to reach their customers within these networks. Considering high investment costs and long construction periods, the

848 Essential Facility, https://www.concurrences.com/en/droit-de-la-concurrence/glossary-of-competition-terms/Essential-facility (accessed: 1 June 2019).

849 Evrard, 2004.

850 European Commission, Guidance on the Commission's enforcement priorities in applying Article 82 of the EC Treaty to abusive exclusionary conduct by dominant undertakings, 2009, para. 81.

851 Case COMP/39.402, *RWE Gas Foreclosure*, Commission Decision of 18 March 2009, para. 22; Case COMP/39.317, *E.ON Gas*, Commission Decision of 4 May 2010, para. 32.

Commission concluded that the transport infrastructure could not easily be replicated by competitors.[852]

In all cases, the Commission determined that the gas incumbents not only controlled the markets for gas transport but all of them held dominant positions in one or more gas supply markets and, moreover, could maintain, or reinforce, their position by foreclosing access to the transmission grid.[853] The refusal was in all cases found to be likely to hinder competition, and given the importance of the pipelines for the dramatically underdeveloped supply competition, there could be no doubt about the existence of the risk of consumer harm.[854] Moreover, the Commission concluded that there was no obvious objective justification for the alleged anticompetitive behaviour.

b. Capacity Hoarding/Capacity Degradation and Margin Squeeze

The above-mentioned practices of RWE, ENI and ČEZ constitute typical examples of an abuse by vertically integrated undertakings. In these cases, the Commission gathered evidence indicating that the above-mentioned companies pursued a systematic strategy aimed at keeping barriers for preventing new entrants from getting access to capacity on their networks. From the perspective of a dominant undertaking, indeed, it can make economical sense to avoid competition in the downstream business in order to protect their own supply business from competitive pressure through alternative offers.[855] The Commission found that RWE, ENI and ČEZ performed a great variety of abusive behaviours, such as primary and secondary capacity hoarding, capacity degradation, capacity mismanagement, margin squeeze or strategic underinvestment strategies, in order to favour their own supply business.[856]

"Capacity hoarding" and "capacity degradation" are not defined as legal terms. While "capacity hoarding" usually refers to refusal to grant access to capacity available on the transport network, "capacity degrada-

852 Case COMP/39.317, *E.ON Gas*, para. 33.
853 Cardoso et al., 2010, p. 10.
854 Ibid., p. 10; Koch & Gauer, 2011, p. 224.
855 Koch & Gauer, 2011, p. 215.
856 Hofmann, 2013, p. 263.

tion" refers to the granting of access to capacity in a less useful way.[857] According to the Commission, there are two types of capacity hoarding, namely primary and secondary capacity hoarding. Primary capacity hoarding is defined as practices by which an undertaking makes less transport capacities available than it could. Secondary capacity hoarding concerns a strategy according to which energy companies "hoard" capacities they actually do not need.[858] In both the RWE and the ENI Cases, the Commission found indications for an understatement of the available transport capacity by the TSO (primary capacity hoarding). The actual quantity of the capacity on RWE and ENI's gas networks was different than set out in their statement.

According to *Koch & Gauer*, the main obstacle to establishing primary capacity hoarding is, from a competition law enforcement perspective, related to the complexity of capacity calculation in gas transport pipeline systems. Particularly, capacity calculation in complex transport systems with numerous entry points is not just an equation that depends on simple technical parameters which can easily be verified by competition authorities. Capacity calculation may require a highly complex analysis not only of the technical setup but also of the possible and actual gas flows in the entire grid.[859] Although it may be difficult for a competition authority to recalculate the exact capacity available at different entry points, there are certain indications to determine the understatement of the available capacity. In order to establish capacity understatement, the actual gas flows at a given entry or exit point can be analysed. If gas flows exceed systematically and significantly the indicated maximum available capacity, it may indicate a primary hoarding strategy.[860] In ČEZ Case, the Commission concluded that ČEZ hoarded capacities it actually did not need (secondary capacity hoarding).

As regards capacity degradation, the concept of abusive capacity degradation was first applied by the Commission in its ENI Decision. The Commission found evidence that ENI might have intentionally

857 European Commission, Antitrust: Commission confirms sending Statement of Objections to ENI concerning the Italian gas market, 2009.

858 Koch & Gauer, 2011, p. 216.

859 Ibid.

860 Ibid.

delayed allocation of new available capacity or fragmented it into sales of short-term capacity even when it could have been offered on a longer-term basis.[861] The Commission alleged that ENI's allocation procedures caused separate and uncoordinated capacity sales on complementary pipelines.[862] Moreover, the Commission found that the capacity offered by ENI was interruptible and not firm.[863] As mentioned above, the Commission determined that such practice led to a foreclosure of competitors trying to supply gas into Italy and therefore restricted competition on the downstream gas supply markets.[864]

As mentioned above, there were concerns raised by the Commission that RWE might have abused its dominant position at the downstream level by means of a margin squeeze. The Commission found evidence that RWE followed a strategy whereby it could squeeze margins of its competitors on the downstream gas supply markets by setting its transmission tariffs at an artificially high level. Such a conduct could limit competitors' or potential entrants' ability to enter the market or maintain their position within the market, which could prevent even an efficient competitor from competing effectively.[865] The establishment of a margin squeeze usually requires a detailed calculation of the dominant undertaking's cost base (e. g. its long-term average incremental costs).

c. Long-term Capacity Booking

The GDF Suez and E.ON Gas decisions dealt with the issue that E.ON and GDF booked almost the entire capacity on their gas networks on a long-term basis for their own supply businesses, leaving virtually no place for a third party to transport gas.[866] The issue of lack of transport capacities in Europe was discussed in the course of an energy sector inquiry. According to the inquiry, the vast majority of the primary ca-

---

861 Case COMP/39.315, *ENI*, para. 51.
862 Ibid., para. 53.
863 Ibid., para. 54.
864 Ratliff & Grasso, 2012, p. 5.
865 Case COMP/39.402, *RWE Gas Foreclosure*, para. 30.
866 Cardoso et al., 2010, p. 8. In other words, the incriminated behaviour consisted in the booking of large parts of capacities through GDF Suez' and E.ON's supply businesses on their "own" transmission network. See: Koch & Gauer, 2011, p. 221.

pacity is typically held by only one or two market players, which are incumbents in their home markets.[867] Mostly, integrated gas or electricity suppliers sign long-term capacity bookings with their downstream affiliate, which leave rather smaller capacities available to their competitors.[868] Consequently, the competitors are not able to gain access to the pipelines necessary to reach their gas customers. The refusal leads to the prevention of the development of effective competition in the downstream market. The energy sector inquiry found that the newly created third-party access rights and non-discrimination rules, intended to open up the incumbents' transmission networks, often had only limited or no effect, as most or even all gas transport capacities had already been booked through the vertically integrated owner of the networks.[869] This issue was, for the first time at all in competition law, tackled by the Commission in the GDF Suez and E.ON decisions.

In the GDF Suez and E.ON cases, the Commission focused on these two companies as shippers, not as transmission system operators, unlike the cases with RWE and E.ON. The GDF Suez and E.ON cases concerned reservations of capacity through the shipper of an integrated company on its own transmission network. In other words, the incriminated behaviour consisted in the booking of large parts of capacities through GDF Suez' and E.ON's supply businesses on their "own" transmission network.[870]

While the commitments of RWE and ENI aimed at eliminating the incentive to discriminate and at the correction of market distortion in the long-run, the commitments of GDF Suez and E.ON resulted in an immediate and long-term release of network capacity. However, given the duration of the commitments and the developments in the sector-specific regulation, the commitments of GDF Suez and E.ON would, if properly overseen, also lead to a permanent change in the structure of gas markets.[871]

867 European Commission, Energy Sector Inquiry, 2007, p. 74.
868 Fumagalli et al., 2018, p. 469.
869 Cardoso et al., 2010, p. 8.
870 Koch & Gauer, 2011, p. 222.
871 Talus, 2011, p. 279.

d. Strategic Underinvestment

For the first time, the Commission referred in the GDF Suez and ENI cases to "strategic underinvestment" in the energy markets. It stated that an undertaking in a dominant position which holds an essential facility is under an obligation to take "all possible measures to remove the constraints imposed by the lack of capacity and to organise its business in a manner that makes a maximum amount of capacity of the essential facility available".[872]

In the GDF case, the Commission concluded that the strategic underinvestment prevented another shipper, which had submitted a capacity request in the open season procedure, from reserving capacity on a long-term basis and hindered competitors' access to the infrastructure for several years.[873] It can be stated that, in the Commission's view, an undertaking which holds an essential facility may be obliged to share the existing capacity, or even to make specific investments to expand the capacity, of its facility if there is appropriate demand and it makes economic sense to do so, looking at the facility concerned on a stand-alone basis.[874]

B. Exclusionary Abuses (Customer Foreclosure)

1. Distrigas

a. Subject Matter

The case[875] is related to the competition-restricting conduct of Distrigas S.A./Distrigas N.V. (hereafter "Distrigas") in the Belgian gas market. Distrigas was the largest incumbent gas supplier and importer in the Belgian wholesale market. It was also operating in the gas supply markets in other European countries, such as Germany, France and the Netherlands, as well as in the gas transit and LNG markets. Distrigas was a subsidiary of Suez Group until it was sold to the Italian company ENI in May 2008.

---

872 Case COMP/39.315, *ENI*, dipnot 43.
873 Merlino & Faella, 2013, p. 528.
874 Ratliff & Grasso, 2012.
875 Case COMP/37.966, *Distrigas*, Commission Decision of 11 October 2007.

On 26 February 2004, the Commission initiated antitrust proceedings against Distrigas concerning its gas supply agreements with industrial clients. The Commission expressed concern that Distrigas prevented consumers from switching supplier and, hence, restricted them from entering into contracts with other gas suppliers through its long-term gas supply contracts. In this way, Distrigas foreclosed the entrance of its rivals into the Belgian gas supply market.[876]

b. Relevant Market and Dominant Position

According to the Commission, the relevant product market was the supply of high-calorific gas to customers having a gas consumption of over 1 million m^3 per annum and connected to the transport network or the distribution network.[877] The Commission furthermore determined Belgium as the relevant geographical market. It identified the relevant geographical market, based on its assessment of the legal and the regulatory regime, the structure of the market and the price differences between Belgium and neighbouring Member States.[878]

According to the preliminary assessment, Distrigas had a dominant position in the market related to gas supply for large clients in Belgium.[879] With very few exceptions, customers only had one gas supplier; therefore, competition in the gas supply market solely took place when a contract expired and a new contract was concluded.

c. Preliminary Assessment and Decision

On 30 June 2005, the Commission adopted the preliminary assessment regarding the gas supply contracts with various customers such as the industrial users, electricity producers and resellers. Given that Distrigas had a dominant position in the Belgian supply market, the Commission expressed concern that access to customers could be foreclosed due to the duration of the contracts and the volumes of gas tied to Distrigas.[880]

876 Ibid., para. 2.
877 Ibid., para. 11.
878 Ibid., para. 12.
879 Ibid., para. 13.
880 Ibid., para. 18.

With respect to the duration of the contracts, in Belgium the standard duration of a gas transport contract with the network operator was generally one year. As for the volumes of gas, the contracts between Distrigas and its customers could be generally divided into two categories:

- contracts which contained explicit clauses requiring the customer to buy all their gas from Distrigas, and
- contracts which contained a fixed annual contractual quantity or an annual minimum quantity.[881]

The Commission found that some contracts had tacit renewal clauses. In other words, the contract was renewed automatically when it expired, until one of the parties explicitly terminated it. Other contracts did not even have a specific termination date, and the contract remained in force unless one of the parties explicitly terminated it. Thus, the Commission considered both those types of contracts to be of indefinite duration.[882]

In this case, the Commission took a conservative approach when calculating the level of foreclosure in the market. Since the customers concerned in the relevant markets were industrial buyers and the gas they bought represented a significant part of their overall costs, it was assumed that they would terminate a contract if it was in their economic interest and if they were able to do so. Customers thus were considered to be tied to their contracts until the first opportunity they had to terminate the contract.[883]

Distrigas offered various commitments to open the Belgian gas market. On 11 October 2007, the Commission decided that the commitments of Distrigas were legally binding.[884] Distrigas undertook not to include tacit renewal clause in any new Gas Supply Agreement. The parties agreed that no new contract with industrial users and/or electricity producers would be longer than five years. Moreover, Distrigas undertook not to conclude any gas supply agreements with resellers with

881 Ibid., para. 19.
882 Ibid., para. 22.
883 Ibid.
884 European Commission, Antitrust: Commission opens Belgian gas market to competition, 2007.

a duration of over two years. In addition, Distrigas committed to ensure that for each calendar year a minimum of 65% and on average for all calendar years a minimum of 70% of the gas volumes to be supplied by itself and related undertakings to industrial users and electricity producers in Belgium would return to the market.[885] In other words, only 30% of total volumes sold by Distrigas could be tied to contracts with a duration longer than a year.[886] This would allow alternative suppliers to make a competing offer to the customers concerned.

2. EDF

a. Subject Matter

The case[887] is related to the competition-restricting practices of EDF, the incumbent electricity supplier largely owned by the French State, in the French electricity market. On 18 July 2007, the Commission initiated antitrust proceedings against EDF with the claim that EDF abused its dominant position and thus infringed Article 102 TFEU. The alleged infringement took the form of long-term contracts concluded by EDF with final consumers of electricity in France, in particular large industrial consumers. It was suspected that these contracts prevented customers from switching suppliers, thereby significantly foreclosing the markets concerned.[888]

b. Relevant Market and Dominant Position

Taking into consideration the previous decisions of the Commission concerning the electricity sector, it can be observed that the Commission divided the relevant market into three groups, based on the retail supply of electricity to end users:

885 Case COMP/37.966, *Distrigas*, para. 27.
886 Talus, 2011, p. 155.
887 Case COMP/39.386, *EDF (Long Term Electricity Contracts in France)*, Commission Decision of 17 March 2010.
888 European Commission, Opening of Proceedings, 2007.

- the supply of electricity to large industrial and commercial customers,
- the supply of electricity to small industrial and commercial customers, and
- the supply of electricity to residential customers.

Concerning the market for the supply of large industrial and commercial customers, the Commission distinguished customers who have exercised their eligibility and other customers. The relevant market concerned only customers who have exercised their eligibility[889]. As for the relevant geographical market, the Commission concluded the geographic dimension of the market for the supply of electricity to large industrial customers was national, thus rejecting a wider geographical scope.[890]

As a result of its investigation, the Commission decided that EDF, which had a near-monopoly of the production, transmission, distribution and supply of electricity in France before liberalisation, held a dominant position in the market for the supply of electricity to large industrial customers in France.[891]

c. Preliminary Assessment and Decision

According to the preliminary assessment, the Commission took the view that EDF may have abused its dominant position in the relevant market and thus infringed upon Article 102 TFEU by means of:

---

889 In order to differentiate large customers who have exercised their eligibility from smaller customers, the Commission took the view that a distinction should be made on the basis of the volume of consumption and that the relevant market should be limited to the supply of large customers for sites with an annual consumption of 7 GWh or more. Case COMP/39.386, *EDF*, para. 19.

890 Ibid., para. 23. The Commission's decision regarding the relevant geographical market was in line with its previous decision-making practice. See, for example, COMP/M.4180, *GDF/SUEZ*, Commission Decision of 14 November 2006, para. 169; COMP/M.3883, *GDF/Centrica/SPE*, Commission Decision of 7 September 2005; COMP/M.3318, *ECS/Sibelga*, Commission Decision of 19 December 2003, para. 8; COMP/M.3075 – 3080, *ECS/Intercommunales*, Commission Decision of 13 February 2003, para. 7; COMP/M.2857, *M.Ecs/IEH*, Commission Decision of 23 December 2002, para. 5.

891 Case COMP/39.386, *EDF*, para. 25.

- concluding contracts with large industrial customers which foreclosed the market of electricity supply to large industrial customers both to undertakings wishing to operate as principal suppliers or as secondary suppliers in France, due to their scope, duration and nature of the contracts, and
- imposing resale restrictions in its contracts for the supply of electricity to large industrial customers in France.

The Commission found that contracts concluded by EDF with industrial customers made it more difficult for alternative suppliers enter into the French market and to acquire EDF's customers. Consequently, customers were not able to switch suppliers, which led to market foreclosure.[892]

The vast majority of EDF contracts indeed contained restrictive clauses either explicitly requiring the customers to exclusively source their electricity from EDF (de jure exclusivity) or through the application of a set of clauses having the same effect, thereby creating strong incentives for customers to source their electricity exclusively from EDF (de facto exclusivity).[893] Moreover, the Commission stated that EDF imposed clauses in its supply contracts that restricted the resale of electricity by large industrial customers. According to the Commission, these clauses restricting the use of electricity by the customer were widespread and had been so for a number of years.[894]

EDF submitted commitments addressing the Commission concerns, and on 17 March 2010 the Commission decided that the commitments of EDF were legally binding. Within the scope of those commitments, EDF undertook that, as of 1 January 2010, for each calendar year during which the commitments apply at least 60%, and on average for all the calendar years during which the commitments apply at least 65%, of the electricity supplied to large industrial customers, either directly or through a buying group, would be returned to the market.[895] Moreover, EDF pledged that the maximum duration of new contracts for the supply of electricity to large industrial customers

892 Ibid., para. 31.
893 Ibid., para. 32.
894 Ibid., para. 36.
895 Ibid., para. 43.

would not exceed five years and that EDF would offer two alternative types of contract, one of which will effectively allow the customer to contract for additional supplies with another supplier of its choice.[896] As for the restricting clauses, EDF undertook to cease restricting the resale of volumes of electricity bought from it by large industrial customers.[897]

3. Summary

While the RWE, ENI, ČEZ, GDF Suez and E.ON cases dealt with the competition-restrictive conduct of undertakings dominant in their relevant markets which led to the foreclosure of access to their gas transmission networks, the Distrigas and EDF cases concerned anticompetitive practices by which energy incumbents essentially tried to keep their customer base for themselves through supply contracts with an extremely long-duration (customer foreclosure).[898]

Long-term supply contracts are bilateral energy exchange agreements between a seller and an end customer that are characterised by long-term commitments with exclusive purchasing obligations or exclusive supply obligations. These long-term contracts aim at binding the customer as long as possible, as a result of which switching the provider or market participation by third-party supplier becomes impossible. These long-term supply contracts (so-called downstream supply contracts) are to be used to delimit the long-term gas import contracts (so-called upstream supply contracts) concluded between the natural gas producer (e.g. Gazprom) and the regional gas companies (e.g. E.ON Ruhrgas). These gas import contracts are also characterised by take-or-pay clauses and long-term ties.[899] Such long-term gas import contracts have so far been considered a necessary component of EU security of supply. Due to the increasing flexibility that LNG, spot markets and other unconventional opportunities for gas production

896 Ibid., para. 45–46.
897 Ibid., para. 49.
898 Koch & Gauer, 2011, p. 228.
899 Through long-term contracts, the buyer, in many cases the national energy supply monopoly, could secure the national energy supply in the medium and long-term and make investment decisions based on predictable transportation needs. Talus, 2011, p. 277; Hofmann, 2013, pp. 252–253.

(e.g. shale gas) provide, this traditional structure is currently undergoing a transformation.[900]

The Commission set out its antitrust policy regarding long-term energy supply contracts in its Distrigas and EDF decisions. Distrigas was the first decision by which the Commission pursued long-term gas supply contracts under Article 102 TFEU. The Distrigas decision established a system for long-term supply contracts, also known as the Distrigas model. With the EDF decision, this model was transferred equally to the electricity sector. Long-term energy supply contracts between suppliers and large industrial consumers are not prohibited by EU competition rules per se.[901] On the contrary, each case must be assessed on its merits.[902] In order to determine whether long-term contracts foreclose markets, the following five criteria must be taken into account[903]:

- the market position of the supplier;
- the share of the customer's demand tied under the contract;
- the duration of the contracts;
- the overall share of the market covered by contracts containing such ties;
- efficiencies.

The Commission concluded that Distrigas and EDF both clearly held a dominant position on the relevant supply markets and might have abused their dominant position under Article 102 TFEU, because their long-term and/or exclusive supply contracts prevented customers from switching, which led to a restriction of the scope for other gas suppliers to conclude contracts with customers and so foreclosed their access to the market. It should be noted that the Commission did not refer to a possible infringement of Article 101 TFEU in its decision, unlike the Bundeskartellamt.[904] In its E.ON decision, the Bundeskartellamt con-

900 Talus, 2011, p. 263.
901 Hofmann, 2013, pp. 254.
902 Spanjer, 2009, p. 199.
903 European Commission, Antitrust: Commission increases competition in the Belgian gas market – frequently asked questions, 2007; Hauteclocque, 2009, p. 98.
904 Koch & Gauer, 2011, p. 229.

sidered that a long-term supply contract can be an anticompetitive (vertical) agreement in violation of Article 101 TFEU.[905]

C. Exclusionary Abuses (Destination Clauses)

1. BEH

a. Subject Matter

The case[906] is related to the infringement of Article 102 TFEU through the abuse of a dominant position in the Bulgarian wholesale electricity market and concerns territorial restrictions incorporated in supply agreements entered into by Bulgarian Energy Holding's (BEH) subsidiaries in the electricity wholesale market in Bulgaria. BEH is a vertically integrated energy company owned by the Bulgarian State. BEH's activities include the acquisition, sale and participation in the management of companies active in the upstream markets (e.g., generation, production) and downstream markets (e.g., transmission, distribution, transit, storage) as well as the sale and purchase of electricity, natural gas, coal and other types of raw materials used for the production of electricity.

The Commission had opened the investigation against BEH in late 2012, accusing the company of abusing its dominant position in the Bulgarian wholesale electricity market. The Commission was concerned that competition in the wholesale electricity markets in Bulgaria and neighbouring Member States might be restricted due to territorial restrictions included in the supply agreements by BEH.[907]

b. Relevant Market and Dominant Position

Concerning the relevant product market, the Commission distinguished between the wholesale supply of electricity at regulated prices and the wholesale supply of electricity at freely negotiated prices in the preliminary assessment. According to the Commission, in this case the

905 Bundeskartellamt, *E.ON Ruhrgas*, Decision of 13 January 2006, B8–113/03–01.
906 Case AT.39.767, *BEH Electricity*, Commission Decision of 10 December 2015.
907 European Commission, Antitrust: Commission opens proceedings against Bulgarian Energy Holding, 2012.

relevant product market is the market for the wholesale supply of electricity at freely negotiated prices.[908] In the preliminary assessment, the Commission provisionally concluded that BEH holds a dominant position in the market for the wholesale supply of electricity at freely negotiated prices in Bulgaria.

c. Preliminary Assessment and Decision

According to the preliminary assessment, BEH was abusing its dominant position in the free wholesale market for the supply of electricity in Bulgaria by way of destination clauses in the contracts entered into by BEH's subsidiaries for the wholesale supply of electricity at freely negotiated prices to entities other than end users.[909] The territorial restriction clauses reduced the possibility of independent customers purchasing electricity from production subsidiaries of BEH to resell it to customers outside Bulgaria. The clauses could therefore lead to an increase in trade barriers between Bulgaria and other Member States, which would distort the allocation of electricity within the common market and adversely affect the liquidity and efficiency of its electricity markets.[910]

The Commission took the preliminary view that, as a result of the territorial restrictions, purchasers of electricity are deprived of the possibility to organise the trading of electricity in the wholesale market for the supply of electricity at freely negotiated prices in accordance with their own and their customers' demand.[911] Moreover, the Commission highlighted that the territorial restrictions impede trade in electricity between Bulgaria and other Member States and hinder the development of a wider regional wholesale market within the European Union.[912]

On 10 December 2015, the Commission accepted the commitments offered by the BEH to resolve competition concerns in the wholesale electricity markets in Bulgaria. Firstly, BEH and BEH's subsidiaries undertook not to include destination clauses or any measure of equiva-

908 Case AT.39.767, *BEH Electricity*, para. 33–35.
909 Ibid., para. 49.
910 Subiotto et al., 2016, p. 289.
911 Case AT 39.767, *BEH Electricity*, para. 65.
912 Ibid., para. 67.

lent effect in their contracts for the sale of electricity on the market for the wholesale supply of electricity at freely negotiated prices.[913] Secondly, BEH committed to set up an independent and liquid power exchange in Bulgaria through which electricity can be traded anonymously, with no possibility of checking where it is resold. Thirdly, BEH committed to offer certain volumes of electricity on an independently operated day-ahead market on a newly created power exchange in Bulgaria.[914] A novelty of this case is that the commitments offered by BEH envisage the creation of new market infrastructure rather than the provision of access to existing assets.[915]

2. Gazprom

a. Subject Matter

The case[916] is related to the infringement of EU antitrust rules by pursuing an overall strategy to partition gas markets along national borders in eight Member States (Bulgaria, the Czech Republic, Estonia, Hungary, Latvia, Lithuania, Poland and Slovakia). The Commission opened formal proceedings to investigate accusing Gazprom of hindering competition in the Central and Eastern European gas markets. It was concerned that Gazprom might be abusing its dominant position in the upstream gas supply markets in the Central and Eastern European Member States and therefore might infringe Article 102 TFEU.

Gazprom is an open joint stock company founded in 1993 to take over the State Gas Group Gazprom. Its major business activities are geological exploration, production, transportation, storage, processing and marketing of gas. The Russian State owns a 50.23% controlling stake in Gazprom.

913 Ibid., para. 76.

914 European Commission, Antitrust: Commission accepts commitments by Bulgarian Energy Holding to open up Bulgarian wholesale electricity market, 2015.

915 Ibid., p. 290.

916 Case AT 39.816, *Gazprom – Upstream gas supplies in Central and Eastern Europe*, Commission Decision of 24 May 2018.

The Commission's investigation focused on three alleged anticompetitive practices:

- hindering cross-border gas sales through destination and export ban clause,
- unfair pricing policy, and
- preventing the diversification of the supply of gas.[917]

b. Relevant Market and Dominant Position

The Commission divided the wholesale supply market into the upstream and the downstream wholesale market. It considered that the relevant product market is the market for the upstream wholesale supply of natural gas by producers and exporters to importers and wholesalers.[918] The Commission preliminarily concluded that Gazprom is dominant in all five Central and Eastern European markets[919] for the upstream wholesale supply of gas.[920]

c. Preliminary Assessment and Decision

According to the Commission's preliminary assessment, Gazprom may have infringed EU competition law by pursuing an overall strategy to divide Central and Eastern European gas markets through reducing its customers' ability to resell the gas cross-border. This strategy allowed Gazprom to charge unfair prices in certain Member States. Moreover, by making the supply of gas and gas prices dependent on obtaining unrelated gas transport infrastructure commitments from wholesalers, Gazprom might have abused its dominant position in the wholesale gas supply market.[921]

917 European Commission, Antitrust: Commission sends Statement of Objections to Gazprom for alleged abuse of dominance on Central and Eastern European gas supply markets, 2015.

918 Case AT 39.816, *Gazprom*, para. 3.

919 Bulgaria, Czech Republic, Estonia, Lithuania and Slovakia.

920 Case AT 39.816, *Gazprom*, para. 34.

921 European Commission, Antitrust: Commission sends Statement of Objections to Gazprom for alleged abuse of dominance on Central and Eastern European gas supply markets, 2015.

On 22 April 2015, the Commission sent a statement of objections to Gazprom alleging that Gazprom infringed Article 102 TFEU through some of its business practices in the Central and Eastern European gas markets.[922] The Commission accused Gazprom of abusing its dominant position by imposing territorial restrictions in its supply agreements with gas wholesalers. These territorial restrictions include:

- export ban clauses (which explicitly prohibit the export of gas),
- destination clauses (which stipulate that the customer [wholesaler or industrial customer] must use the purchased gas in its own country or can only sell it to certain customers within its country) and
- other measures preventing the cross-border flow of gas[923].

In addition, according to the Commission's preliminary findings, these territorial restrictions allowed Gazprom to pursue an unfair pricing policy in five Eastern EU Member States by charging prices to wholesalers that are significantly higher compared to Gazprom's costs or to benchmark prices.[924] Furthermore, the Commission was concerned that Gazprom leveraged its market dominance in Bulgaria and Poland by making gas supplies conditional upon obtaining certain infrastructure-related commitments from wholesalers.[925]

In its preliminary assessment, the Commission highlighted that a contract imposing on the purchaser a territorial restriction in the form of an export restriction or a restriction regarding the territory into which goods can be resold may be regarded as a restriction of competition.[926] As mentioned in the BEH decision, the list of abusive practices set out in Article 102 TFEU is not exhaustive. Any practice that leads to a segmentation of the internal market (market partitioning) can be seen as

922 Case AT 39.816, *Gazprom*, para. 34.

923 Ugarte & Di Masi, 2016, p. 22.

924 European Commission, Antitrust: Commission sends Statement of Objections to Gazprom for alleged abuse of dominance on Central and Eastern European gas supply markets, 2015.

925 Ibid.

926 Case AT 39.816, *Gazprom – Upstream gas supplies in Central and Eastern Europe*, Statement of Objections, para. 823.

infringement of EU competition rules by the CJ.[927] According to the Commission, a contract clause restricts competition if such a measure – by artificially altering the conditions of competition – is obviously capable of inducing traders to prioritise to the national market over exports, thereby giving rise to a segregation[928] of the internal market in contrast to the economic interpenetration desired by the Treaty.[929]

The Commission concluded that Gazprom might have infringed Article 102 TFEU based on the above-mentioned reasons[930] and recalled that, for the purpose of proving an abuse of a dominant position within the meaning of Article 102 TFEU, it is sufficient to show that the abusive conduct tends to restrict competition or that the conduct is capable of having that effect.[931]

Even though Gazprom did not agree with the Commission's preliminary view, it offered the following commitments:

- Removal of territorial restrictions and measures of an effect equivalent to such restrictions to the free flow of gas: Gazprom committed not to apply and not to introduce any contractual provisions in its gas supply contracts that may, directly or indirectly, prohibit, restrict or make economically less attractive the customers' ability to re-export or resell gas.
- Establishing a structured process to ensure competitive gas prices: Gazprom committed to extend the scope of the price revision clause by offering this clause also to new customers and by covering contracts with a total duration of at least three years (instead of four years).[932] Relevant Gazprom customers are given an effective tool to make sure their gas price reflects the price level in competitive Western European gas markets, especially at liquid gas hubs.

927 Even though market partitioning cases have mainly been assessed under Article 101 TFEU so far, the Commission in this case applied Article 102. Case AT 39.816, *Gazprom*, Statement of Objections, para. 834.

928 The division of something into sections or categories.

929 Case AT 39.816, *Gazprom*, Statement of Objections, para. 838.

930 Ibid., para. 1238.

931 Ibid., para. 841.

932 Ibid., para. 153.

- No leveraging of dominance in gas supply[933]: Gazprom cannot act on any advantages concerning gas infrastructure which it may have obtained from customers by having leveraged its market position in gas supply.
- Facilitating gas flows to and from isolated markets: Gazprom will enable gas flows to and from parts of Central and Eastern Europe that are still isolated from other Member States due to the lack of interconnectors, namely the Baltic States and Bulgaria.[934]

On 24 May 2018, the Commission adopted a decision making the commitments legally binding on Gazprom after reviewing comments of all stakeholders. According to the Commission's view, the commitments offered by Gazprom have addressed all substantiated concerns in respect of territorial restrictions, prices and infrastructure. The Commission stated that the commitments would contribute to improving the competitiveness and liquidity of the gas markets in the Central and Eastern European countries covered by the investigation.[935]

3. Summary

The first step to creating an internal EU energy market is to remove the major barriers to cross-border energy trade. However, destination clauses and territorial sales restriction clauses, traditionally inserted in long-term upstream gas supply contracts, restrict the territorial area in which gas can be resold by buyers. These clauses involve two different restrictions:

- prohibiting the buyer from reselling the gas into other countries or other areas than those for which it is intended;

933 The Commission was concerned that Gazprom leveraged its dominant market position on the gas supply market to obtain advantages with regard to the access to or control of gas infrastructure. European Commission, Antitrust: Commission imposes binding obligations on Gazprom to enable free flow of gas at competitive prices in Central and Eastern European gas markets, 2018.

934 Ibid.

935 No fines for Gazprom's monopolistic practices in Central Europe?, 2017, https://www.osw.waw.pl (accessed: 1 June 2019).

– preventing a buyer from reselling gas to other customers in the same geographic area.[936]

While allowing for differentiated price setting by giving large gas producers the possibility to sell gas to different buyers at different prices and conditions at the same delivery point, these clauses limit the freedom of the buyer to resell the gas, thus reducing liquidity in the market.

The basis of these clauses is the horizontal and vertical segmentation of the EU energy markets. Traditionally, large producers sold the gas indirectly to end customers through national incumbent suppliers within the area where these incumbents controlled the pipelines as well. These areas were typically the vertically integrated incumbent supplier's immediate home state. These clauses enable suppliers to maintain different price areas for the same product, as they reduce the opportunities of the buyers to resell the gas outside a specific geographic area. Moreover, they also decrease liquidity in the energy markets, making it easier to identify individual transactions and facilitating collusion between market players. Due to the above-mentioned effects in the markets, EU competition law prohibits destination and territorial sales restriction clauses.[937]

The Commission has traditionally reviewed destination clauses within the meaning of Article 101 TFEU.[938] In its GDF/ENI Decision[939], the Commission concluded that the destination clause in the gas transport agreement between GDF and ENI was a restriction of competition and consequently an infringement of Article 101 TFEU on the grounds that it prevented ENI from selling in France the gas that was being

936 Stern, 2005, p. 133.

937 Talus, 2011, p. 159; Murphy, 2014, p. 47.

938 According to Regulation 330/2010 (on the application of Article 101(3) of the Treaty on the Functioning of the European Union to categories of vertical agreements and concerted practices), restrictions of the territory into which a buyer may sell the contracted goods were considered to be a restriction under Article 101 TFEU that remove the benefit of the block exemption. Moreover, it is clear from previous judgments of the CJ that clauses that restrict the buyer's freedom to use the supplied goods in accordance with his own economic interests or restrict the territory into which goods can be resold may be regarded as a restriction on competition, within the meaning of Article 101 TFEU. Case C-319/82 *Société de vente de ciments et béton de l'Est SA v Kerpen & Kerpen GmbH und Co. KG*, [1983] ECR 04173, para. 6; Subiotto et al., 2016, p. 289.

939 Case COMP/38.662, *GDF/ENI*, Commission Decision of 26 October 2004; Case COMP/38.662, *GDF/ENEL*, Commission Decision of 26 October 2004.

transported through France, which precluded customers in France from purchasing that gas.[940] Moreover, the clause caused isolation of the French market, which is incompatible with the creation of an integrated European gas market.[941]

However, for the first time the Commission used Article 102 to investigate these territorial restrictions in the BEH and Gazprom cases. In its BEH decision, even though the practices that were the subject of the Commission's concerns were set out in the contracts that the BEH's subsidiaries entered into with purchasers, the Commission decided to assess these practices under Article 102 TFEU. According to the preliminary assessment of the Commission, its dominant position on the relevant market allowed BEH to impose such conditions on its purchasers. Similarly, in the Gazprom Case, the Commission noted that the fact that an agreement may fall within Article 101 TFEU does not preclude the application of Article 102 TFEU, since this latter Article is *"expressly aimed in fact at situations which clearly originate in contractual relations"*.[942] Admittedly the Commission did not fit the case within one of the established categories of abuse under Article 102 TFEU.[943] However, while Article 102 TFEU does not explicitly refer to the imposition of restrictions regarding destination, the list of abusive practices set out in Article 102 TFEU is not exhaustive.

940 However, according to the settled case-law of the Court of Justice of the European Communities, clauses which restrict the freedom of one of the parties to use the delivered goods in accordance with his own economic interests constitute restrictions of competition within the meaning of Article 81 of the Treaty. In particular, ruling on export bans, the Court ruled that a clause of this kind *"by its very nature [...] constitutes a restriction of competition [...], the objective of which the contractors have agreed to try to isolate part of the contract"*. Case COMP/38.662, *GDF/ENI*, para. 67.

941 Ibid., para. 69.

942 Case AT 39.816, *Gazprom – Upstream gas supplies in Central and Eastern Europe*, para. 832.

943 Subiotto et al., 2016, p. 290.

D. Exploitative Abuses

1. E.ON Electricity

a. Subject Matter

The case[944] is related to the competition-restricting conduct of E.ON AG and its subsidiaries, E.ON Ruhrgas AG and E.ON Gastransport GmbH, in the German gas supply and transmission markets. Believing that E.ON infringed upon EU competition law, the Commission carried out an unannounced inspection at the premises of E.ON on 12 December 2006.[945] The Commission required E.ON to submit very extensive data from the undertakings concerned to establish whether some capacity had effectively not been offered on the short-term market.[946]

Based on the information it obtained during the inspections, the Commission opened two antitrust proceedings against E.ON in 2008. Under the first case, the Commission was concerned that E.ON abused its dominant position by withholding available generation capacity offered on the short-term market with a view to raising the price above competitive levels in the German electricity wholesale market. The second case was related to the German electricity balancing market[947]. The Commission had expressed concern that E.ON might have granted preferential treatment to its generation affiliate in the access to the German electricity transmission network by purchasing secondary balancing power rather than tertiary balancing power.[948]

944 Case COMP/39.388, *E.ON*, Commission Decision of 26 November 2008; Case COMP/39.389, *E.ON*, Commission Decision of 26 November 2008.

945 Case COMP/39.388 & Case COMP/39.389, *E.ON*, para. 41; European Commission, Competition: Commission has carried out inspections in the German electricity sector, 2006.

946 Chauve, 2009, p. 52.

947 According to the ENTSO-E Network Code on Electricity Balancing, the balancing market is "*the entirety of institutional, commercial and operational arrangements that establish market-based management of the function of Balancing*", while "Balancing" being defined as "*all actions and processes, on all timelines, through which TSOs ensure, in a continuous way, to maintain the system frequency within a predefined stability range*".

948 Tapia & Mantzari, 2013, p. 616.

b. Relevant Market and Dominant Position

Under the first case, the relevant product market was considered to be the wholesale market for electricity (imports and the generation of electricity for further resale)[949], and the geographic market was considered to be the territory of Germany.[950] In its preliminary assessment, the Commission found that E.ON, RWE and Vattenfall collectively dominated the German wholesale electricity market. The Commission took a view that the specific characteristics of the electricity sector may allow each of the largest power generators within the same market to be individually dominant even with limited market presence.[951] Under the second case, the relevant product market was the market for the demand of secondary balancing power (secondary balancing reserves).[952] The geographically relevant market was the network area of each transmission system operator.[953]

Concerning the dominant position, the Commission concluded that E.ON held a dominant position within the meaning of Article 102 TFEU on the market for the demand of secondary balancing reserves in the E.ON network area, where the TSO (E.ON Netz, a subsidiary of E.ON) acted as a monopsonist[954].[955]

c. Preliminary Assessment and Decision

The Commission provisionally concluded that E.ON might have infringed Article 102 TFEU in two ways. Firstly, E.ON might have abused its dominant position on the German electricity wholesale

949 Case COMP/39.388 & Case COMP/39.389, *E.ON*, para. 11.

950 Ibid., para. 12.

951 In the market test, the Commission received a submission stating that Vattenfall should not be considered part of the collectively dominant group of undertakings. Therefore, the question was left open whether RWE, E.ON and Vattenfall are to be considered collectively dominant as described in the preliminary assessment or whether only RWE and E.ON are to be considered collectively dominant. Under both alternatives E.ON would be considered part of the collective dominant position. Case COMP/39.386, *E.ON*, paras. 13–24.

952 Case COMP/39.388 & Case COMP/39.389, *E.ON*, para. 46.

953 Ibid., para. 47.

954 One who is a single buyer of a product or service offered by many sellers.

955 Case COMP/39.388 & Case COMP/39.389, *E.ON*, para. 48.

market as a wholesaler in the electricity market by developing a strategy to withdraw available generation capacity with the aim to raising electricity prices to the detriment of consumers.[956] In addition, the Commission was concerned that E.ON might have complemented this with a medium and long-term strategy of hindering actual or potential competitors from entering the generation market and thereby limiting the market volume in electricity generation.[957]

Secondly, according to Article 102 TFEU E.ON might have abused its dominant position as a transmission system operator on the market for the demand of secondary balancing reserves[958] in the E.ON network area by increasing its own costs with a view to favouring its production affiliate and passing the costs on to the final consumer, on the one hand, and by preventing power producers from other Member States from exporting balancing energy into the E.ON balancing market, on the other hand.[959]

E.ON proposed very far reaching commitments to address the Commission's concerns in both cases[960]:

- In order to remedy the Commission's concerns on the wholesale electricity market, E.ON offered to divest significant volume of generation capacity (around 5000 MW, about 20% of E.ON's German generation portfolio) in Germany from different types of technology and fuels, i.e., run-off-river, lignite, hard coal, gas, pump storage and nuclear, to independent competitors.[961]
- In order to address the Commission's concerns on the electricity balancing markets, E.ON offered to divest its entire transmission system business consisting of its Extra-High-Voltage (380/220 kV) line network and the system operations run by E.ON Netz. The High-Voltage (110 kV) line network, which was also operated by

956 Ibid., para. 26.
957 Ibid., para. 41.
958 Balancing energy is last-minute energy necessary to maintain the frequency of the current in the grid.
959 European Commission, Antitrust: Commission market tests commitments proposed by E.ON concerning German electricity markets, 2008.
960 Koch & Gauer, 2011, p. 235.
961 European Commission, Antitrust: Commission opens German electricity market to competition, 2008.

E.ON Netz, would remain with E.ON under this commitment proposal.

The Commission decided that the commitments offered by E.ON were sufficient to meet the competition concerns expressed in the preliminary assessment. Following this decision of 26 November 2008, for the first time in the history of European antitrust law a company sold significant assets to eliminate competition concerns. Both commitments were major structural interventions in the form of ownership unbundling.[962]

2. Swedish Interconnectors

a. Subject Matter

The case[963] is related to the curtailment of export transmission capacity for electricity[964] by Svenska kraftnät (SvK) to address internal congestion since at least 2002.[965] SvK is an authority that is operated in the form of a state-owned undertaking. It is designated as a TSO by Sweden for its national electricity system[966] and is responsible for maintaining, operating and developing the national high-voltage electricity grid including all the state-owned interconnectors with neighbouring countries. After Dansk Energi[967] submitted a complaint to the Commission in July 2006 concerning an alleged restriction of transmission capacity on the Öresund interconnector linking Southern Sweden and Eastern Denmark by SvK, the Commission opened proceedings with the abuse claim against SvK on 1 April 2009.

The Commission suspected that SvK had abused its dominant position in the Swedish electricity transmission market by strategically

962 Hofmann, 2013, p. 317.

963 Case COMP/39.351, *Swedish Interconnectors*, Commission Decision of 14 April 2010.

964 The curtailment of export transmission capacity means that domestically generated or imported electricity is reserved for domestic consumption contrary to the objective of creating an internal market for electricity. Mäntysaari, 2015, p. 131.

965 Case COMP/39.351, *Swedish Interconnectors*, para. 1.

966 Ibid., para. 3.

967 Dansk Energi is a non-commercial lobby organisation for Danish energy companies operating in Denmark.

limiting the amount of export transmission capacity available on electricity interconnectors situated along Sweden's borders from January 2002 to April 2008 with the objective of relieving internal congestion on its network.[968] Reserving domestically produced electricity for only domestic consumption resulted in favouring consumers in Sweden over consumers in neighbouring EU or EEA Member States.[969]

b. Relevant Market and Dominant Position

The relevant market was considered to be the 220–400 kv transmission grid including the interconnectors connected to it.[970] As a relevant geographic market, the Commission applied the territory of Sweden. According to the preliminary assessment, the Commission concluded that SvK held a dominant position within the meaning of Article 102 TFEU on the Swedish electricity transmission market.[971]

c. Preliminary Assessment and Decision

According to the preliminary assessment, the Commission had concerns that SvK might have infringed Article 102 TFEU through abusing its dominant position on the Swedish electricity transmission market by curtailing the amount of export capacity on the Öresund interconnector linking Southern Sweden and Eastern Denmark when it anticipated internal congestion problems on the national transmission system. It reserved domestically produced electricity for only domestic consumption and thereby discriminated between different network users. The Commission found that SvK artificially segmented the domestic market and thereby prevented industrial and other users located outside Sweden

968 European Commission Antitrust: Commission opens proceedings against Swedish Electricity Transmission System Operator concerning limiting interconnector capacity for electricity exports, 2009.

969 Akman, 2015, p. 233.

970 Case COMP/39.351, *Swedish Interconnectors*, para. 16.

971 Ibid., para. 24. The dominant position of SvK in the relevant market was self-evident. SvK was a monopoly, as the Swedish State granted an exclusive concession to SvK to operate the electricity transmission network. Therefore, it held a dominant position on the electricity transmission network in Sweden. Hauteclocque & Hancher, 2011, p. 21.

to benefit from the internal market by treating requests for transmission for the purpose of consumption within Sweden differently from requests for transmission for the purpose of export.[972]

SvK had several different bottlenecks in its network, especially at the cross-border points where demand for transmission capacity exceeds network capacity. Sweden exports electricity to the continent to satisfy demand in the south, while in the north it imports electricity from Norway since there is cheap hydro power often in excess of demand in Norway. According to the assessment, the lines in one or more of the bottlenecks, but particularly in the North, could not accommodate North-South flows of electricity in or into Sweden. Because of the lack of network capacity, congestion often occurred in the Swedish electricity network[973] and SvK needed to manage this congestion.[974] While these bottlenecks could be remedied in the long term by expanding network capacities, in the short term there were three types of measures which could be adopted by SvK to relieve internal network congestion[975]:

- Market splitting: to split the Swedish market into separate price zones on both sides of the bottleneck and hence give price signals to increase production and decrease consumption in the higher-priced side of the bottleneck.
- Congestion shifting: to curtail available transmission capacity for trade with another zone in order to relieve the anticipated congestion on the bottleneck within its network.
- Countertrading: to pay individual generators on both sides of the bottleneck to change their planned production (or consumption), which effectively reduces the transmission flow on the bottleneck, or to pay large energy consumers to change their consumption patterns.

972 Case COMP/39.351, *Swedish Interconnectors*, para. 27. Internal demand was satisfied whenever capacity was available, whereas external demand was refused despite availability during a substantial number of hours during the year. Hautecloque & Hancher, 2011, p. 21.

973 Sadowska & Willems, 2012, p. 1.

974 Case COMP/39.351, *Swedish Interconnectors*, para. 36.

975 Ibid., para. 37. Sadowska & Willems, 2012, p. 3.

SvK chose the third option and curtailed the export capacity on several interconnectors during a significant number of hours in the period January 2002 to April 2008.[976] The Commission subsequently found that average prices in the neighbouring countries were significantly higher than prices in Sweden due to capacity limitation and congestion on the interconnectors.[977] The prices had been lower when more capacity had been available for the transfer between Sweden and the control areas. The Commission therefore considered that SvK's behaviour of artificially restricting the capacity of interconnectors led, *de facto*, to discrimination between the customers in Sweden, on one side, and customers in Member States and contracting parties to the EEA Agreement importing electricity from Sweden, on the other side.[978] In view of such discrimination, the Commission considered that Article 102 TFEU had been infringed. As mentioned above, SvK's behaviour contributed to the segmentation of the markets, which was incompatible with the European internal market.

On 4 September 2009, SvK proposed commitments to address the Commission's concerns. It primarily committed to subdivide the Swedish transmission system into two or more bidding zones[979].[980] SvK offered the commitment to manage internal congestion in the Swedish transmission network through countertrade until the bidding zones become operative, as it can be cheaper to make the necessary adjustments in Sweden than in neighbouring countries. With this commitment it was intended to reduce the limitation of capacity on the interconnectors.[981] On 14 April 2010, the Commission decided that the commitments of SvK were legally binding.

976 Case COMP/39.351, *Swedish Interconnectors*, para. 38.

977 Ibid., para. 41.

978 Ibid., para. 42.

979 A bidding zone is the largest geographical area within which market participants are able to exchange energy without capacity allocation.

980 Case COMP/39.351, *Swedish Interconnectors*, para. 47.

981 European Commission, Antitrust: Commission market tests commitments proposed by Svenska Kraftnät concerning Swedish electricity transmission market, 2009.

3. Summary

a. Capacity withdrawal

The E.ON case addressed an alleged strategy by E.ON to withdraw available generation capacity with the intention of increasing electricity wholesale prices to the detriment of consumers. The distortion of competition through capacity withdrawal was based on the economic concept of the so-called "merit-order"[982], which explains the price setting mechanism on short term electricity markets.[983] Since electricity cannot be stored, it is always necessary to produce just enough electricity to meet demand. Fluctuations in electricity demand can be regulated by turning power plants on and off. Thus, on the one hand, it is sufficient, e.g., to run on low demand the most cost-effective power plants (e.g., hydropower and nuclear power). In the case of greater demand, on the other hand, more cost-intensive power plants (e.g., coal or gas) must be switched on and added to the grid. On the electricity exchange, the electricity price is based on the short-term market after the last power plant needed to meet the demand (marginal power plant). If, as the E.ON decision suggests, more cost-effective power plants are shut down, more costly power plants have to be added. This results in an increase in electricity prices. The losses suffered by the withdrawn capacity are compensated by additional profits through higher contribution margins. The electricity price is thus driven up by manipulation of the supply of products.[984]

Some specific features of the electricity markets make them particularly vulnerable to manipulations by capacity withdrawal: As the production costs between different power plant types (e.g., gas and nuclear plant) differ significantly, the cost curve is quite steep on its right

982 According to the merit order concept, prices are set by the (short-run) marginal cost of the plant producing the last unit of electricity required to meet demand. The last unit ("marginal unit") needed to meet the demand at a given moment is the one with the highest marginal costs of the units running at a given point in time. It follows from this concept that the costs of the "price setting" power plant also determine the revenues of all other power plants from other producers called to produce in any given hour. Koch & Gauer, 2011, p. 232.

983 Due to the dramatic price increasing effect of such behaviour, this abuse form can be particularly harmful for energy customers. Ibid.

984 Hofmann, 2013, p. 308.

side. Due to the fact that electricity demand is almost inelastic and that electricity cannot be stored, withdrawing some of the generation almost automatically raises the price in the (short-term) electricity market. The costs of the withdrawal (foregone profits of the unsold generation) are usually compensated by significantly increased profits of all the generation which continues to be produced.[985]

Capacity withdrawal should not be confused with capacity hoarding – subversion of the refusal to supply – in which the network operators provide less network capacity than could be available. The E.ON case is about the production capacity which is held back by the energy producer in the electricity wholesale market in order to increase the electricity price.

The Commission found evidence that E.ON might indeed have pursued a strategy to withdraw available generation capacity on the German short-term market in order to raise prices between 2002 and 2007. It should be noted that a "short-term" withholding strategy in hours of high demand is also likely to have an effect on the long-term wholesale market, as prices on the long-term market are driven by the corresponding trend in short-term prices. The withholding strategy may therefore not only increase prices on the short-term market but cause buyers to buy also long-term ("forward") products at higher prices.

b. Purchase of overpriced balancing energy

The second E.ON Electricity case concerned an alleged abuse on the balancing markets. Due to non-storability of electricity, such balancing or control by the transmission system operator of the respective balancing zone is necessary to compensate for unexpected fluctuations in the network in the short term. In order to ensure system stability and maintain the appropriate tension level in their grids, the TSO needs balancing energy. There are three types of control/balance energy: primary, secondary and tertiary balancing energy[986]. The Commission

985 Koch & Gauer, 2011, p. 232.

986 Primary balancing energy has to be available within seconds; secondary and tertiary balancing energy kick in after longer periods (usually after 15 seconds and 15 minutes, respectively).

discovered evidence indicating that E.ON's TSO accounted for almost all purchases of balancing energy within its grid area and that the main seller of such energy was E.ON's generation branch (E.ON Supply & Trading). While E.ON Supply & Trading hold a strong position in the secondary balancing energy market, the tertiary balancing energy market was more competitive. The Commission found that E.ON Netz might have systematically bought secondary reserves from E.ON Supply & Trading instead of procuring cheaper tertiary reserves from other national or foreign generators. By favouring its own production affiliate, E.ON might have artificially increased costs for the TSO and, ultimately, for the final consumer.[987]

The E.ON wholesale case concerned an alleged strategy by E.ON to withdraw available generation capacity (limiting the production of certain power plants) with an aim to increase electricity wholesale prices. With regard to the overpriced balancing energy, the Commission remains vague in its subsumption and, in this case, refers only in general to Article 102 TFEU. According to *Koch & Gauer*[988], as both, capacity withdrawal and purchase of overpriced balancing energy, are not directed against competitors but directly effects customer prices (and, accordingly, E.ON's revenues), it would be appropriate to consider such conducts as exploitative abuses under Article 102 (2)(a) TFEU ("unfair selling prices"). Even though, the Commission did not set out in detail the reasons for its judgement on the "unfairness" of the prices, and despite the fact that it is difficult to establish the "benchmark" between fair and unfair prices, the Commission's decision to consider prices "unfair" seems plausible in the present case, given the massive effect of the manipulative strategy on consumer prices.[989]

c. Discrimination through congestion management and market segmentation

The antitrust cases examined above primarily targeted TSOs for abuses related to the existence of a vertically integrated undertaking favouring its affiliated supply arm in related markets (RWE, ENI, GDF Suez, E.ON Gas and E.ON Electricity). By contrast, SvK was not a vertically

987 Koch & Gauer, 2011, p. 233.
988 Ibid., p. 234.
989 Ibid.

integrated company. It was already a completely unbundled TSO and had no interest in supply activities. [990] Moreover, in the SvK case the Commission took action against an undertaking that was in fact a central administrative authority having no objective of profit maximization. Unlike the situation in the above cases, SvK also did not limit capacity to maximize profits but rather to maintain a single price zone in Sweden. SvK claimed that Sweden should not be divided into subareas due to lack of sufficient liquidity and lack of competition both on the day-ahead market and on subsequent intraday and balancing markets.[991]

In this case, the Commission concluded that SvK's behaviour would constitute an abuse of a dominant position for two reasons. The Commission alleged an abuse namely that the restriction of capacity discriminated against certain network customers. The Commission viewed the first abuse as discrimination on grounds of nationality[992]. The customers who imported electricity from Sweden had to pay a higher price for electricity than customers in Sweden, which was considered discrimination because of their nationality. Moreover, the Commission pointed out that the domestic market was artificially segmented by SvK, thus preventing foreign industrial and other users located outside Sweden to benefit from the internal market.[993] By limiting the amount of export transmission capacity available on electricity interconnectors, SvK indeed artificially maintained significantly higher prices in the neighbouring countries, such as Denmark, than in Sweden.

The importance of the SvK case is that it primarily established that unbundling, even full ownership unbundling, might not abolish all barriers to an internal energy market.[994] It should be noted that the Commission reviewed the SvK case based on EU competition law, whereas the case could have also been addressed under Regulation 1228/2003 and the congestion management guidelines. The case was

990 Hauteclocque & Hancher, 2011, p. 20.

991 See the explanations of SvK's Director General to the Commission in a letter of 22 May 2008, Case No 39.351 – *Øresund interconnector*, 356/2006/MA30.

992 Case COMP/39.351, *Swedish Interconnectors*, para. 42.

993 Ibid., para. 27; Hofmann, 2013, p. 321; Hauteclocque & Hancher, 2011, p. 21.

994 Ibid, p. 22.

indeed very regulatory in nature. The Commission's approach shows that it may also be willing to use competition rules to solve problems related to non-compliance with the sector-specific legislation.[995]

III. Article 107

A. PreussenElektra

1. Subject Matter

The case[996] is related to the German electricity scheme, which required distribution companies to buy electricity from renewable energy sources at a fixed minimum price, and to the question whether such a scheme is compatible with EU state aid rules. While PreussenElektra operated more than twenty conventional and nuclear power plants in Germany and fed electricity to regional electricity suppliers, medium-scale local undertakings as well as industry, Schleswag was a regional electricity supplier that bought electricity almost exclusively from PreussenElektra – which also owned 65.3% of Schleswag's shares – for customers in the region of Schleswig-Holstein.[997]

The "Stromeinspeisungsgesetz" (Law on feeding electricity from renewable energy sources into the public grid, hereinafter "StrEG") obliged the electricity supply undertakings which operated a general supply network to buy the electricity that is generated exclusively by renewable energy sources within their areas and to pay the (private) providers a fixed minimum price which was considerably higher compared to the electricity produced from non-renewable resources. The additional costs were borne by the suppliers and passed on to upstream network operators/providers if the energy thus purchased exceeded 5% of the energy supplied by the former to end users.

This scheme had been notified to the Commission within the scope of Article 108(3) TFEU, and it was duly approved in accordance with the

995 Ibid.

996 Case C-379/98, *PreussenElektra*, [2001] ECR I-2099, para. 10.

997 Thieme & Rudolf, 2002, p. 226; Case C-379/98, *PreussenElektra*, [2001] ECR I-2099, para. 17–18.

procedure. However, it was modified during the legislative process and the "hardship clause" was added.[998] According to the hardship clause, the supplier had the right to receive compensation from the network operator for its additional costs where the proportion of the renewable energy purchased under this scheme exceeded 5% of the energy supplied to end customers by the supplier.[999]

At the end of 1998, the share of electricity supplied through renewable sources reached 5% of Schleswag's total sales. Schleswag invoked the hardship clause from the StrEG and invoiced PreussenElektra for the additional costs caused by the obligatory purchase of wind-generated electricity from PreussenElektra. PreussenElektra transferred the instalment for May 1998, reserving the right to claim the money back at any time. Later it made an application to the German Court of First Instance (the Landgericht Kiel) for the part of the sum paid to Schleswag.[1000] PreussenElektra argued that the sum claimed had been paid to Schleswag without a valid legal reason since Paragraph 4 of the StrEG, on which that payment was based, was contrary to the TFEU's directly applicable provisions on State aid.[1001] The German Court of First Instance requested the CJ to decide whether Paragraph 4(1) of the StrEG was compatible with Article 107 TFEU concerning subsidies.

2. Decision

The CJ examined the question whether the rules on payment and compensation for supplies of electricity constitute state aid for the purposes of Article 107 TFEU.[1002] During its review, the CJ took into consideration the criteria set forth in Article 107 TFEU regarding state aids.

998 Paragraph 4 of the StrEG; Talus, 2013, p. 142.

999 *"[...] in so far as the kilowatt hours to be compensated for exceed 5% of the total kilowatt hours supplied by the electricity supply undertaking through its network during a calendar year, the upstream network operator shall be obliged to reimburse the electricity supply undertaking in respect of the supplementary costs resulting from the kilowatt hours exceeding that share."* Case C-379/98, *PreussenElektra*, para. 10. See: Armenteros & Lefevere, 2001, p. 344.

1000 Case C-379/98, *PreussenElektra*, para. 22.

1001 Ibid., para. 23.

1002 Ibid., para. 27.

It recalled that Article 107(1) TFEU provides that any aid granted by a Member State or through State resources in any form whatsoever which distorts or threatens to distort competition by favouring certain undertakings or the production of certain goods is, insofar as it affects trade between Member States, incompatible with the common market.[1003]

The CJ stated that an obligation to purchase electricity produced from renewable energy sources at minimum prices indisputably conferred a certain economic advantage on producers of that type of electricity, since it guarantees them, with no risk, higher profits than they would otherwise realise.[1004] Similarly, the criteria regarding the distortion of competition and effects on trade among Member States were considered to be met, although it was not stated clearly. However, the CJ clearly expressed that the fourth criteria, namely that aid must be granted by a Member State or through state resources in any form whatsoever, has not been fulfilled. It adopted a very narrow interpretation of the concept of "state resources"[1005] and determined that the obligation imposed on private electricity supply undertakings to purchase electricity produced from renewable energy sources at fixed minimum prices did not involve any direct or indirect transfer of state resources to undertakings which produce that type of electricity.[1006] The CJ took the view that support measures financed by private companies cannot be considered to be state aid within the scope of Article 107(1) TFEU even though such measures were established by the State.[1007]

1003 *"Any aid granted by a Member State or through State resources in any form whatsoever which distorts or threatens to distort competition by favouring certain undertakings or the production of certain goods shall, in so far as it affects trade between Member States, be incompatible with the common market."* Cf. Case C-206/06, *Essent Netwerk Noord*, [2008] ECR I-5497, para. 64.

1004 Case C-379/98, *PreussenElektra*, para. 54.

1005 Talus, 2013, p. 143.

1006 Case C-379/98, *PreussenElektra*, para. 59.

1007 Ibid., para. 58–62.

B. EDF

1. Subject Matter

The case[1008] is related to whether tax breaks granted by France to EDF was compatible with EU state aid rules. EDF is a French electric utility company which operates in France as well as in several other European countries. The majority of the ownership belongs to the French State. On 16 October 2002, the Commission initiated a formal investigation against EDF claiming that tax breaks granted to EDF were incompatible with EU rules on state aid.

2. Decision

During its in-depth examination, the Commission found that the French government did not levy all the corporate tax which would ordinarily be payable by EDF. In 1956, the French Government granted a concession to EDF to manage the high-voltage transmission network for 75 years. In 1997, the Government established that EDF was deemed to have owned the network since 1956. Therefore, the French authorities reorganised EDF's balance sheet and certain accounting provisions were reclassified as capital injections without being subject to corporation tax.[1009]

During its examination, the Commission took into consideration the criteria used by the CJ regarding state aids:

– an intervention through state or state resources;
– the possibility of this intervention to affect the trade between Member States;

1008 C(2003)4637, *EDF*, Commission Decision of 16 December 2003.

1009 Previously, assets allocated to the high-voltage transmission network were classified as "assets under concession" under the balance sheet. "*No 97-1026 of 10 November 1997 provided that 'as at 1 January 1997, the value of the assets in kind allocated under concession to the RAG appearing as liabilities on EDF's balance sheet shall be entered, net of the corresponding revaluation differences, under the item 'Capital injections". The share of the provisions corresponding to grantor rights was therefore to be reclassified as capital injections without being subject to corporation tax.*" C(2003)4637, *EDF*, Commission Decision of 16 December 2003, para. 28.

- an advantage for the recipient;
- distortion of competition.

The Commission highlighted that besides positive benefits, such as subsidies, the notion of aid includes financial advantages granted by the public authorities and reducing the charges that are normally included in an undertaking's budget. It can be stated that such advantages would have the same effect as subsidies. The CJ also repeated in numerous occasions that the non-collection of taxes which should normally have been collected is equated to the consumption of state resources.[1010] It has been observed that the non-collection of the full amount of corporation tax due in respect of the 1997 financial year derived directly from a measure adopted by the State.[1011] The Commission noted that this tax exemption conferred on EDF an undue economic advantage compared with other operators on the market and thus distorted competition.

The Commission also established that EDF was already in a firm position in certain markets in other Member States in 1997 and that the aid resulting from the non-payment of corporation tax by EDF on some of the accounting provisions created free of tax for the renewal of the high-voltage transmission network inevitably affected trade between Member States.[1012] Therefore, the Commission concluded that the tax exemption constituted state aid that was incompatible with the internal market as it had the effect of strengthening EDF's competitive position in relation to its competitors.[1013] The Commission also requested France to recover this aid.[1014]

On 15 December 2009, the General Court annulled the Commission's decision on the grounds that, when re-examining the French au-

1010 Ibid., para. 101. The collection of a tax is revenue attributed to the state. Thus, a non-collection of taxes would be considered forgone state revenue and would thus involve state resources.

1011 Ibid.

1012 Ibid., para. 115.

1013 Ibid., para. 154.

1014 European Commission, State aid: Commission reopens inquiry into the tax aid awarded to EDF following Court judgment, 2013. "*[…] The Commission's investigation confirmed that EDF received an individual, unjustified tax exemption which gave it an advantage to the detriment of its competitors, in breach of EU state aid rules.*" European Commission, State aid: Commission orders France to recover €1.37 billion in incompatible aid from EDF, 2015.

thorities' reclassification of the provisions as capital, the Commission had not checked whether a private investor would have invested a comparable amount under similar circumstances.[1015] Specifically, a private investor test helps to determine whether a state incentive constitutes an economic advantage and whether it actually distorts or endangers competition. Article 107(1) TFEU prohibits any aid granted by a Member State or through state resources in any form whatsoever which distorts or threatens to distort competition by favouring certain undertakings, or the production of certain goods, insofar as it affects trade between Member States.[1016] Under certain circumstances, however, financial benefits granted by Member States are not prohibited. If the same measure would have been adopted by a private investor operating in normal market economy conditions and being in a situation similar to the State's, the measure in question would not be considered state aid.[1017]

The General Court's judgment was confirmed by the CJ in June 2012.[1018] According to the CJ, the applicability of the private investor test ultimately depends on the Member State concerned having conferred, in its capacity as shareholder and not in its capacity as public authority, an economic advantage on an undertaking belonging to it.[1019] The CJ stated that the application of such a test would make it possible to determine whether, in similar circumstances, a private shareholder would have made an additional investment in an undertaking in a situation comparable with that of EDF and in an amount equal to the tax due.[1020]

After the CJ's decision, the Commission reopened the inquiry into tax exemptions which were granted to EDF with the aim to reaching a decision in accordance with the criteria laid down by the European Courts. During its investigation, the Commission was unable to gather evidence proving that the French Government in the past acted as a

1015 Ibid.

1016 Article 107(1) TFEU does not distinguish between state intervention in public undertakings or in private undertakings. Werner, 2012.

1017 Ibid.

1018 Case C-124/10 P, *EDF v Commission*, [2012] 3 CMLR 17.

1019 Ibid., para. 81.

1020 Ibid., para. 95.

shareholder or that any *ex ante* study had been undertaken to demonstrate the profitability of the investment. Furthermore, the Commission noted that the private investor test was not met, in particular because at the time the profitability that could reasonably be expected of such an investment was too low. It follows that the tax exemption granted to EDF cannot be considered an investment made on economic grounds.[1021] Moreover, the Commission expressed that the French Government granted the aid in a manner which was essentially infringing upon Article 108(3). It reiterated its previous statement and recalled that the exemption from the corporate tax through the reclassification of certain accounting provisions as capitalisation constituted an aid and was incompatible with the internal market as it distorted competition.[1022] The Commission stated that the EDF should refund the aid unlawfully paid in the form of an exemption from corporation tax in order to restore the competition environment which had been tainted due to the tax exemption.[1023]

EDF was dissatisfied with the Commission's new decision and brought an action before the General Court for its annulment.[1024] On 16 January 2018, the General Court upheld the Commission's decision. It recalled that neither in its judgment of 2009 nor in CJ's judgment of 2012 was it assumed that the private investor test was applicable in EDF case, thus leaving the Commission to determine whether the private investor test was applicable.[1025] The General Court noted that the private investor test only applies if the Member State concerned granted the economic advantage as a shareholder and not as public authority. According to the General Court, the private investor test was not applicable, and it highlighted that, when a Member State relies on the private investor test, it is incumbent upon the Member State to establish unequivocally and on the basis of objective, verifiable and contem-

1021 European Commission, state aid: Commission orders France to recover €1.37 billion in incompatible aid from EDF, 2015.

1022 SA.13869, *EDF*, para. 216.

1023 Ibid., para. 220.

1024 Case T-747/15, *EDF v Commission*, Judgment of the General Court of 16 January 2018.

1025 General Court of the European Union, The General Court of the EU upholds the Commission's decision ordering France to recover €1.37 billion in the context of State aid granted to EDF, 2018.

poraneous evidence that it acted as a private investor.[1026] The General Court noted that neither EDF nor France submitted evidence sufficient to demonstrate the applicability of the private investor test.[1027] On 27 March 2018, EDF submitted an appeal against the General Court's decision of 16 January 2018 to the CJ. On 13 December 2018, the CJ dismissed EDF's appeal and reconfirmed that the aid which had been granted back in 1997 had to be recovered.

The EDF decision can be considered as one of the most significant decision concerning state aid since the European Courts attempted to define, for the first time, the necessary criteria to distinguish between the state acting as shareholder and the state exercising public power.

IV. Merger Regulation

A. ENI/EDP/GDP

1. Subject Matter

The case[1028] is related to the assessment of whether a proposed concentration by EDP and ENI was compatible with the common market. EDP is the ex-incumbent electricity company with main activities consisting of the generation, distribution and supply of electricity in Portugal. EDP also controls the Spanish company HC Energía, which is operating in electricity and gas markets. GDP is the ex-incumbent gas company in Portugal. It is a wholly owned subsidiary of the Portuguese company Galp Energia, which is jointly controlled by the Portuguese State and ENI, active in both the oil and the gas sectors. GDP and its subsidiaries cover all levels of the gas chain in Portugal. GDP imports natural gas into Portugal through its subsidiary Transgas, which is responsible for the transportation, storage, transport and supply through the high-pressure gas pipeline network. ENI is an Italian state-controlled company mainly operating in the natural gas and oil markets. On 9 July 2004, EDP, along with ENI, notified the Commission regarding a proposed concentration

1026 Case T-747/15, *EDF*, para. 136.
1027 Ibid., para. 347.
1028 Case COMP/M.3440, *ENI/EDP/GDP*, Commission decision of 9 December 2004.

by which EDP and ENI would acquire joint control of GDP by way of a purchase of shares.[1029]

During its initial investigation, the Commission realised that the merger might remove GDP as a potential competitor of EDP in the Portuguese electricity markets.[1030] The elimination of a potential competitor could strengthen EDP's dominance in Portuguese electricity markets. Having concerns that the proposed acquisition could significantly strengthen EDP's dominant position in the electricity wholesale and retail markets in Portugal, the Commission decided to open an in-depth inquiry.[1031]

2. Decision

The Commission analysed the possible impact of the proposed transaction on the gas and electricity supply markets in Portugal. In its 9 December 2004 decision, the Commission concluded that the proposed transaction would strengthen EDP's dominant position in the electricity wholesale and retail markets in Portugal[1032], which would significantly impede effective competition in this market.[1033] Moreover, gas was considered at that time as one of the most efficient ways to produce electricity, so that the concentration would have made current and possible future power producers in Portugal dependent on their main competitor, namely EDP. As for natural gas markets, the proposed transaction would also strengthen GDP's dominant position in the relevant gas markets in Portugal[1034] through the foreclosure of a signifi-

1029 Ibid., Prior notification of a concentration, 2004.
1030 European Commission, In-depth investigation into EDP/ENI's proposed acquisition of GDP, 2004.
1031 Ibid.
1032 EDP held 70–80% of generation capacity, accounts for 70–80% of generation and is the largest importer of electricity. COMP/M.3440, *ENI/EDP/GDP*, para. 282.
1033 Prior to the merger, there were strong incentives for GALP/GDP to enter the wholesale electricity market and to develop as EDP's main competitor. However, the proposed transaction would eliminate the potential competitor. Ibid., para. 335.
1034 The Commission observed that, through Transgas, GDP controlled all the available entry capacity of the international pipeline coming from Algeria. It also owned and operated the Sines LNG terminal and the Carriço storage facility. GDP/Transgas could thus significantly limit access by third parties to the Portuguese network even

cant part of the gas demand (controlled by EDP) and the elimination of EDP as the most likely entrant in the gas markets.[1035]

The Commission rejected the remedies submitted by the parties on 26 November 2004 and stated that they did not fully and unquestionably address the competition concerns.[1036] Consequently, the Commission declared the proposed transaction incompatible with the common market and prohibited it because effective competition would be significantly impeded in a substantial part of the common market.[1037] On 21 September 2005, the General Court upheld the Commission's decision to prohibit the proposed transaction.[1038] The General Court's decision showed that undertakings must propose adequate remedies in due time with a view to addressing fully the competition concerns identified by the Commission.

B. E.ON/MOL

1. Subject Matter

The case[1039] is related to the assessment of whether a proposed concentration by E.ON and MOL was compatible with the common market. E.ON is a German energy company which focuses on the supply of electricity and gas. Prior to the concentration, E.ON was already active on the gas and electricity retail markets in Hungary through its control of several regional distribution companies. MOL is a vertically integrated oil and gas group primarily active in Hungary. It is in particular the

---

if national regulations ultimately impose rules on third parties' access to the gas infrastructures. Ibid., para. 495.

1035 As an electricity incumbent, EDP had strong advantages in entering the market for the supply of gas to small customers; the ownership of a local distribution company could give it further advantages and proved its ability to enter/expand. However, the potential transaction would lead EDP's elimination as an immediate and potential competitor. Ibid., para. 561–595, 914; European Commission, Mergers: Commission prohibits acquisition of GDP by EDP and ENI, 2004.

1036 Case COMP/M.3440, *ENI/EDP/GDP*, para. 912.

1037 European Commission, Mergers: Commission prohibits acquisition of GDP by EDP and ENI, 2004.

1038 Case T-87/05, *EDP v Commission*, 2005, Judgment of the General Court of 21 September 2005; European Commission, Mergers: Commission welcomes CFI ruling in EDP/ENI/GDP case, 2005.

1039 Case COMP/M.3696, *E.ON/MOL*, Commission decision of 21 December 2005.

incumbent gas supplier in Hungary.[1040] On 2 June 2005, the Commission received a notification of a proposed concentration by which the undertaking E.ON Ruhrgas would acquire control of the whole of the undertakings MOL WMT and MOL Storage, at the time solely controlled by MOL Hungarian Oil and Gas Plc (MOL), by way of the purchase of shares. E.ON Ruhrgas would also acquire MOL's shareholdings in Panrusgáz, a joint venture company between OAO Gazprom and MOL.[1041]

The Commission opened a detailed investigation into the planned acquisition of the gas wholesale and storage activities of the Hungarian oil and gas group MOL by E.ON within the scope of the EU Merger Regulation.[1042] On 7 July 2005, the Commission decided to initiate proceedings in the above-mentioned case after finding that the notified concentration raised serious doubts as to its compatibility with the common market.[1043] After its initial market investigation, the Commission concluded that the proposed concentration could cause serious concerns regarding competition at all levels of the electricity and gas supply chain in Hungary, given the vertical and horizontal overlaps between the two undertakings' business activities.[1044] Therefore, the Commission decided to open an in-depth inquiry.

2. Decision

The Commission established on the basis of its investigation and its economic assessment that such transaction would directly lead to the creation of a vertically integrated undertaking, active both in electricity generation, wholesale and retailing, and in gas, equally wholesaling and retailing. The Commission's investigation revealed that access to gas resources is crucial for electricity retail activities as dual offers are expected to play an important role in electricity retail markets.[1045] The

1040 European Commission, Mergers: Commission opens an in-depth investigation into E.ON's acquisition of Hungary's MOL gas business, 2005.

1041 Case COMP/M.3696, *E.ON/MOL*, Prior notification of a concentration, 2005.

1042 European Commission, Mergers: Commission opens an in-depth investigation into E.ON's acquisition of Hungary's MOL gas business, 2005.

1043 Case COMP/M.3696, *E.ON/MOL*, Initiation of proceedings, 2005.

1044 European Commission, Mergers: Commission opens an in-depth investigation into E. ON's acquisition of Hungary's MOL gas business, 2005.

1045 Case COMP/M.3696, *E.ON/MOL*, para. 719.

proposed transaction might have strengthened the control of the new entity over all the gas resources available in Hungary, both domestic and imported.[1046] Moreover, the new entity would have the ability and the incentive to significantly hinder competition on the downstream electricity and gas markets by raising rivals' costs or by foreclosing its actual and potential competitors on these markets, as its competitors would necessarily have to rely on the new entity to procure their wholesale gas.[1047] The Commission concluded that the proposed transaction would thus lead to higher prices on all electricity retail markets.[1048]

In order to address the concerns identified by the Commission, E.ON offered comprehensive and far-reaching remedies with a combination of both structural and behavioural measures. Firstly and most notably, MOL undertook to divest its remaining minority interest in the wholesale and storage subsidiaries acquired by E.ON (MOL WMT and MOL Storage), thereby ensuring the structural separation of the various gas activities (from production to distribution) in Hungary.[1049] Through this commitment, a full ownership unbundling of gas production and transmission activities from gas wholesale and storage activities has been achieved. Secondly, E.ON offered to release gas quantities through yearly public auctions (gas release programme) and to assign half of the supply contract for the Hungarian domestic production of gas to a third party (so-called contract release).[1050] Thirdly, E.ON undertook to release significant volumes of gas on the market at competitive conditions (so-called gas release) and to implement an 8-year gas release programme. Fourthly, E.ON committed to grant access to storage capacities at regulated price and conditions to end users and wholesalers who would

1046 European Commission, Mergers: Commission approves acquisition by E.ON of MOL's gas business, subject to conditions, 2005.

1047 Ibid.; Case COMP/M.3696, *E. ON/MOL*, para. 719–733.

1048 Case COMP/M.3696, *E.ON/MOL*, para. 707.

1049 According to the commitments, MOL would divest its remaining shareholdings of 25% in MOL Storage and MOL WMT within six months following the date of closing. In addition, MOL would not acquire direct or indirect minority stakes in MOL WMT and MOL Storage for a period of 10 years as long as E.ON is a majority shareholder of these companies. Ibid., para. 735–736.

1050 European Commission, Mergers: Commission's conditional approval of E.ON's acquisition of MOL's gas business – frequently asked questions, 2005.

purchase gas directly through the gas release programme or the contract release.[1051]

The Commission concluded that the commitments submitted by E.ON and MOL were sufficient to address the competition concerns raised by this concentration.[1052] A novelty of this case is that the Commission has, for the first time within the context of merger control, accepted gas release and contract release as measures aimed at remedying competition concerns in the energy sector.[1053]

There are two main differences between the EDP/GDP merger and the E.ON/MOL merger. First, unlike the former, the latter did not create a national champion. The EDP/GDP merger would have left one undertaking with strong state connections dominant in both the electricity and gas markets in Portugal.[1054] Secondly, while EDP/GDP merger raised significant horizontal competition concerns[1055], the E.ON/MOL merger did not raise any horizontal competition concerns, because the involved companies were not active in the same markets. The main competition issues were actually of a vertical nature (companies active in downstream/upstream markets). E.ON and MOL were operating in different segments of gas and electricity markets in Hungary. E.ON had essentially a strong market position at the level of retail gas and electricity supply, at the distribution of gas and electricity, through its control of regional distribution companies, and at the electricity generation, while MOL was active at the upstream level, in gas production, transmission, storage and wholesale.[1056] Therefore, the Commission was concerned that the proposed merger would create a fully vertically integrated entity.[1057]

1051 In particular, E.ON undertakes to offer access to 158 sufficient storage capacities for such end users and wholesalers even if they purchase gas for the first time or develop an increased demand for storage when buying gas quantities through the gas release programme or the contract release. Case COMP/M.3696, *E. ON/MOL*, para. 755.

1052 Ibid., para. 824.

1053 Bartok et al., 2006, p. 11.

1054 Tatcher, 2014, p. 459.

1055 Both companies were potential competitors.

1056 European Commission, Mergers: Commission's conditional approval of E.ON's acquisition of MOL's gas business – frequently asked questions, 2005.

1057 Case COMP/M.3696, *E.ON/MOL*, para. 282.

C. GDF/Suez

1. Subject Matter

The case[1058] is related to assessment of whether a proposed concentration by GDF and the Suez Group was compatible with the common market. GDF operated on all levels of the gas sector, and additionally it was active in electricity production and retail. GDF was active mainly in France, but also in Belgium, Germany, the United Kingdom, Luxembourg, Hungary and Spain. Along with Centrica, GDF exercised control over SPE, the second largest firm in the Belgium gas and electricity markets. The Suez Group mainly operated in the gas and the electricity sector, in energy services and water services in France and Belgium. Furthermore, Suez consisted of bodies such as Electrabel (electricity and gas), Distrigas, Fluxys and Suez Energy Services. On 10 May 2006, the Commission received a notification concerning a proposed concentration by which GDF would enter into a full merger with the Suez group by way of an exchange of shares. Through the proposed merger, GDF would fully acquire Suez, which would cease to exist as a legal entity.[1059]

The Commission raised doubts, on the basis of its initial market investigation, as to the proposed transaction's compatibility with the common market[1060] as it might cause serious competition concerns at all levels of the gas and electricity supply chain in Belgium and at all levels of the gas chain in France, given the vertical relationships and the horizontal overlaps between the two undertakings' business activities.[1061] The Commission noted that the proposed transaction fell within the scope of the Merger Regulation. In June 2006, the Commission decided to open a detailed investigation into the planned merger between GDF and the Suez Group of France within the scope of the EU Merger Regulation.[1062]

1058 COMP/M.4180, *GDF/Suez*, Commission Decision of 14 November 2006.
1059 Ibid., Prior notification of a concentration, 2005.
1060 Ibid., para. 11.
1061 European Commission, Mergers: Commission opens in-depth investigation into merger between Gaz de France and Suez group, 2006.
1062 Ibid.

2. Decision

The Commission identified serious risks namely that the proposed transaction might result in a significant impediment to competition as it would combine the supply activities of the two main gas and electricity operators in Belgium with two of the three main gas operators in France. Furthermore, it would give the new entity control of most gas imports into both Belgium and France. Finally, the Commission found potential vertical problems stemming from the parties' control over essential infrastructure (e.g., transmission and transport networks, storage facilities).[1063]

In the Belgium gas market, the Commission concluded that the merger as notified would significantly impede effective competition in the various gas markets, particularly by enhancing the dominant position of Distrigas. Due to the dual impact of the following two factors, Distrigas's position would be enhanced because:

- GDF's operations in Belgium would be absorbed by Distrigas and
- the transaction would remove the strong competitive pressure hitherto exerted by GDF. GDF was Distrigas's main competitor and also had huge potential for growth.

The Commission noted that, due to the fact that it was already extremely difficult to enter the Belgian gas markets and the merger would raise entry barriers even further, it would be unlikely for competitors to be able to take over GDF's position and compensate for the competitive pressure which would be eliminated as a result of the proposed merger.[1064]

Regarding the French gas market, the Commission concluded that the notified merger would considerably hinder effective competition in the various markets for the supply of gas in France, particularly because of the strengthening of GDF's dominant position.[1065] Contrary to the situation in the Belgium market, GDF would incorporate Suez's activities in France (in particular the elimination of current competition). Moreover, the transaction would eliminate the strong competi-

1063 Ibid.
1064 COMP/M.4180, *GDF/Suez*, para. 107.
1065 Ibid., para. 386.

tive pressure exerted by Suez (through Distrigas) in the French gas markets.[1066]

As for electricity markets, the Commission established that through the notified merger Suez (Electrabel) would also strengthen its already dominant position, as GDF would be eliminated as a potential entrant on the market for the gas supply to electricity producers in Belgium.[1067]

The parties offered comprehensive remedies in order to eliminate the Commission's concerns concerning competition, which included[1068]:

- the divestiture of Suez Group's holding in Distrigas,
- the divesture of GDF's stake in SPE,
- the restructuring of the activities of Fluxys S.A. and the relinquishing of all control over the company,
- a series of additional measures (most notably investments) relating to gas infrastructure in Belgium and France (the parties endeavoured to make a series of investments to increase Belgian and French gas infrastructure capacity), and
- divestment of the Cofathec Coriance and the district heating networks operated by Cofathec Services.

Considering these structural remedies, the Commission decided that the concerned merger would not significantly impede effective competition in the common market or a substantial part of it and that the merger should therefore be declared compatible with the Merger Regulation.[1069]

D. EDF/British Energy

1. Subject Matter

The case[1070] is related to assessment of whether a proposed concentration by GDF and the Suez Group was compatible with the common market. British Energy was active in the generation, wholesale trading and supply

1066 Ibid., para. 391.
1067 Ibid., para. 840.
1068 Ibid., para. 1147–1166.
1069 Ibid., para. 1229.
1070 COMP/M.5224, *EDF/British Energy*, Commission Decision of 22 December 2008.

of electricity as well as in the provision of other electricity related services in Great Britain. On 3 November 2008, the Commission received a notification of a proposed concentration by which the undertaking EDF through Lake Acquisitions Ltd (Lake Acquisitions) would acquire control of the undertaking British Energy plc (British Energy) by way of the purchase of shares.[1071] During its first phase investigation, the Commission found that the transaction, as initially notified, would have been likely to raise serious competition concerns.

2. Decision

The Commission had concerns regarding four main points:

- the changed ability and incentive for strategic capacity withdrawal with the intention to increase prices;
- the reduction in wholesale market liquidity;
- a high concentration in the ownership of sites most likely to be suitable for new nuclear build;
- the potential for the combined entity's holding of three National Grid connection agreements in relation to Hinkley Point to act as a barrier to entry for other competitors in the relevant region.[1072]

EDF and British Energy submitted remedies to address the Commission's concerns. Further to the results of the market test of these remedies and in its own assessment, the Commission concluded that the remedies proposed were not sufficient to remove the two first areas of concern mentioned above. However, the parties subsequently submitted an enhanced remedy package. Overall, the commitment included the agreement to divest two "flexible plants" (EDF's power generation plant at Sutton Bridge and the British Energy's generation plant at Eggborough), to sell certain minimum volumes of electricity into the wholesale market over a period of time, to divest a site potentially suitable for building a new nuclear power station located at either Dungeness or Heysham and to end one grid connection agreement with

1071 Ibid., Prior notification of a concentration, 2008.
1072 Ibid., para. 7.

National Grid at Hinkley Point.[1073] The Commission concluded that the revised remedy package submitted by the parties in phase I was sufficient to remove all identified competition concerns. That enabled the Commission to clear the deal without opening a phase-II investigation.[1074]

1073 European Commission, Mergers: Commission clears proposed acquisition of British Energy by EdF, subject to conditions, 2008; COMP/M.5224, *EDF/British Energy*, para. 198.

1074 Drauz et al., 2010, p. 18.

Part 5 Conclusion

For the first time since the reforms of the Treaty of Lisbon, energy related matters are covered by a separate title (Title XXI in Part Three, Article 194 TFEU) and energy policy is considered an area of EU competence in the EU's founding Treaties. Article 194 TFEU states the objectives of EU's energy policy, including parameters such as ensuring the functioning of the energy markets, ensuring security of the energy supply in the EU, promoting energy efficiency along with energy optimisation, developing new and also renewable forms of energy and consequently improving the interconnection of the energy networks.

§ 10. Liberalisation of EU Energy Markets

I. Development of the Regulatory Framework

Energy markets can be either state monopolies or liberalised markets. Prior to the 1990s, the first option was prevalent. After the Second World War, large national monopolies were created; this movement was supported by the theory that the whole energy sector should be regarded as a natural monopoly. The reason behind this assumption was the high costs implicated by the construction and operation of energy facilities and grids. It was more cost efficient to have a monopoly than to provide these services through numerous competing entities. However, there was always the possibility that undertakings which constitute natural monopolies would abuse their position. Although the aforementioned risk was acknowledged, there was a common belief that the introduction of competition would lead to shortages.

The second option, liberalised markets, is based on the principle of free competition. Liberalised markets allow several undertakings to participate in the sector, while the final user has the right to freely choose its supplier taking into consideration the price and the quality of services. This procedure, namely the gradual implementation of competition rules, is termed "liberalisation" or "deregulation of the market".

The EU has endeavoured to realise the objective of establishing an internal market and opening energy markets to competition through the regulatory reforms. The Commission set up a three-step process to complete the internal energy market. The EU initially adopted three Directives with the aim of integrating European energy markets. In 1990, Directive 90/377/EEC was introduced as a first measure. It aimed at eliminating discrimination against users by increasing their freedom to choose between different energy sources and different suppliers through increasing the transparency of gas and electricity prices charged to industrial end users. This Directive was followed by Directive 90/547/EEC and Directive 91/296/EEC with the aim to facilitate the transmission of electricity and natural gas. As a second step, the Directive on the conditions for granting and using authorisations for the prospection, exploration and production of hydrocarbons (Directive 94/22/EC) was adopted on 30 May 1994.

After these first steps towards the integration of the European energy markets, the Commission enacted the first Electricity Directive (Directive 96/92/EC) in 1996 and the first Gas Directive (Directive 98/30/EC) in 1998, thereby constituting a cornerstone regarding the liberalisation of the electricity and gas markets. Both Directives aim at increasing efficiency in the energy markets by opening them to competition and increasing the competitive capacity of the EU economy through decreasing energy costs. The first Directives intended to liberate entry to, or exit from, the energy markets and gradually sought to open them to competition. The electricity and natural gas exchange over transmission lines between Member States was considered especially important.

Although nearly all Member States fulfilled the requirements of the aforementioned Directives by September 2000, the EU could not obtain the desired results from the first Directives. It was clear that they were not sufficient to create a functioning internal energy market. The new reform package entered into force in 2003 and included two Directives (Directive 2003/54/EC and Directive 2003/55/EC) and two additional Regulations. The EU attributed specific significance to these

Regulations including the conditions of transmitting high voltage electricity and high-pressured natural gas from one country to another. The aim was to increase energy trade among Member States by disintegrating the lasting resistance related to ownership transfer in national markets.

Primarily, the Second Energy Package aimed at accelerating the process of creating competitive electricity and gas markets. The new package contained more detailed sector-specific provisions on regulated third-party access, functional and legal unbundling, and regulatory authorities. The intention was to achieve further liberalisation of EU energy markets. The countries were provided a deadline of July 2004 to open their markets to non-household consumers and subsequently of July 2007 to include the household consumers so as to let consumers select their own suppliers. Another important feature of this package was that it required at least the legal unbundling of the production, transmission, distribution and supply activities. The purpose was to prevent the discriminative attitudes towards the other undertakings which endeavour to use the transmission and distribution components of such undertakings and to increase competition. Moreover, the supervision of the aforementioned types of activities through the independent national regulators was undertaken in a planned manner.

In retrospect it can be said that the Second Energy Package did not yield the expected benefits either. In general, it has been observed that consumers have not been provided with as many options as were expected in terms of the alternative electricity and the natural gas suppliers. There were several complaints even in nations with a wide variety of options, pertaining to unsatisfactory service quality. This led to the investigation of the energy sector activities in terms of competition rules.

In 2005, a sector inquiry was carried out by the Commission after receiving several complaints concerning entry barriers and limited possibilities to access customers. The energy sector inquiry published in 2007 stated that the Directives of the Second Energy Package were insufficient for the purpose of solving the problems peculiar to the energy markets (especially regarding competition) and could not respond to the desired goals. It identified serious shortcomings in the electricity and gas markets, such as high market concentration, lack of liquidity and lack of integration between Member States' markets. The energy sector inquiry had the following results:

- The amount of concentration was very high in the national markets.
- There was a liquidity deficiency which prevented new entries to the markets.
- The integration of the Member State markets was very weak.
- A transparent information flow system had not been created to easily access information related to both electricity and natural gas markets.
- Pricing mechanisms were unreliable.

All of the above-mentioned issues constituted serious obstacles to the establishment of competitive energy markets. It was acknowledged by the Commission that the benefits of competition would remain out of reach without comprehensive changes in the EU energy markets. In order to address these issues, the Commission developed a strategy which included adopting a new legislative package to improve the regulatory framework and using the full range of competition tools to pursue individual cases setting precedents that could significantly help to increase the level of competition in the EU energy markets.

The Commission put forth new proposals in order to compensate for the gaps existing in the first Electricity and Gas Directives enacted at the end of the decade of the 1990s and the Second Energy Package in 2003. The Third Energy Package adopted in 2009 included two Directives (Directive 2009/72/EC and 2009/73/EC) and three Regulations (Regulation 713/2009, Regulation 714/2009 and Regulation 715/2009).

Unlike the two previous reform packages, the Third Energy Package included further concrete provisions on vertical unbundling and ownership transfer in order to enable the easy access of the new and relatively small energy companies to transmission and distribution networks and to prevent the anticompetitive conduct of dominant undertakings in the electricity and gas markets. Inasmuch as legal unbundling did not create the necessary motivation for competition, the Commission adopted three new options; one radical and the other two less radical. The first option endeavours to force full ownership transfer. Ownership unbundling requires a structural separation of transmission activities from generation, production and supply activities. Certain Member States, such as Germany and France, considered this option to be immensely radical. Therefore a second option, independent system operator, which is an intermediate solution, is included in the Electricity and Gas Directives. With this option the supplier and the network can remain in the same group, but the network operator must be an entirely separate legal entity. This permits the vertically integrated company to still own the network even though the network must be managed by an independent system operator. Under the third option called independent transmission operator, the vertically integrated company retains ownership of the network; however, the network must be operated by another undertaking.

Additionally, new provisions were added to the Third Electricity Directive in order to enable transparency by disclosing the necessary information to the public regarding issues such as usable transmission, interconnection capacities, production and system balancing. The Agency for the Cooperation of Energy Regulators (ACER), which has authority to take a decision with respect to cross-border issues, was established with the aim to develop integration among Member States. Through ACER, it is intended to create an effective cooperation mechanism among the national regulatory authorities. Furthermore, the vertically integrated incumbents are required to be effectively unbundled in order to achieve the goal of establishing liberalised, competitive electricity and gas markets. The EU introduced various unbundling regimes in order to separate the transmission and distribution activities from other activities. The concept of ownership unbundling is put forth as a default option, and alternatively, as other possible options, the independent system operator and independent transmission operator have been created. Aside from the provisions regarding unbundling and third-party access, certain additional regulations have been integrated into the new Directives in order to promote the cooperation between national regulatory authorities (NRA) and increase their authority. The NRAs are granted new powers to engage in monitoring as well as *ex post* control and enforcement.

The Commission aimed at ensuring that the Third Energy Package – once fully transposed by Member States into their respective national laws – would eliminate undertakings' incentives to further conduct anticompetitive practices and promote the development of cross-border competition within the EU. However, it can be observed that these reforms are taking longer than expected to have a real impact on European energy markets.

Originally, Member States were required to transpose the third Energy Directives into their national law by 3 March 2011. However, complete and accurate implementation of the Directives was quite a challenge for several Member States', whereby none of them had achieved full transposition by the deadline. The Commission warned Member States that they had not fully transposed the third Electricity and Gas Directives into their national laws, subsequently initiating legal actions. Moreover, the Commission began to systematically take all necessary measures in order to assist Member States in fulfilling their obligations. Furthermore, by September 2011, the Commission had opened 38 infringement proceedings against 19 Member States for not transposing or for transposing only partially the Directives. These proceedings accelerated the transposition process and motivated Member States to take the necessary steps in order to complete the process.

As a second step, the Commission began to determine the obstacles which resulted from incorrect transpositions or inconsistent application of the Directives. In order to resolve these problems, the Commission undertook systematic non-conformity checks of national measures in almost all 28 Member States and as a consequence opened pilot cases on several occasions against Member States. The Commission gave priority to violations having the highest impact on the functioning of the internal market. On this basis, following the conclusion that a number of Member States' national laws were not compatible with the Third Package, the Commission initiated "EU-Pilot" cases. As of 1 July 2016, eight of these EU-Pilot cases have resulted in infringement proceedings where, inter alia, the violation of the EU Electricity and Gas Directives is alleged. Further EU-Pilot cases remain open and might lead to more infringement proceedings.

Recent reviews regarding the Third Energy Package show how far the EU rules in the energy sector evolved in the last twenty-year period and demonstrate that the process of establishing a competitive single EU energy market, although it began slowly, has evolved in a very rapid manner. However, despite the Commission's attempts, i.e. energy reforms, further steps have to be undertaken in order to enable full competition in European energy markets, especially at the retail level. The tendency of consumers to resist change makes it difficult to create a competitive environment. Although ten years have passed since the development of the Third Energy Package, several Member States still face obstacles as regards competition. These obstacles and discrepancies between different regulatory schemes endanger the integration of European energy markets.

While provisions set forth by the Third Energy Directives are thought to be sufficient, in practice Member States have only been partially successful in implementing such provisions. Furthermore, not all of the problems identified in the energy sector inquiry have been addressed. The liberalisation process in Central and Eastern Europe is relatively slow, which negatively affects the integration process. It can be observed that dominant incumbents in these countries continue to abuse their market power.

II. Assessment on the Current State of the Liberalisation

Although certain crucial steps have been undertaken since the 1990s aiming at liberalising and opening the electricity and the natural gas markets to competition, the establishment of competitive single electricity and natural gas markets has not yet been fulfilled. The current situation demonstrates that energy markets have not been liberalised at the desired level, thus creating a substantial obstacle to competition. Electricity and gas markets continue to exhibit potential shortcomings which might affect competition within the energy markets, including:

- In terms of wholesale and retail segments, electricity and gas markets are quite concentrated, which creates an activity area that can be used by the incumbents. A high level of vertical integration between energy suppliers and a high level of concentration in the energy markets lead to market distortions, i.e. lack of free and open competition in energy markets, limit efficiency, reduce consumer choice and lead to higher prices.

- Today, new entrants still encounter difficulties and barriers concerning their integration in the supply market, such as lack of access to customer and market information for suppliers, lack of price transparency, and differences in processes and standards. Competition will remain limited as long as there are barriers to entry to the market.
- Liberalisation of the energy markets is varying in the Member States. In many Member States, the unbundling of infrastructure activities from supply activities has not been fully realised.
- State ownership of first-generation producers in electricity and gas markets in Member States still continues.
- Former state monopolies, which can be considered as incumbents with few incentives to allow for market opening, often maintain a significant influence on national decision-making processes.
- National grids are not well connected to one another, and this requires significant investment.
- Uncoordinated national policies also hamper the integration of markets.
- It can also be seen that electricity and gas prices have increased for consumers and there are high price rises. Moreover, in terms of households, there are price differences across Member States.
- Across EU Member States, supplier-changing rates of consumers have remained low due to high switching costs and limited transparency, which both constitute a competition issue. It can be observed that consumers still lack awareness in respect of their ability to switch suppliers and also in respect of certain information that is crucial to make informed decisions.
- Cross-border trade of electricity remains low compared to natural gas. The reason behind this is that in some Member States electricity is seen as part of state sovereignty, and reluctance to open the electricity market can be still observed.
- Congestion in the transmission and distribution networks causes reduction in efficiently allocated capacity to transport electricity. Inasmuch as it constrains the ability of remote suppliers to compete with each other, it limits competition in the electricity markets. Moreover, congestion management of the transmission networks and balancing markets are currently predominantly nationally or-

ganised, which is in contradiction with the goal of an internal energy market. Cross-border integration and the opening up of these markets to new market players require a certain degree of harmonisation across Member States. To this end, harmonisation, open access to markets and a level playing field for (new) market players should be ensured by sector-specific regulations.

It can be observed that the main challenges continue to be high energy prices, the slow pace of investment in the energy sector due to the lack of incentives for investing, and security of supply. These issues mostly stem from lack of competition in the market.

Contrary to their objective, the regulatory measures aimed at opening and liberalising electricity and natural gas markets hardly have had a positive effect in terms of reducing energy prices, both electricity and natural gas, for industrial consumers and households. Although they have contributed to an increased number of suppliers active in the market and consequently have increased the competitiveness in the market, this has barely been reflected in the prices. It can be argued that the EU is having difficulties in finding a regulatory approach concerning energy markets that fits all its currently 28 Member States.

Realising the EU's aforementioned objectives will be possible as and once the experience obtained during the liberalisation process is reflected in the EU-level regulations and when a dynamic yet stable legal infrastructure for the markets is established alongside effective *ex ante* and *ex post* implementation of competition principles and rules. Competition law and sector-specific regulations can help to address all of the above-mentioned issues. Consistent enforcement of these two legal instruments gives investors the certainty and predictability they need. Opening infringement procedures against undertakings that harm their competitors by threatening to close to new entrants or blocking energy flows from one EU country to another might deter other incumbents. It is apparent that European energy markets need competition, transparency on pricing and genuine choice for consumers.

EU competition law and sector-specific regulations address those challenges in several ways. Competition enforcement and sector-specific regulations play a key role in establishing a properly functioning internal energy market. While competition law protects competition through prohibiting collusion, abuse of a dominant position and mergers, all of which hamper effective competition, sector-specific regulations help to establish and maintain competition in the energy markets through unbundling and third-party access regimes. Both competition law and sector-specific regulations contribute by lifting obstacles to competition and barriers to trade between Member States. Moreover, they lead to opening markets to new players, creating a level playing field between competitors and ultimately promoting investment and innovation. The Commission continues to challenge practices that hamper the competitive environment of the internal markets. This anticompetitive conduct leads to higher energy prices. A more efficient Europe-wide grid would help to reduce prices for households and companies.

§ 11. Sector-Specific Regulations and Competition Law

The legal and regulatory framework of the energy sector is established by two different instruments at the European level: competition law and sector-specific regulations. Although these instruments can be seen as similar in terms of their purposes, they are quite distinctive. On the one hand, both aim at developing and protecting competition; on the other hand, sector-specific regulations pursue certain other objectives in addition, such as sustainable development or consumer protection.

In theory, competition law protects the market, while sector-specific regulations create the market. As a consequence, in order for competition law to function, first the sector-specific regulations must be implemented in a successful manner, which should result in the creation of the market. Competition law assumes that the market functions properly under the conventional market conditions, whereby the operational decisions are freely taken by the undertakings in the market. From the competition law perspective, in order to enable effective competition in the market, undertakings must have a level playing field and be able to take their decisions independently. The actions of undertakings can be limited by EU competition rules and merger control.

Sector-specific regulations are implemented based on the assumption that the market requires the direct or indirect supervision of the state. Sector-specific regulations can interfere with the undertakings' decision-making procedures and, hence, require justification. For example, the intervention of sector-specific regulations in the energy sector is justified by the natural monopoly feature of networks. It has been acknowledged that the most convenient way to create a competitive environment on the network level is implementing sector-specific regulations.

Another difference between these two instruments is the timing of their application. While sector-specific regulations are implemented *ex ante*, competition law is implemented *ex post* except for merger control. It has been acknowledged that in energy markets *ex post* measures, i.e. competition law, are not sufficient to ensure effective functioning of the market. In order to establish effectively functioning energy markets, *ex ante* measures, i.e. sector-specific regulations, are required.

There are also differences between competition law and sector-specific regulations with respect to their institutions. The primary duty of competition authorities is detecting anticompetitive behaviours, but they do not have the competence to impose *ex ante* obligations or to implement certain policies. Sector-specific regulators can, however, take prospective measures to ensure efficient competition. In other words, competition authorities instruct undertakings on what not to do, while regulators instruct them on what to do. Therefore, while the prohibitions of competition law are put forth in a general manner, regulations define a behavioural framework for undertakings.

In an environment in which it is unclear whether competition law or sector-specific regulations has precedence concerning competition-related issues, there is a perpetual risk of overlaps in terms of jurisdiction or in terms of each institutions' reluctance to take initiatives with respect to intervention. An institution's intervention is likely to be solved in an efficient manner by the means of another institution. This situation may cause regulatory inconsistencies as well as jurisdictional confusion. In order to prevent such conflicts, the allocation of competencies between sector-specific regulators and competition authorities is required in the energy sector. This allocation is an ongoing challenge in most Member States and often a highly controversial issue. It can be observed that different Member States adopt different approaches.

There are several ways to allocate competencies between competition authorities and sector-specific regulators:

- Competition authorities have competence to enforce both competition law and sector-specific regulations.
- Sector-specific regulators can have full competence to enforce competition law and sector-specific regulations.
- Competition authorities and sector-specific regulators simultaneously have jurisdiction over industries, with competition law being allocated to competition authorities and sector-specific regulations being allocated to sector-specific regulators.

It can be said that competition law and sector-specific regulations should be seen as complementary legal instruments. Both instruments deal with a common problem, namely the illegitimate acquisition of market power and the likelihood of it being abused, and both try to achieve a common aim: establishing a competitive internal market. Only through a combination of both tools can it be ensured that market power does not distort and hamper the development of competition in the markets.

The above discussion shows that the concept of concurrent jurisdiction is the best model, since it is a practical and pragmatic solution to managing the interface between competition law and sector-specific regulations. This model has real potential to help overcome many tough challenges, e.g., the overlap between competition law and sector-specific regulations or determining what the respective roles of competition authorities and sector-specific regulators should be. For example, the networks constitute natural monopolies and therefore the owners of the networks mostly have a dominant position in the market. Generally, sector-specific regulations handle the access regime to the network. However, refusal to grant access to the network can be considered an abuse of a dominant position on the market; therefore, the competition authorities should deal with it. In case of an overlap, authorities must consult with each other in specified areas. In this model, the functional separation of competition authorities from sector-specific regulators is necessary in order to ensure that both policies are administered by authorities suited to their enforcement powers.

In order for this model to work properly, the competition authorities and the sector-specific regulators have to co-ordinate with each other, with the respective governments and with the Commission. These complex regulatory bodies have no choice but to try to co-operate, even if the manner of such co-operation and the subjects on which co-operation occurs are determined on a pragmatic, case-by-case basis rather than a rule-based system.

As regards energy markets, the objectives as well as the roles of sector-specific regulators in the energy sector are specified clearly in the third Energy Directives. These objectives include the establishment of a competitive, reliable and environmentally sustainable internal energy market, opening up the market effectively within the EU for all consumers and suppliers, enabling the efficient and reliable operating of gas and electricity networks, eliminating limitations on gas and electricity trade among Member States, empowering the integration of national markets, encouraging an effective competition environment and, finally, protecting consumers. Several duties have been allocated to the sector-specific regulators for the purpose of fulfilling the aforementioned objectives. The competition authorities aim at enabling the continuous effective operation of free competition with respect to the effective use of resources. Whilst they pursue the realisation of those objectives, they protect the independence of the economic activities of the actors in the market.

It can be said that competition law and sector-specific regulations are effective if they work together. The establishment of competitive electricity and natural gas internal markets in the EU is solely possible through the effective implementation of rules on competition and sector-specific regulations in these markets. Within this context, it is necessary that sector-specific regulations should be developed for electricity and natural gas markets which should include *ex ante* measures to prevent competition infringements and abuse of dominant position. Moreover, if competition infringements and an abuse of a dominant position are given in the market, *ex post* measures should be implemented. In other words, the establishment and conservation of competition in these markets requires a "two-layered" process.

> *"European competition policy provides a series of powerful tools to enforce conditions of fair competition in liberalised markets [...]. But competition enforcement is just one partner, one half of a 'pas de deux'. It dances not alone, but in step with regulation. Regulation opens the market – and com-*

petition policy makes sure that the opened markets really work [...]. And both have to adjust their movements in parallel, in line with the pace of the music. And when it comes to redefining the dancefloor – in this case fundamental restructuring of the energy marketplace – both dancers need to step into motion." (Neelie Kroes, 2007).

§ 12. Competition in Energy Markets

Considering the decisions discussed in Chapter 9, it can be concluded that the Commission did not only apply EU competition rules but also took into account, in order to justify intervention in the energy markets, the regulatory framework which supports liberalisation in the energy sector. The liberalisation of energy markets has led to a process of convergence between EU competition law and sector-specific regulation. The liberalisation process of the EU energy markets is realised by EU Treaty Law and the secondary EU legislation, i.e. Directives. Institutional structures established by EU Treaties enable the Commission to play a key role regarding the implementation of both instruments.

As mentioned before, opening energy markets to competition began at the end of the 1990s with the introduction of sector-specific regulations, i.e., Electricity and Gas Directives. After it was realised that the second Directives did not yield the expected benefit, the Commission launched the energy sector inquiry. With the inquiry it became apparent that EU electricity and gas markets were still not competitive at the desired level. The structure of these markets and the behaviours of the dominant undertakings hinder progress. It can be observed that European energy markets are essentially comprised of fragmented national markets with incumbents in dominant positions which often own both the supply business and the transmission network. These vertically integrated undertakings do not have incentives to invest in the grid infrastructure and in long-term capacities, since this would expose them to more competition which results in lower market entry, more limited choices, lower security and lower sustainability of supply than would otherwise be the case.

Since the energy sector inquiry, the Commission has opened several antitrust proceedings against energy companies in the EU energy markets. These antitrust proceedings fell into three broad categories:

- collusion between undertakings;
- exclusionary abuses by undertakings in a dominant position;
- exploitative abuses by undertakings in a dominant position.

The first category encompasses the alleged collusion between undertakings (GFU, DONG/DUC and E.ON/GDF decision). Three main examples of infringement under Article 101 TFEU are:

- joint selling,
- joint marketing and
- market sharing.

The most notable example of anticompetitive joint selling agreements is the GFU case, which is related to the joint sales of Norwegian natural gas through a single seller. The case highlighted that introducing competition into the upstream sector is important for the successful creation of an internal gas market in Europe. Moreover, it established that the Commission is able to take into consideration the commercial interests of the concerned undertakings whilst ensuring that EU competition law is protected.

With regard to anticompetitive market sharing agreements, the Commission initiated an investigation against E.ON and GDF for market-sharing in breach of the rules on cartels and restrictive business practices (Article 101). Market-sharing agreements constitute a very serious infringement of EU competition rules. In its E.ON/GDF decision, the Commission issued for the first time a fine for the antitrust infringement in the energy sector.

As concerns the second category, namely exclusionary conduct, the Commission investigated whether undertakings in a dominant position had conducted the following activities:

- capacity hoarding: refusing to grant access to capacity available on the transport network (RWE, ENI and ČEZ cases);
- capacity degradation: granting access to capacity in a less useful way (ENI case);
- capacity mismanagement: understating technically available capacity and managing the scarce transport capacities on its network (RWE case);

- margin squeeze: excluding rivals by inflating network costs and imposing stringent balancing requirements in small balancing zones (RWE case);
- strategic underinvestment: failing to increase capacity in major import pipelines to protect a dominant position on supply markets (GDF and ENI cases);
- long-term capacity booking: foreclosing access to markets by a combination of long-term upstream supply contracts and long-term capacity reservations (GDF and E.ON cases);
- long-term supply contracts: trying to foreclose customers through supply contracts with an extremely long duration (Distrigas and EDF cases).

The third category, namely exploitative abuse, includes conducts carried out by undertakings in a dominant position to harm customers directly, e.g., increasing prices to the detriment of consumers via withholding available generation capacity or discriminating certain type of consumers.

To ensure that competition in the energy sector is not distorted, the Commission also focused on state aid which is not compatible with the internal market. The Commission takes into consideration the criteria used by the CJ regarding state aids, the presence of an intervention through the state or state resources, the potential of this intervention to affect trade between Member States, an advantage for the recipient and the distortion of competition. Moreover, the Commission applied the "private investor test" to determine whether or not aid distorts or threatens to distort competition.

In addition to the infringements within the scope of Articles 101, 102 and 107 TFEU, the Commission also focused on mergers which may have anticompetitive effects, e.g., ENI/EDP/GDP, E.ON/MOL and GDF/Suez. In order to eliminate the anticompetitive effects of a transaction – for example when such a transaction would directly have resulted in the creation of a vertically integrated company –, the Commission usually imposed structural remedies such as ownership unbundling or divesture of certain market segments. Moreover, if the remedies offered by the parties to the transactions did not seem to be sufficient to address competition issues, the Commission did not hesitate to prohibit the transaction.

Together with Article 101 and 102 TFEU, EU merger control is an important instrument to develop a market structure in which competition is respected and to reduce horizontal and vertical integration in energy markets. In the decisions of the Commission regarding energy markets, it can be seen that concentrations are not banned. In many cases, the Commission applied remedies to eliminate the potential competition-restricting effects of mergers. Moreover, these remedies also contributed to the support of liberalisation in energy markets. In most of the decisions, concentrations that significantly affected competition were permitted only on certain conditions. This method enables the realisation of concentration without allowing it to prevent the market's proper functioning. Hence, the market develops, and the competitive structure is protected. Even new entries to markets with the characteristic of dominant position become possible. Consideration of the conditions set out in commitments given by undertakings who are parties to concentrations enables the functioning of this mechanism. Such commitments address the concerns of the Commission and are in accordance with the capabilities of the parties concerned. The Commission exercises control mechanisms after the decision. This practice increases the rate of correct implementation of the conditions by the parties to the concentration. The favoured conditions in the decisions regarding the energy markets include ownership unbundling, transfer of long-term agreements, natural gas sale and granting access to third persons. In other words, these conditions are the most effective measures applied to eliminate the anticompetitive effects that concentrations in the energy markets have. With these methods permitted by EU competition law, the aim is to establish a single energy market through the entry of new actors into a market which has high entry obstacles, the facilitation of third-party access to the system and the prevention of discriminatory practices. In practice, the Commission handled around 540 merger and anti-trust cases in the gas and electricity markets across Europe in the time period between 1994 and 2019.

Based on the above-mentioned cases, it can be stated that, even though the Commission can achieve significant results in terms of opening EU energy markets to competition by using the competition tools, some issues in the energy sector may be best dealt with by means of sector-specific regulations rather than enforcing competition rules. It should be noted that one of the most important outcomes of the energy sector inquiry was that the Commission was able to determine where regulatory changes would be necessary to enhance competition in the EU energy markets and where it could achieve better results by enforcing competition rules.

The initiatives regarding the liberalisation of energy markets have had a varying success, and the establishment of a competition environment takes a long time. As mentioned above, despite past efforts of the Commission to liberalise EU electricity and gas markets and subsequently open them to competition, entry barriers still exist and are leading to market concentration. The impact of these barriers is especially severe with regard to new market players. For this reason, the Commission uses all possible competition law instruments for developing the functioning of the energy markets.

The energy markets have been highly regulated historically and will remain so in the future. The already significant role of sector-specific regulations will become even more important in the near future, given the ambitious policy objectives outlined by the EU. The role of competition law instruments has been and will continue to be important to protect and maintain effective competition as well as to achieve the EU's objective concerning the establishment of an internal energy market.

FSC
www.fsc.org
MIX
Papier | Fördert
gute Waldnutzung
FSC® C083411

Kolibri 360 GmbH
Ferdinand-Jühlke-Straße 7
99095 Erfurt, Deutschland
produktsicherheit@kolibri360.de